LETTERS FROM UNCLE DAVE:
The 73-Year Journey to Find a Missing in Action
World War II Paratrooper

Phil Rosenkrantz

Rose & Crown Outreach

PLACENTIA, CALIFORNIA

This is a masterful weave of military history, family history, and insights into the means whereby we try to recover or identify our fallen. It was informative and poignant all at the same time...It would be a great thing if each of our veterans could be so appropriately memorialized!

Brigadier General John S. Brown (retired), former Historian of the Army

Phil Rosenkrantz in "Letters From Uncle Dave" could not have written this WW II story any sooner, because it just recently ended. You must read this book. It is so much more than the title suggests. My cousin, S/Sgt Ross Carter, served in a sister company of the 504th Parachute Infantry Regiment 82nd Airborne with "Uncle Dave", and honored their sacrifices in "Those Devils In Baggy Pants" published in 1951. It was binary. There were those heroes who didn't make it. There were those who were "refugees from the law of averages" who did and came home. There was another group of heroes: Missing In Action. "Letters From Uncle Dave" is the story of one MIA who floated through time, bereft of a final resting place, and the journey of his family. Great job...I feel like Uncle Dave is my uncle, too. You have done a fabulous job blending all the parts of his life and the parts after his life ended to ensure that he will never be forgotten. In the Navy, we say Bravo Zulu or Well Done.

David Ross Fraley (cousin to author Ross Carter "Those Devils in Baggy Pants" about the 504 Parachute Infantry Regiment)

What an amazing journey and wonderful story on so many levels! I cannot commend you enough on your perseverance to find out about your uncle's story, to discover his remains, and to bring closure for you and

your family...Hopefully, your book will be an inspiration to others who wish to discover their veteran's story. Bravo!

Steve Snyder, author of the
award-winning book, *Shot Down*

"Arriving into H Company, I found a tremendous group of fine soldiers and officers," recalled Colonel (ret.) Elbert F. Smith after the war. The men of the 504th Parachute Infantry Regiment were the first U.S. Paratroopers to experiment with a new way of making a more safe and thus adequate drop into enemy territory. One of Smith's 'fine soldiers' was David Rosenkrantz from Los Angeles."

Frank van Lunteren, Author and
Historian

Two of our best lieutenants...died of wounds. 11 more had been killed, among them Sergeant Rosie Rosenkrantz of Company "H" who was one of the finest mortar non-coms in the regiment and an old friend from Fort Bragg days. I was greatly moved by his death.

From the Journal of Corporal
George "Mickey" Graves Jr.

This is an engrossing story of an ordinary person and his family, called upon by his country to do extraordinary things. These are the people that won World War II. It is asked what do you get out of the effort to read this book? What you ultimately get is a micro history lesson about the war from a soldier's perspective, a look at leadership and the grieving process for over 70 years. Most importantly, you will get a new friend, SSG David Rosenkrantz.

Rosey is someone you know, an "average Joe", who was drafted into the Army to defend his country. You will read his letters to his family and marvel how he endured the hell of war. The only hint of dissatisfaction is his recommendation to his family to join the Navy.

At the end of the book you will mourn the loss of your new friend and rejoice that SSG David Rosenkrantz was returned home to his family.

Stanley G Phernambucq
COL (R) US Army

www.philrosenkrantz.com

Book Layout © 2017 BookDesignTemplates.com

Interior Design and Editorial Services: Remembering the Time

Letters From Uncle Dave/Phil Rosenkrantz – 1st ed.
ISBN 978-1-7351950-2-5

Dedication

It was not until the last twenty years that I truly understood the remarkable sacrifices and accomplishments of the US military in WWII. This book is dedicated to the men, women, and families of 82nd Airborne Division and the 504 Parachute Infantry Regiment where my uncle, S/Sgt David Rosenkrantz served. The members of the 504 have become known as those "Devils in Baggy Pants." My uncle was one of those H Company paratroopers at Anzio who earned the regiment that name. My thanks to all of you.

— PHIL ROSENKRANTZ

CONTENTS

FOREWARD

"Arriving into H Company, I found a tremendous group of fine soldiers and officers," recalled Colonel (ret.) Elbert F. Smith after the war. He was the platoon leader of the 1st Platoon in H Company: "In our barracks, we deliberated the ways and means of getting these weapons, machine-guns and BAR's (Browning Automatic Rifle), out with the men. (...) Our final idea was to disassemble the weapons and strap the parts to each gun crewmember in a manner in which he could safely jump with it." In doing so, the men of H Company of the 504th Parachute Infantry Regiment were the first U.S. Paratroopers to experiment with a new way of making a safer and thus more adequate drop into enemy territory. One of Smith's 'fine soldiers' was David Rosenkrantz from Los Angeles – better known to his family as Dave, or "Rosie."

Dave joined H Company as it was being formed in the Summer of 1942. His unique letters and drawings up until his untimely death in the Holland Campaign two years later provide a unique insight in the life of a young paratrooper. Like his buddies in H Company, Dave had chosen to become a paratrooper and went overseas in April 1943 from Camp Edwards, Massachusetts to an improvised Camp Leautey, 15 miles from the port of Casablanca. The paratroopers had to march the entire length since the trucks that should have been there had not arrived.

From Camp Leautey a train journey followed days later to "a living patch of hell" – a very basic bivouac in Oujda, Algeria in the blazing sun. Food was scarce and even the Regimental Commander – who used to eat with his Regimental Staff in the 3rd Battalion Mess, chose to have dinner elsewhere. But the 3rd Battalion troopers like Sergeant Dave Rosenkrantz improvised and by late June 1943 they found themselves in Kairouan, Tunisia.

First action was the jump on Sicily – which was scattered for the 3rd Battalion. Their battalion commander was captured after a day of fierce fighting as well as a few dozen others. However, a German company of Tiger Tanks was held up by them until the evening of July 10, enabling the famous Colonel James Gavin and his 505th PIR to prepare defenses on Biazza Ridge. It was also here that a photograph was made later that month of Dave Rosenkrantz and several 505th PIR troopers. Yet, his landing in Sicily is one of the fascinating stories which his nephew, Dr. Phil Rosenkrantz, uncovered over two decades of dedicated research for his missing uncle.

Letters From Uncle Dave is a fascinating read about the Rosenkrantz family and their sons and daughter who served their country in a time when the Axis Powers threatened humanity in both Europe and Asia. Dave was the only one who, after fighting also in the Salerno and Anzio Beachhead and the Italian mountains near Venafro, did not return from the Holland Campaign. Just about a week before he was killed in action, he was last interviewed by a war correspondent. His last words were recorded – on newspaper instead of the V-Mail papers he had sent home. But his body was missing in action until early 2018.

I first met Phil Rosenkrantz in October 2003 as a twenty-one-year-old historian student and had the honor a year later to cross on 20 September 2004 with them during a commemoration event across the broad Waal River in a DUKW amphibious craft. Although I was familiar in crossing the river by car and train, I was astonished how broad the river actually is when you have to paddle across....and the distance from the river edge to the summer dike. Staff Sergeant Dave Rosenkrantz lived through that courageous action and gave the best example of leadership in his new role of platoon sergeant as the platoon was surrounded in Heuvelhof farm.

Phil has undertaken a mammoth task in writing such a complete and touching overview of his uncle's life and his family in World War II. Although I could never meet his uncle Dave Rosenkrantz, I am sure he would have been proud of the persistence and dedication of Phil's efforts to not only find him, but also to serve as his biographer. When Phil placed a rosette behind the name of his uncle on the Wall of Missing in Margraten Cemetery in September 2019, I thought the full circle had ended. Now I realize I was wrong – this book is the keystone to the project. Uncle Dave has been located and is no longer missing. It is time to read about his life.

Strike and Hold,

Frank van Lunteren
Honorary Member 504th PIR
Historian of the 504th PIR in WWII

PREFACE

*Greater love has no one than this: to lay down
one's life for one's friends.*
John 15:13

I have been very fortunate in my life to have a beautiful family, a
rewarding career, great friends, good health, and a meaningful
spiritual life. However, twenty years ago I began the journey of
learning about my Uncle Dave and added a rich dimension to
my life. Pursuing his story and discovering his heroic service in
World War II resulted in a greater appreciation of history and
for the sacrifices that have been made—both at home and
abroad—to help preserve our freedom.

With the advent of the internet, starting in the late 90s, I
decided to use search engines to find out more about Uncle
Dave's unit and—with any luck—what happened to him. I never
dreamed that I would learn much more than where he served or
how he died. By the grace of God, we were able to not only find
out what happened but see him returned home to be buried
with his brothers.

Throughout this book, my uncle is referred to as Dave, David,
Uncle Dave, and his nickname Rosie/Rosy. His life story is filled
with examples of loyalty, sacrifice, and leadership. From
beginning to journey's end, people from around the world, who
we would never have connected with otherwise, have entered
our lives in meaningful ways. I hope to pass along a portion of
this richness in the pages of this book. Although his life was
tragically cut short, Dave left gifts behind for us if we are willing
to follow his journey and pick them up along the way.

Two very large "Why?" questions loomed throughout this 73-
year saga. The first is: Why volunteer to become a paratrooper?
This displays Dave's purpose and character. He sacrificed the
last 32 months of his life before paying the ultimate price to
defend his country and his fellow paratroopers. Similarly, his

younger brother, Launie, gave six years of his life serving in the US Navy, enduring multiple battles and an ocean rescue. Launie returned to a life plagued by the effects of post-traumatic stress disorder, PTSD[i], and grief over the loss of many comrades. Both uncles developed purpose and character over their lifetimes based on values, teaching, and training.

The second question is: Why devote so much time, money, and effort to find our dead and bring them home? The US is one of the only countries that allocates significant resources to bring home our war dead. Why is this important? The reasons we do this include forensic needs, morale, family, politics, and morality. These topics affect everyone in some way and are discussed throughout the book.

American paratroopers were new to the military arsenal in World War II and played a major role in Europe's liberation. How paratroopers were trained, deployed, and fought heroically is woven throughout the whole story of Uncle Dave's service and even the long, winding road to closure. It is my hope that readers will appreciate not only the events of World War II, but also the significance of the American paratroopers and the leadership and training that prepared them.

For free supplemental materials, go to:

www.philrosenkrantz.com/studyguides

ACKNOWLEDGEMENTS

Many people have been part of the 73-year journey to find out what happened to Uncle Dave and bring him home. Friends, relatives, Dutch men and women, researchers, veterans, government and military officials, and other 504 relatives have contributed to this fantastic adventure. The acknowledgments contain a rich story all by themselves. It has been a long journey to this point, learning as I go, so I apologize for omitting anyone.

First and foremost, I need to acknowledge my Uncle David, his brothers and sisters, and my grandparents for their sacrifices over the decades and for providing such a rich legacy. The examples they set—as did others of their time—will be felt for generations to come. Their legacy is humbling, and much appreciated. Had I passed on this journey; I would have missed one of the most satisfying endeavors of my life.

Next, I would like to thank my immediate family for their support. My wife, Judy, has been at my side for the many trips to the Netherlands and other events. She has supported me all along the way. My son, David, and his wife, Elizabeth, have been sounding boards whenever I needed a second opinion. They helped with assembling the letters and photos in the book and taking pictures on our trips in 2009 and 2019. My daughters Julia and Sarah have been supportive and helpful, including assisting us on our journey to the Netherlands in 2009. My daughter, Debi, has helped in other ways by keeping my life in balance and accompanying me to Disneyland hundreds of times over the last 20 years.

My sisters, Gina and Sandy, and brother, Harry, Jr., have been very supportive and encouraging as well. Gina and her husband, Russ, accompanied us to the Netherlands in 2009 and the DPMO Family meeting in Scottsdale in 2011. My sister Sandy helped with researching military records and editing some of the writing. All of them helped with our uncle's funeral in 2018.

I would like to thank my cousins Doni Satorhelyi, Alan Rosenkrantz, Bill Clabaugh, Rudy Rosenkrantz, Ruby Alcaraz Rosenkrantz, Olivia Vasquez, Lisa Alcaraz Rosenkrantz, Yolanda Topete, and Rudy Topete and their families for their encouragement, support, editorial reviews, and for providing letters, photos, and other memorabilia.

I cannot thank enough Dutch researcher and battlefield expert, Ben Overhand, and author and historian, Frank van Lunteren for their untiring dedication and support for finding Uncle Dave and bringing him home. Ben actively searched and researched what happened to Uncle Dave for 35 years. His battlefield knowledge amazes me. Likewise, Frank's understanding of the men and events of the 504 Parachute Infantry Regiment and Operation Market Garden is unparalleled. I have been around enough brilliant people in my life to say they are geniuses at what they do. It has been a blessing to get to know both men and their families.

There are many other Dutch men and women who contributed in various ways. This is one place where I am sure I have forgotten some names. I would like to thank Jan Bos, Johan van Asten, Anton van Ensberger, Jos Bex, Anja Adriians, Doreen Steenbergen, Hans Veders, and Michiel van Manen for their kindness and contributions. I would like to acknowledge the many Dutch people who have contacted me and helped me learn more about the photograph of my uncle after the jump into Holland, including Mirjam Claus-Blenk, Ronald Peters, Theon Ariens, and Peter Pouwels.

I had the good fortune to meet and spend time with many 504 paratroopers who served in World War II, many of who went through battles with my uncle. Most have passed on, so I was fortunate to meet them when I did. My grateful thanks go to veterans Fred Thomas, Ted Finkbeiner, T. Moffatt Burris, James "Maggie" Megellas, Albert Tarbell, Larry Dunlop, Roy Hanna, Francis Keefe, Albert Clark, Fred Baldino, James Kiernan, Robert Devinney, and Walter Littman, for their friendship and assistance.

One of the highlights of this journey has been making friends, traveling with, and learning from other relatives of 504 paratroopers. We cherish these friends and I apologize for omitting any names. They include Kathleen & Ray Buttke, Catherine Metropoulos, Bud & Eileen Kaczor, Cooper Beverly-Meise, Dain Blair, Mary Gagliano, Tom Ryan, David Ross Fraley, the Peggy Shelly family, the Keefe family, the Smits family, the Blankenship family, the Hanna family and the Mandle family.

Many others from the 82nd Airborne and 504 Parachute Infantry Regiment assisted in various ways. We appreciated being included in the 504 Reunion at Fort Bragg in February 2017. I would like to thank Major Richard Ingleby from Ft. Bragg and his paratroopers for their assistance during the 75th Anniversary of Operation Market Garden and for attending Uncle Dave's Rosette ceremony. Others from the 82nd Airborne family I would like to thank are Chloe Gavin Beatty (daughter of General James Gavin) and her son, James Gavin Beatty, for their friendship and interest in the book. Thanks to Tyler Fox, for sending me a newspaper article from WWII about my uncle that turned out to be very useful.

Finding Uncle Dave would not have been possible without the help and expertise of those behind the scenes at various government agencies. I would like to recognize the ones who I worked with personally and met either at a DPMO Family Meeting (Scottsdale, AZ, or San Diego, CA) or on-site in the Netherlands. From the Defense POW Missing Personnel Office (DPMO)/Defense POW-MIA Accounting Agency (DPAA): Drs. Ed Burton, Jeff Johnson, and Ian Spurgeon. From the Joint POW/MIA Accounting Command (JPAC), I want to thank Heather Harris.

Many people helped bring Uncle Dave's remains back to Los Angeles and ultimately lay him to rest at the Riverside National Cemetery. We are very thankful to William "Shorty" Cox, CMAOC Fort Knox, KY, for visiting our family and personally relating the story of finally identifying Uncle Dave's remains. We also want to thank SFC Miguel Cesena, US Army NG, Casualty Assistance Officer, for coordinating the delivery of Uncle Dave's remains from the Army side. Likewise, we would like to thank Greg Welch, Barbara Risher Welch, and Nancy Valdez from Risher Mortuary for their excellent handling of the mortuary and funeral affairs for our family. They went the extra mile to help us. We also thank the Patriot Guard Riders and local veteran's organizations for their assistance during the arrival at Los Angeles International Airport and the funeral in Riverside. The friendly staff at Riverside National Cemetery was very accommodating.

Sometimes, you don't know you need help until someone shows up to provide that help. That is the case with Laura Herzog and her organization, Honoring Our Fallen. Laura provided transportation for us when Uncle Dave arrived at Los Angeles International Airport and again for family members the day of the funeral at Riverside National Cemetery.

Lt. Col Joe Buccino, 1st Sgt Douglas Smith, and Sgt Christopher Gallagher from the 82nd Airborne Division came from Ft. Bragg, NC, to present the eulogy and awards the family had never received. I would like to thank my cousin, Pastor Rudy Topete, from the Tribe Church, and Rabbi David Becker, Chaplain from the California National Guard, for helping with the funeral service. I would like to thank James "Woody" Woods for providing photographs.

I would also like to recognize the Grove Community Church in Riverside, for graciously donating the space, food, and servers for our family reception after the funeral service. We also appreciate the kind visit from the Grove church leadership to offer their sympathy and thanks to the family.

I would like to thank Superintendent Shane Williams, Deputy Superintendent Juan Guttierez, and the staff at the Netherlands American Cemetery for their cooperation and support for the Rosette Ceremony on September 19, 2019. It was significant. Thanks to Ton Hermes from the Foundation for Adopting Graves American Cemetery Margraten for coordinating the event. We were pleased that we could meet Marion and Eddie Gilissen from the family who adopted Uncle Dave's unidentified grave for many decades.

The local press was very kind to us. *Los Angeles Times* reporters Paloma Esquivel, Gina Ferrazi, and Laura Newberry visited our family gatherings and ceremonies. They collaborated to put together an impressive front-page tribute to Uncle Dave and other articles, as well as a thoughtful documentary. Our family appreciates their professionalism and kindness.

Writing and publishing a book like this turned out to be a lot more work than anticipated. The good thing is that there are no regrets. I had the pleasure to meet and work with some fabulous editors, authors, and experts. I would like to thank my editors: Jennifer Holik and Karen Ray, for their enthusiastic dedication to making this book possible and worth reading. I also want to thank Jennifer's husband, Johan van Waart, for reviewing the manuscript. Their friendship, advice, and expertise are much appreciated. The World War II remembrance community includes lovely, caring people filled with insight and generosity.

Many friends helped along the way as reviewers or contributors. Their suggestions were invaluable. I would especially like to thank Catherine Strommen, Jerry Carlos, and Stan Phernambucq for their helpful and insightful remarks and ideas. My thanks also go to several authors who generously assisted in various ways: Steve Snyder, Janelle Kaye, Michelle Cahill, and Dr. Jack ReVelle.

Finally, I would like to thank God for this insightful voyage into family and world history. I believe the experience has made me a better person and allowed me to help others who are on a similar journey.

INTRODUCTION

On the night of July 9, 1943, the liberation of Europe from Nazi control began. American paratroopers of the 82nd Airborne Division were dropped into Sicily to secure important locations and defend the coast so that Allied landing forces could safely come ashore and deploy. Paratroopers were mis-dropped all over the island, including my uncle, Sergeant David Rosenkrantz, and Corporal Lee Black from Tennessee, a medic. Both paratroopers were in the 82nd Airborne Division, 504 Parachute Infantry Regiment, H Company. They landed and were quickly captured by 200 Italian soldiers. After a conference, the Italians decided that they should surrender rather than suffer the wrath of oncoming American forces only a few kilometers away. After celebrating, the two paratroopers accompanied the Italians to their surrender.

The story was quickly publicized in Rosenkrantz's hometown of Los Angeles. And he became an instant hero. People everywhere clamored for news from the front, and this story of victory involving a local soldier was just what they hoped to hear. No one was more relieved than David's mother (and my grandmother), Eva Rosa Rosenkrantz. She was born in Russia (today Poland) in 1884 and immigrated to the US on a passenger ship in 1902. She had four sons serving in the military during World War II. After hearing the capture story, Eva Rosa was quoted in a big article in the Los Angeles Daily News saying, *"I just knew he would do something big. Everybody liked him. He could do anything."* The newspaper even made up a song about the four Rosenkrantz brothers:[1]

And wherever there is action,
Rosenkrantzes will be seen,
In the Army, Navy, Air Forces,
United States Merchant Marine

The newspaper quoted David's sister, Goldie, "*...doesn't seem like there is a graveyard big enough to get and hold us Rosenkrantzes for a long while.*"

Despite David's assurances in letters to his mother that he would come home safe, the happiness would not last. Approximately 14 months later—on a Sunday in late 1944—the family was gathered at the house on 92nd Street in Watts for the usual Sunday dinner prepared lovingly by Grandma. Family and friends were enjoying each other around the dinner table when a vehicle drove up and officers delivered terrible news. They told the family that David was Missing-In-Action (MIA) and the report was he had been killed. However, there were no details about his death. The news devastated the family. My Uncle Max told me it was the worst day of his life. My father never talked about his own pain. I regret now never directly asking him about it.

David's mother, Eva Rosa, was never the same for the rest of her life. She went to her grave in 1960, still grieving, without closure, and in denial that he was dead. It would be 39 more years before the family would discover what happened to David. It would be another 20 years before his remains would be identified, brought home, and buried with his brothers at Riverside National Cemetery in California.

This book is a series of compelling stories explaining the journey and mystery of those years. Over 49 surviving letters Dave wrote home to his parents and siblings are included in these pages along with photographs and endnotes providing further detail. Dave's engaging personality, rich descriptions, and intricate sketches of paratrooper life are reflected in his writing. Please do not skip past the letters and miss the opportunity to get to know Dave on a deeper level.

From Dave's first accounts of paratrooper training in July 1942 "*When they said the paratroops would be tough, they weren't kidding.*" to his thoughts as a seasoned soldier not quite a year later in April 1943 "*In any case we are prepared for anything and afraid of nothing*" his transition into a respected leader is chronicled through his own words and others' memories.

The twists and turns of his story form a compelling drama full of adventure and history. The story begins with an immigrant family. Two young people left their homeland, crossing the ocean to start a new life, and ultimately raising eleven children. Profiles of each of their children illustrate the determination and toughness of immigrant families in our country.

One of the original *"Devils in Baggy Pants"*, paratrooper David Rosenkrantz fought in historic battles in Sicily, Italy, and Holland. He was eventually Missing in Action (MIA) and the story follows the 73-year journey to find his remains and bring him home. A critical aspect of this journey was the family's grief and struggle for closure, and this is discussed with the goal of helping others who face similar challenges.

Leadership is an integral part of the paratroopers' story during World War II. The impact of their training and accomplishments on modern leadership theory is critical. General James M. Gavin, commanding officer of the 82nd Airborne and the impact of his leadership during and after World War II is explored. The Army and the Marines both teach *Leaders Eat Last*. Many leadership gurus today teach methods and attitudes that have their roots in military leadership dating back over 200 years. References at the end of the book provide resources for those who want to delve deeper into this topic.

World War II impacted several generations of our family, along with millions of others. Similar stories continue to emerge as we send our young men and women off to serve and protect our country. This book relays a story of hope for those in comparable circumstances who may be looking for closure in their own family's journey.

Estimated deaths in World War II for military personnel and all civilian victims range from 60 to 70 million, representing about 3% of the world population at that time. The number of American servicemen and women killed is over 400,000, and the number wounded is over 600,000. These sobering statistics are difficult to wrap our heads around. This book relates the history and long-term effects of the loss of just one of those 400,000 Americans. Studying the story of one person who died and multiplying it by tens of thousands gives us a more accurate understanding of the damage of World War II.

I chose these excerpts from his April 15, 1943, letter for several reasons. It marks a major milestone—the last letter from the US and announces heading to fight. He mentions his promotion to Sergeant and gives colorful descriptions of his weapons. The letter is also an attempt to minimize his family's worries.

You are invited to enter the world of S/Sgt David Rosenkrantz through his own words. In his last letter from Ft. Bragg, NC, before heading for North Africa, he penned these historic assurances to his parents.

April 15, 1943
Dear folks,

This is the last letter I'll be writing from Fort Bragg. It won't leave here until after I do which won't be later than Tuesday so that when this letter finally reaches you I will be on my way to some port of embarkation, on the East Coast here somewhere. You understand that the reason the letter is held is so that no information will leak out to the wrong people.

Gee, why I forgot to mention it but now I got my other stripe. It's sergeant now. It took a long time but finally got here. It's better late than never.

I wish you could see me all ready to fight. I have my Tommy gun and a carbine and a machete. The machete is a heavy knife about a foot-and-a-half long that I will use to clear brush out of the way so that I can fire my mortar, and it can be used for other things too. I also have a jump knife. It is a large pocket knife with a blade that jumps out when you press a button and the knife is kept in a secret pocket on the jumpsuit. We will also have a trench knife. It is a wicked weapon and can do a lot of damage. I can either use the blade or the knuckles, and they're all bad. That's enough stuff for anyone to fight with, so you see we're a pretty rough outfit. Besides that our company carries other weapons like a rocket launcher that shoots rockets at tanks and which causes a lot of damage and we also have rifles that shoot grenades which are also pretty wicked. We also carry twice as many machine guns as any other outfit.

Don't think we use all those guns at once though. Being parachuters means that we might fight anywhere or anything so that one time we might use only one kind of gun or another time some other kind. In any case we are prepared for anything and afraid of nothing.

Maybe one of these days you'll get a letter from me from Berlin or Tokyo and I hope it isn't too long away but I'm afraid it is.

There, now I've given you a lot of military information that you didn't know before but I want you to be sure that we will be able to take care of ourselves when the time comes which I don't expect to be for a couple of months yet. So I will close with love to Ma and Pa and the rest of you. Don't think about my future too much because this baby is taking no chances if he can help it.

Well, be careful and don't catch any cold.

Dave

These are words you use when you are about to enter the gauntlet of war, but don't want the family at home to worry. They illustrate his maturity and character, allowing the reader to know him on a personal level.

PART ONE

AN IMMIGRANT FAMILY STORY

*Hyman & Eva Rosa Rosenkrantz around 1910
shortly after moving to Los Angeles. Children L-R:
Ben, Julius (Blackie), and Hannah (Rosenkrantz
family photography)*

CHAPTER ONE

IMMIGRANTS

Hyman and Eva Rosa Rosenkrantz, my grandparents, were Russian Jews who immigrated to the United States through Ellis Island separately as teenagers in 1902. They were from what is known today as Łódź, Poland.[2] The movie *Fiddler on the Roof,* [3] provides a glimpse of their life and culture in Russia They met in New York City, got married, and had two children there. Shortly after their second child was born, Hyman traveled to Los Angeles to obtain work as a tailor. Eva Rosa and the children, Hannah and Ben, traveled by train to join him in downtown LA. His specialty was suit making and he worked as a tailor his entire career.

My cousin Donetta gave me a copy of her father's birth certificate. Julius, nicknamed Blackie because of his hair, was the first child to be born in Los Angeles. He was born at home on what was to become a famous street—Bunker Hill, now a major street in downtown LA—The Music Center stands there today. My wife, Judy and I have been there many times for concerts. We didn't realize we could have been sitting on the same spot where my grandparents first lived.

Watts

The family later moved to the suburb of Watts at 1633 E. 92nd St., where they finished raising their family. Around 1953, their home was sold and sadly burned down sometime later in the 1950s.

Uncle Dave spoke fondly of Watts in his letters home. Today, many know of Watts because of the Watt's Riots in 1965 and 1992. During the 20s and 30s, the neighborhood became part of the southern edge of the City of Los Angeles and by the 40s the demographics had changed, from Caucasian to primarily African American. Today Watts is primarily Hispanic.[4]

Watts Towers, a famous landmark[5] built by Italian immigrant Sam Rodia, during the early 1920s, was less than two miles from my grandparents' home. I remember my father taking us there when I was very young. The two tallest towers are just under 100 feet tall. From 1967 – 1982 I worked at the General Motors Assembly Division Plant in South Gate, California,

bordered by Watts. I worked in the Industrial Engineering Department there for 10 years and had occasion to be on the roof of the plant and view Watts Towers standing tall just a few miles away. My father grew up only a few miles from where I worked for 15 years.

The couple produced nine more children for a total of three girls and eight boys. Their names, in chronological order are: Hannah, Benjamin (Ben), Julius (Blackie, Jule), Max, Lawrence (Larry), David (Dave, Rosie), Frieda, Launie, Goldie (Janet), Jack, and Harry (my father).

David was the middle child and had a personality that

Hyman & Eva Rosa Rosenkrantz around 1910 shortly after moving to Los Angeles. Children L-R: Ben, Julius (Blackie), and Hannah (Rosenkrantz family photograph) endeared him to everyone. He was the most extroverted of the eight Rosenkrantz brothers. Many of the children graduated from David Starr Jordan High School in Watts. Hyman and Eva Rosa observed many Orthodox Jewish traditions and ceremonies. However, the Jewish community in Los Angeles was small and they did not raise their children with any religious training.

Hyman died in 1952, after which Launie moved Grandma a few miles further east to Santa Fe Springs, where they lived until 1958. They relocated to Canoga Park on the other side of Los Angeles County in 1958 when Launie was transferred to Rocketdyne. I was too young to remember my Grandpa Hyman but did get to know my Grandma, Eva Rosa during the 50s. Until I was nine, we lived in Norwalk, only 1.5 miles from Grandma's house. It was a short bicycle ride to visit her any time. During my childhood in the 50s, we went for Sunday dinner at her house almost weekly. It was always an excellent kosher meal. I didn't realize until much later why we didn't have traditional gravy after understanding more about the meaning of kosher.

According to my dad, his father, Hyman, had an after-work routine, which consisted of sitting in a chair in the living room, playing solitaire, listening to the radio, and smoking cigarettes. He would talk to whoever came through the living room but did not participate actively in anything in my father's life. My father remembers his mother constantly chewing out Grandpa for smoking cigarettes. Grandpa had several siblings who lived in New York City and at least one of his brothers visited once while we lived in Norwalk. Other than that, not much was said about Grandpa or Grandma's relatives.

According to my father, when Grandma was a little girl she traveled around Russia with her father, a knife smith. My father claimed that she spoke Russian and Yiddish. She was an amazing woman managing to raise 11 children on a tight budget and save money on top of that. In the early 30s, she had saved up $500 and bought 160 acres of Mojave Desert property at El Mirage Dry Lake. She purchased it from some homesteaders who had failed to make a go of it, speculating that someday it would be worth something. When she passed away in 1960, the acreage was divided among her living children. Each one inherited a 20-acre parcel. Some sold the property right away to get whatever money they could. However, those who held onto their plots for speculation purposes were never significantly rewarded. Eventually, the State of California declared eminent domain and purchased all the property at a disappointing price per acre to use for a state recreational area.[6]

Grandma also applied for a patent for something she had invented at one point, but nothing ever came of that.

One thing the family could always count on was food on the table for whoever was there. If you showed up with a friend, they were welcome to eat also. My mother told me about going over for dinner after she started dating my father. Grandma always accused her of being too skinny and encouraged her to eat more.

Around 1959

Grandma needed to move into a nursing home and stayed there for the last year or so of her life. I visited her once, but my father went often. One time he bought some lox (salmon) and bagels to take to the nursing home. I had never seen that before and didn't think it was very appealing. He explained that it was lox and bagels and that Grandma would love it.

She went to her grave never knowing what happened to her son, David, and where his remains ended up.

Grandma went through a lot of tragedy in her life, mixed in with some good things. She went to her grave never knowing what happened to her son, David, and where his remains ended up. She would have been comforted to know the facts and put his memory to rest.

The stress and fear Grandma and thousands of other mothers across the country must have gone through during WWII are difficult to imagine today. She had four sons who actively served during the war years. She was a *Four-Star Mother,* and they were a *Four-Star Family.*[7] Three of her sons were in harm's way, and two saw massive death and destruction. We don't hear much about families that have sons and daughters in combat situations. Perhaps we need to.

Last summer, my wife, Judy, and I attended a nearby art festival along with other Gold Star Families (the Gold Star indicates a military family member had died). Tickets had been donated to the non-profit organization Honoring Our Fallen, and we were invited to attend. We met and spoke with other Gold Star Families and Gold Star Mothers. It was an eye-opening experience to hear their stories and understand their grief. One woman had lost her father during the Vietnam War when she was a young girl, and then, tragically, her son was killed in the Gulf War. Coincidentally, her son was in the 504 PIR like Uncle Dave. She commented on how she hadn't understood what her mother went through until she lost her own son. Hearing her story—and that she was still grieving—helped me realize that the pain and suffering my family, especially my grandmother, went through during and after World War II was more than I had imagined. Wartime deaths are not just a statistic, they represent lives gone forever and even more that are changed permanently.

CHAPTER TWO

COMPOUNDED FAMILY TRAGEDY

To understand the full impact of my Uncle Dave's loss in World War II, it is important to consider preceding family tragedies. David was the middle child of 11, and his oldest sibling was Hannah, who died from pneumonia in 1918 at the age of 12. Her loss was devastating to my grandmother. Grandmother's next five children were boys: Ben, Julius ("Blackie" and sometimes "Jule" in Dave's letters), Max, Lawrence, and then David. After David was the next girl, my aunt, Frieda.

Frieda was a dancer but also worked in the defense industry for a short time. She married very young and her son Billy, was Hyman and Eva Rosa's first grandchild. Frieda divorced and was later killed on a trip to Buffalo, New York to visit her new fiancé's family in the summer of 1942. Bill eventually went to live with his father. The family kept in touch with Bill for a while, but ultimately, the contact dwindled to practically nothing. Grandma's loss of both her second daughter and meaningful contact with her first grandchild must have taken a heavy toll.[8]

1943

1943 must have been a hard year for my grandmother. In addition to grieving Frieda, many other stressful events occurred. On January 30, the *USS Chicago* was sunk in the Battle of Rennell Island. My uncle Launie was on that ship. News of the sinking probably reached the US shores before news of the fate of individual sailors. Fortunately, Launie survived the sinking,

Uncle Jack entered the Army Air Forces in 1943 and Uncle Lawrence joined the Merchant Marine. Grandma now had four sons serving. Life was not to get easier for her, in July, Uncle Max lost his eye in an industrial accident and on July 9, the invasion of Sicily began. Uncle Dave was part of the initial invasion when the Third Battalion of the 504 Parachute Infantry Regiment joined with the 505 PIR to drop into Sicily to protect the beach during the shore landing. Anxiety was high at home until news reached the family that Dave was alive. He continued to fight in Sicily and Italy during 1943 and early 1944.

The terrible losses and accidents would take a toll on any mother. Ultimately, all the previous losses combined with the loss of David in late 1944 were more than my grandmother could take. I believe the compounding effect of losing her first two daughters, and then her favorite son was just overwhelming and affected her and the family for many decades.

Another factor in the aftermath of World War II was the effect of Launie's PTSD on the family. He was Radioman 1st Class (RM1C), US Navy, and lived through eight naval battles. Launie cared for his mother after Grandpa died in 1952 until she died in 1960. Although there aren't specific incidents recorded, based on my observations of him until his death in 1982, the impact of his PTSD on their lives must have been significant.

CHAPTER THREE

DAVID - THE APPLE OF HIS MOTHER'S EYE

October 31, 1915 – September 28, 1944

Dave was the middle child of 11. He was outgoing and had strong relationships with all his brothers and sisters. My father and several of my cousins said that David was the apple of his mother's eye.

During his time at David Starr Jordan High School in the 30s

the school was integrated, with large percentages of white, black, and Asian students. The yearbook from his senior year class of 1934 shows a diverse group of friends.

Dave's nickname, Rosie, was evident even then. The nickname Rosie has been the fate of many generations of the Rosenkrantz men, including myself and my son, (sometimes spelled Rosy or Rosey) at some time in

Dave's Senior Class picture at Jordan High School in Watts.

their lives. During my college and General Motors years I was happily called Rosey by everyone who knew me personally. When I left GM to teach at California State Polytechnic University, Pomona (a.k.a. Cal Poly Pomona) names were more formal, and I left the informal moniker behind.

Dave's high school report cards don't reveal much of a scholarly side. However, he was active in football, glee club, and drama. After graduation he worked for the Civilian Conservation Corps (CCC) for a while. Later, he worked at the General Motors Assembly Plant in South Gate, the same one I worked at later, adjacent to Watts. Dave's job as a driver was to move the cars around after they came off the final line. I did not know he had worked there until long after I left General Motors, but observed drivers performing this job for over 15 years. There were some years when my plant visits would have taken me through his former work area daily. I would have cherished visualizing him driving cars off the line or into one of the repair holes.

Dave in the Civilian Conservation Corp

David was drafted into the Army in January 1942.

Irv Spector

One of Dave's best friends growing up was Irv Spector (Spec), who lived one house away   Dave and Spec both loved sketching and cartooning and each ended up in the Army. However, Irv worked for the Army Signal Corps making training films and doing some cartooning

After the war Irv had a career in the animation industry and became famous working for Hanna Barbera and MGM. He helped produce some notable animated features such as *The Lorax, The Grinch Who Stole Christmas, Scooby Doo,* and *The Jetsons.* During the 50s Irv had a comic strip titled *Coogy.* In several of his strips, he embedded features to honor and remember his friend David Rosenkrantz.

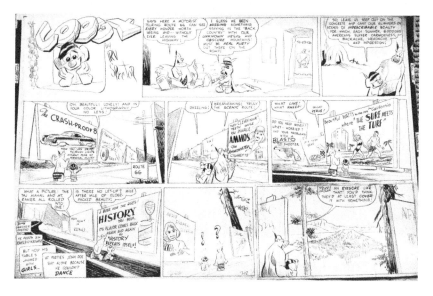

Example of one of Irv Spector's comic strips referencing both David and their hometown of Watts, CA. The lower-left frame mentions "CHEES-O-KRANTZ." The right middle frame mentions WATTS.

Dave and Irv liked to sketch, and Dave sent some home. Dave also drew a wall full of portraits of un-known people; it's obvious he was a talented artist. Irv was stationed in New York City and Dave visited him once while on leave from Ft. Bragg.

Dave drew these sketches in England.
(photo courtesy Ted Finkbeiner)

FOUR SONS IN WWII

My Grandmother had four sons actively serving during World War II. Launie was already a radioman in the Navy when David joined the Army. Lawrence (Larry), served during the war in the Merchant Marine. Jack served in the Army Air Forces training airplane mechanics at Fort Bliss. A fifth son, my father, Harry, joined the Army in 1946 and was sent to Italy as part of the Occupation Forces. Ultimately, five Rosenkrantz brothers were involved with World War II, three of them in harm's way. It must have burdened her greatly.

Eva Rosa was a Four-Star Mother

Dave's WWII Siblings (L-R): Jack (Army Air Forces), Harry (Army), Goldie (Janet) (Douglas Aircraft), Launie (Navy), Lawrence (Merchant Marine). Circa 1950.

Mrs. Rosenkrantz Proud of her Four Servicemen, Los Angeles
Daily News, July 16, 1943

CHAPTER FIVE

MAKING A DIFFERENCE – FAMILY HISTORY AND HIGHLIGHTS

The following brief profiles of Dave's ten brothers and sisters will help readers and relatives learn more about the Rosenkrantz Family and help us value their lives and struggles even more. (in birth order)

Hannah (1906 – June 19, 1918)

Hannah was the firstborn child. Sadly, she did not live very long; her death from pneumonia at age 12 in 1918 probably indicates that she was a victim of the Influenza Epidemic of 1918. This pandemic killed 50 million people worldwide and affected 25% of the US population.[9]

Circa 1914 (L-R Standing: Ben, Max, Julius, Hannah. Seated: Lawrence)

Benjamin (January 12, 1908 – January 6, 1996)

Ben led a fascinating life and has produced the largest family branch to date. He married Ramona (Ramona De la Cruz), a Mexican-American born in Texas. According to my father, Ben learned to speak Spanish fluently as a teenager and loved the Spanish language. Ben and Ramona raised three children, Rudy, Ruby, and Olivia to be bilingual also. The cousins all have close-knit families and cherish their Jewish/Mexican heritage.

Among other things, Ben was a taxi driver in Los Angeles for many years. Ramona owned a clothing store on 103rd Street in Watts. Sadly, her store was burned down during the Watts Riots in August 1965.[10] I visited her shortly after the loss of her store and during that visit a black family stopped by to repay her for some credit she had extended to them at her store. The father apologized for the riot and thanked her for her generosity. Ramona was very compassionate and regularly extended credit to people in the community who needed to buy school clothes for their children. Ben's great-grandson, Pastor Rudy Topete, helped officiate Uncle Dave's funeral in 2018.

Hot Air

To the Editor: My young son, who likes toy balloons, sometimes blows them up too big and breaks them. The other morning, when I found a flat tire on my car, his extraordinary lung power came in very handy.

As shown in the enclosed photo (*see cut*), his sister acted as his assistant. By pumping his leg, she increased the muscular action on the lung tissues, producing a better-balanced and more evenly distributed respiratory condition.

Also, by pumping first one leg and then the other, she raised the nitrogen content of the expelled carbon dioxide, which might otherwise have oxidized the inside of the inner tube and made it wear unevenly.

You may note in the picture that the tire is shown inflated. I found out later that the children had been working on the wrong tire.

Ben Rosenkrantz
Los Angeles, Cal.

Can other readers top this?—Ed.

Letter to the Editor reflecting Ben's sense of humor

Julius (Blackie) (January 27, 1910 – December 3, 1996)

Blackie's first wife was Bonnie; their daughter is my cousin Donetta (Doni). Doni has been very helpful in providing letters and other memorabilia over the 20-year journey of compiling information for this book.

Wedding picture Julius (Blackie) (age 24) and first wife, Bonnie (age 18)

Blackie worked for Universal Studios for 47 years as a Property Master. He worked with many acclaimed actors and on many famous movies; at least 27 films between 1934 and 1973. His name appears in the credits for many of the movies.[11] Like the rest of the Rosenkrantz brothers, Blackie was a very nice, soft-spoken man. He told me once that most of the actors were not easy or fun to work with, but he had become friends with some over the years. My father told me that one of Blackie's friends was the great horror movie actor, Boris Karloff, famous for his roles in the classic films *The Mummy* and *Frankenstein*.[12]. Blackie once introduced my father to Boris Karloff and Dad said Karloff was a very kind, gentle person.

An interesting story I cannot resist passing along was one Uncle Blackie told me once after he had retired and was living in Newberry Springs, CA. Blackie described

Blackie in 1957 on the set with Jimmy Stewart during the filming of the movie The Spirit of St. Louis

Blackie and my Cousin Doni (age 11) on the set of the movie Singapore in 1947

working on a movie with Sidney Poitier during the sixties. Sidney was born in Florida but raised in the Bahamas and was one of the most successful actors of all time, as well as a diplomat.[13] Management at Universal Studios thought that my uncle's name, Blackie, would be offensive to Sidney and other black actors. They decided that everyone should start calling my uncle by his given name, Julius. When Sidney Poitier heard what was going on, he got upset and made it clear to Universal management that my uncle's name was Blackie! According to Blackie, Sidney requested later from Universal that he work on more of Sidney's movies.

Blackie was very close to Dave and was the one who saved most of Dave's surviving letters. As you read Dave's letters, you will see that Blackie sent him many things over the years: candy, fruitcakes, photos, and clothing, to name a few items. Photos from Hollywood were a big hit with Dave's Army buddies.

Blackie had a long marriage to his second wife, Eva. Eva was the only one of his wives I ever met, and she was delightful whenever we were together.

Max (Feb 12, 1912 – March 1, 2006)

Max Rosenkrantz

Max and his wife, Julia, had three children—my cousins Barbara, Alan, and Lucille (Lucy). We lived a half-mile from them from 1958 to 1967 and my cousins and I attended the same junior high and high schools. Max wanted his children to play musical instruments; Barbara played the piano; Alan played the steel guitar and Lucy played the guitar. Alan made a living for many years playing professionally.

Max had lost part of one hand during a fire when he was very young. While working at a factory as an adult, he lost an eye in an industrial accident. He was a gentle, compassionate man with a heart for the Mexican population. Whenever he could, he would help others.

Max tried to enlist and serve his country also, but because of his wounded hand, the military did not think he could handle a rifle and rejected him. He did not let that discourage him, however, and joined the CCC where he became a highly regarded chef. He was an excellent cook all of his life. After losing his eye, the factory promised him a job for the rest of his life. Unfortunately, they shut down and could not keep their promise. Poor Uncle Max, with three little ones at home he had no job.

Once again, he didn't let that get him down. He went into construction and worked on several multi-million-dollar projects, mostly water treatment plants. Max was also a gifted mechanic who kept the fleet of work trucks running for the construction company as well as maintaining the field generators, crane engines, and other equipment. When a truck or crane broke down on site, he was the go-to man. Max was also a gifted carpenter and often built things on the construction site as well as at home, including a patio and huge storage shed/workshop. He was a true man's man. Max converted to

Christianity in his 70s—which is very rare. Max lived to the age of 94...the longest life of any of the 11 Rosenkrantz children. He remained very close to his brother, Lawrence, throughout their lives.

Lawrence (September 29, 1913 – November 19, 2003) US Merchant Marines

Merchant Marine Lawrence Rosenkrantz

Lawrence (a.k.a. Larry) was Dave's next older brother. He led a fascinating life of adventure and entrepreneurial attempts. These endeavors included fighting against the Socialist Dictator Franco in Spain, running a jewelry store, joining the Merchant Marine during World War II, and attempting various entrepreneurial enterprises in Mexico. Lawrence even had a patent for an invention; what is known today as a *seed strip* or *seed tape*. He was never able to sell his idea, and when the patent period ended others were able to use it without paying any licensing or royalty fees.

In 1937, Lawrence traveled to Spain and join up with the Communists to fight against the socialist dictator Franco. On-line records show he ended up working in a hospital for the Communist military.[14] He decided that the Communists were no better than the Socialists, so, according to both historical records and the conversation I had with him, he deserted. His story was that the Spanish underground helped him get out of the country and onto a boat to England. According to him, while on his voyage to England he made friends with an executive from General Motors who was on vacation. The GM executive paid for his voyage home by ship.

Lawrence also spent some time on cargo ships working his way around the world. He told me that he got tired of people stealing his books. Apparently stealing other people's reading material was a common occurrence on ships. He thought it would be a good idea to buy some Spanish language books and a Spanish language dictionary as he figured people wouldn't take them. He said it didn't work because he wasn't able to learn Spanish from the dictionary.

Before joining the Merchant Marine, Lawrence opened a jewelry shop just outside of Universal Studios to sell jewelry to people in the movie industry. The venture was funded by his brother, Blackie. Unfortunately, this was during wartime and not a good time for the jewelry business. My father said disposable income in the movie industry was not enough to sustain Lawrence's jewelry business.

After the jewelry business failed, Lawrence joined the Merchant Marine in 1943. He told me a story once of the Liberty ship he was on being under attack. Somehow, he was involved with the action regarding which way the ship should change direction—but I never fully understood the story. He wrote home about being in the engine room of a Liberty ship, which required him to stay in one hot place and watch some gauges. Although he was bored and uncomfortable, he seemed OK with having a safe assignment.

Lawrence Rosenkrantz at Lawrence Gem & Jewelry Company in Los Angeles, California

While Lawrence's first attempt to learn Spanish failed, he did end up living in Guadalajara, Mexico, for about 20 or 30 years during the 50s to 70s and learned to speak Spanish fluently. It's unknown what he did there other than more attempts to have a successful business venture. One business was selling perfume.

His most unfortunate business venture was probably the purchase of an asbestos mine about one year before asbestos was declared a carcinogen and banned from use in building materials.

Lawrence was a quiet, gentle man who spent his last years living in Los Angeles at various houses and staying in touch with Uncle Max. He died peacefully at age 90 and is at the Riverside National Cemetery with his four brothers who also served in World War II or the Occupation Forces.

Frieda Clabaugh (December 13, 1917 – buried August 17, 1942)

Frieda Rosenkrantz Clabaugh

Frieda was a dancer. She married around age 18 and her son, Billy, was the first grandchild born to Hyman and Eva Rosa. Frieda also worked for the defense industry in Los Angeles. After divorcing her first husband, she engaged to marry again and traveled to Buffalo, NY with her fiancé to meet his family. Tragically she was hit by a car and killed at age 24. She was buried at the Mount Zion Jewish Cemetery in Los Angeles, CA, on August 17, 1942.

Billy initially lived with Frieda's sister, Goldie (Janet) and his grandmother, Eva Rosa. Goldie got sick, and Bill's father took him and raised him. Eventually, Bill lost touch with his mother's family. This was another source of sadness for Eva Rosa. About 20 years ago I was able to locate Bill and reestablish contact with the family. It was wonderful to reconnect and get to know his family.

Frieda Rosenkrantz was a dancer. During WWII she also worked in the defense industry.

Launie (March 19, 1920 – November 3, 1983) US Navy

L-R: Ben, Launie Rosenkrantz

Launie joined the Navy before World War II (April 1940) and served actively until after the war. He was discharged in August 1946. His first ship assignment was on the *USS Chicago (CA-29)*, a heavy cruiser, where he started his career as a radioman. The *USS Chicago* was at sea during the attack on Pearl

Harbor on December 7, 1941—having just sailed out a few days prior.

It was evident that Uncle Launie had PTSD even though the condition was not being treated much in those days. I once asked him if he could tell me about his time in the Navy. His reaction was something I will never forget. He jumped up out of his chair and was out of the room as fast as he could go. I never asked him that question again. Later, I told my dad what happened and learned about Launie's experience with the sinking of the *USS Chicago*.

The *USS Chicago* saw a lot of action in World War II. A Japanese torpedo damaged the *USS Chicago* earlier in the war and the ship was taken to San Francisco for repairs, after which it returned to the South Pacific. The final battle was called the Battle of Rennell Island in the Coral Sea. Shortly after arriving, on January 29, 1943, a couple of torpedoes from Japanese bombers hit and disabled the *Chicago* killing over 50 sailors on board. Launie survived that torpedo hit, but—according to my father—most of his close friends were killed. The ship was disabled and under tow for repairs. The next day another Japanese patrol spotted it and decided to try and sink it. Even though most of the dive bombers were shot down in the attempt, the Japanese succeeded in making several critical torpedo hits that caused the *USS Chicago* to sink within 20 minutes. Those who were able had to abandon ship. Many below decks were unable to get out and perished as the *Chicago* went down. My uncle was lucky enough to be rescued. He survived that experience physically but had severe PTSD for the rest of his life. (More is discussed about Uncle Launie's wartime experiences and how it affected the family in Part 4.)

My father said Launie possessed a wire that came across the radio room announcing that Pearl Harbor was under attack. Unfortunately, I never was able to find it. However, my cousin, Alan (Max's son), discovered a teletype from a Navy ship warning of Japanese torpedo bombers heading toward the *USS Chicago* in January 1943. Those planes eventually attacked the ship. How Launie ended up with that wire isn't known. Perhaps he visited the radio room of the ship that rescued him and somehow obtained the copy.

Other ships he served on (in rough order based on muster rolls and missing some transfers) were the *USS Prince William, USS Midway (CVE-63),* later renamed the *USS St. Lo), USS Fanshaw Bay (CVE-70), USS Cook Inlet, USS Saratoga (CV3), USS Natoma Bay, USS Fanshaw Bay* (again), *USS Casco (AVP-12),* and *USS Chilton.*

I grew up knowing my Uncle Launie and seeing him frequently. He was employed by Rockwell in a research lab working on thin film deposition. He was laid off in the aerospace downturn in the early 70s and never recovered professionally. His last years of work were performing receiving inspection of electronic components.

Launie also suffered from Parkinson's Disease in the last few years of his life. The last year or two he lived with my parents until he passed away at the age of 63. He was generous to his nieces and nephews. He tried many hobbies to fill up his life that was dominated by PTSD. Whenever he got tired of a hobby, he would generously hand over whatever he had to one of us. My siblings, cousins and I accumulated many musical instruments and electronic devices. I ended up with a five-string banjo, electric typewriter, and one of the original Heathkit computers—all in working condition. I still have the banjo and typewriter. Sadly, my parents sold the Heathkit computer (a collector's item by then) at a garage sale without checking with me.

In early 2019, my sister, Sandy, and I obtained the Official Military Personnel File (OMPF) for Uncle Launie and researched some of the ships he was on. One interesting finding related to the *USS Chilton,* his last ship. In the summer of 1946, the *USS Chilton* supported atomic bomb testing at the Bikini Atoll.[15] Further research on the effects of radiation on those exposed during World War II suggests that Uncle Launie's Parkinson's Disease could be related to exposure to radiation in World War II.[16]

Goldie (Janet Norman) (June 25, 1922 – Feb 3, 2011)

Goldie was married three times; the first time to Roland Allaire. Her second and longest marriage was to Tom Woods. Her final marriage was to Matti Nuutinen, a contractor from Finland. They legally changed their names to Matt and Janet Norman.

While married to Tom Woods they adopted my cousin, Frieda Lynne Woods Andros. She was named after Aunt Frieda and was a year younger than me. We grew up together. Frieda didn't like her first name and eventually decided to go by her middle name, Lynne. Janet and Tom divorced when Lynne was a teenager and I didn't see her much after that.

L-R: Eva Rosa, Goldie Woods (Janet Norman), and Frieda Lynne Woods Andros. Frieda was named after her Aunt Frieda. She never liked the name and later went by her middle name, Lynne. (about 1955)

Lynne was happily married with three children and many grandchildren. Her daughter, Angela (Ange), became an NFL cheerleader and is a very successful dance and cheer instructor and coach, with many of her teams performing successfully in national competitions. Tragically, Lynne died of cancer at the age of 59.

During World War II Janet worked in the aerospace industry in Los Angeles, assembling cockpits in fighter planes. I asked her once which models she worked on, but she couldn't remember.

She moved to Las Vegas while married to Matti. After divorcing him, she lived in Big Bear, CA, for a while, but relocated to the Mojave Desert near Barstow to be near Julius. She was very crafty and worked at Calico Ghost Town[17] near Barstow for many years. Janet was also a talented oil painter and was active with the artist community and Chamber of Commerce in Newberry Springs. She won many local awards for her art. In her last few years, my wife, Judy, drove out to Barstow every week or two to check on her. Janet and her boyfriend, Bob, were avid sports fans and watched many games together. She was the last of Dave's siblings to pass away.

Jack (December 8, 1924 – February 15, 2002) Army Air Forces

Corporal Jack Rosenkrantz

Jack was another soft-spoken, gentle Rosenkrantz brother. He joined the Army Air Forces in August 1943 at age 19 and trained in airplane mechanics. After the military, Jack stayed single, working various jobs during his 20s and 30s. He lived with Launie, Lawrence, and Grandma for several years in Santa Fe Springs. He had a motorcycle and sometimes gave me thrilling rides before the days of helmets and safety laws. When I graduated from high school, Uncle Jack took me to a department store and bought me a suit. as a graduation present.

According to my father, Jack had a childhood crush on their neighbor, Betty. Betty's uncle was Irv Spector, one of Dave's best friends. However, when they were young, Betty had no interest in Jack. She married someone else and had two children. When Jack was about 40, he heard that Betty had divorced and looked her up. They fell in love and got married. Betty was a Christian, and somewhere along the way in their relationship Jack converted to Christianity. Jack was a devoted Christian for the rest of his life and touched many people with his gentle spirit. He worked for many years as a custodian at a local hospital. He had several bouts with brain cancer and died at 77. Jack and Betty are buried together at the Riverside National Cemetery.

Harry (January 17, 1928 – November 10, 2009) US Army

Private Harry Rosenkrantz, US Army.

Harry was the youngest of the 11 children and also my father. He told me that growing up, he was just that little kid running around the house with very little concern from anyone else. There was one exception—his brother David. David was very active in making sure my father made it to accordion lessons and practiced diligently. Even after David joined the Army, he would write to my father to make sure he was on track. Dad never offered any information about David or things that happened in his early life. However, if I asked him a specific question, he would answer it if he could. Upon reflection, I realize that my father must have grieved over the loss of David but never let it show too much.

Harry was too young to join the Army during World War II but joined in 1946 at 18. He served in the occupation forces in Italy, guarding the border with Yugoslavia at Trieste. He told me that he was actually in paratrooper training, and one day they asked for volunteers for something. He thought it would look good if he volunteered. They took the volunteers out of paratrooper training and sent them to Italy. He was there for about nine months, then discharged and sent home. He said his biggest regret was not taking advantage of his time in Italy to visit historical sites. For example, he visited Florence but did not take the time to visit the Sistine Chapel.

After serving in the Army, Harry, married, Jeanette Lucille Rand on September 24, 1948. After they got married, they lived with Goldie and her husband, Tom, in South Gate, CA, next to Watts. In 1949, when I was five months old, my parents bought a little house in Norwalk, CA, using the GI Bill. When I was nine years old, they bought the home my Uncle Launie originally owned, and we moved 1.5 miles to Santa Fe Springs. My parents moved to Yucaipa, CA, in 1967 and Highland, CA, in 1971.

My parents were involved in the community when we lived in Santa Fe Springs. The first thing I remember was my father joining the Los Angeles Sheriffs Emergency Reserve. He went through a modified police training course and worked on events and activities to take some of the pressure off of the regular deputy sheriffs.

My parents were active in politics, especially in the anti-communist movement. Then, through some neighbors, they decided to visit the local Baptist church. They ended up becoming Christians, joining the church, and were active Christians for the rest of their lives. My father was a deacon at the church in Santa Fe Springs and an elder in a church in Yucaipa. My sister, Diana, and I had become Christians four years before my parents through attending Vacation Bible School in Norwalk, CA.

Harry ran for elected office three times in his life. He ran for City Council in Santa Fe Springs on the platform of stopping the city from taking of property from homeowners for non-public (a.k.a. urban renewal) use under the claim of eminent domain.[18] He ran for School Board while they lived in Yucaipa, and he ran for Water Board when he lived in Highland. He narrowly lost the city council and school board elections and did not come close to winning the water board election. In both close elections he learned a lot about dirty tricks.[19]

My father deeply loved my mother, Jeanette. For over 51 years, they had a wonderful life together. I was the oldest child with three younger sisters—Diana, Gina, and Sandra (Sandy)—and a younger brother, Harry, Jr. My father worked in production control for several companies and then around 1970, he and my mother bought a Dairy Queen in Highland, CA. They successfully operated it for 11 years before selling it when the market was good. My sister Diana died unexpectedly at the age of 35 from pulmonary emboli. The whole family took this very hard—especially my parents. My mother died in 1999.

My father remained in sales of some sort for the next 20 years after selling the Dairy Queen. He fully retired at age 72—not long after my mother died. He moved up to Klamath Falls, OR, where he lived with my sister, Gina and her family for the rest of his life. He died from cancer at age 81 in Klamath Falls, OR.

My father was a good role model, and everyone who knew him loved him. He grew up in Watts, and most of his childhood friends were black. I am thankful we were raised without racial prejudice. Two incidents have always stuck with me. When I was in high school, my father ran a small printing plant in South Gate for a while. He said at dinner that he needed to hire someone for a job opening. The next day he mentioned that he had hired someone. I was curious about how he did that since I didn't know anything about business or hiring people. I asked him how he found people and his response was, "It's easy. I look in the phone book for a church in Watts. Then I call them up and ask if they know of someone who needs a job."

Diana, Gina, Harry, and Phil Rosenkrantz (abt 1958). This is one of my favorite childhood pictures.

Another interesting story is about my name, Phillip. When I was about 50 years old, I curiously asked my dad why I was named Phillip. His middle name was Phillip, but he had chosen it himself.[20] My father said that one of his friends growing up was Philip Hurlic.[21] Philip was a black child actor who starred in the famous 1938 movie, *The Adventures of Tom Sawyer*[22], as Young Jim. I have liked my name more ever since he told me that.

An interesting note about names is that he also told me my name was going to be David in honor of my Uncle David. However, my grandmother strongly objected. She believed in the tradition (superstition) that it was bad luck to name a child in memory of someone who was still living—which she believed David was. Respectful of her wishes, they named me Phillip instead. Note that a year later my Aunt Goldie (Janet) named her daughter Frieda in memory of her sister who had died.

My father, Harry Rosenkrantz, Uncle Harvey Rand, my mother Jeanette Rand, Aunt Maybelle Rand (abt early 1948)

PART TWO

MILITARY SERVICE

Paratrooper David Rosenkrantz

Dave's letters are rich in personality and context; 49 of the 56 surviving notes are included in chronological order within these pages. The letters are just as he wrote them with only minor spelling corrections. They are interesting, fun, and allow the reader to get to know David on a personal level.

CHAPTER SIX

YOU'RE IN THE ARMY NOW

David was drafted and inducted into the Army on January 29, 1942 at Fort MacArthur in Los Angeles, California. He then went to Camp Wolters in Texas for basic training.[23] After that, he was transferred to Fort Benning, Georgia for airborne training. Upon completing his parachute training, David was assigned to the 82nd Airborne Division, 504 Parachute Infantry Regiment (PIR), H Company.

At Fort Benning David's training was devoted to learning how to jump out of a plane, earn his paratrooper wings, and begin combat training. He was then transferred to Fort Bragg, North Carolina for more combat training. Their training separated Airborne paratroopers from all other military fighting forces such as the infantry and the Rangers. Dave wrote home about his training and thoughts during those periods and related a bit about the weapons they were using and his successes. His fascinating letters provide an exciting perspective on what he and the other paratroopers were going through before their first jump in Sicily in July 1943. Uncle Dave's letters and his military service make me proud to be his nephew and part of the Rosenkrantz Family.

Paratroopers

The Paratrooper was new to the American combat arsenal. General James M. Gavin's opening paragraphs in his 1947 book, *Airborne Warfare* (reprinted 2014) said the following:

Sicily in July of 1943 was the birthplace of American Airborne technique. It was, as well, the crucible into which were thrown the brainstorms, the cocktail celebrations, and the intensely cherished unorthodox combat tactics of a young Army. Theories originally conceived, nurtured and brought to apparent maturity without the test of battle were exposed to their test. How well they fared, how well they fought, and what our airborne forces accomplished are questions not even partially answered to date. But the toddling tot that later became the First Allied Airborne Army was born in Sicily and survived a very rugged delivery.

The plan of invasion called for one parachute combat team of the reinforced 82nd Airborne Division to drop between Caltagirone, where large enemy reserves were known to be, and the 1st Division beaches. After the D-Day landings the combat team was to be built up by successive air and sea lifts in the zone of the Seventh Army and participate in the conquest of the island. (Gavin, Airborne Warfare, 2014)

Paratroopers were a new warfare concept and some military leaders were skeptical of their benefit. General Gavin was expert in figuring out how and when to deploy paratroopers. During the year before the invasion of Sicily, many tactics and equipment options were developed and tested. Several of Dave's letters talk about how the paratroopers figured out how to jump with their weapons ready to fight.

The 504 PIR had a year of training at Fort Bragg and in North Africa to prepare for their first combat jump. Dave was trained in the use of mortars and eventually led a top-rated mortar squad. He was also rated Expert marksman—one of the few in H Company who earned that distinction; his letters talked about that as much as the censors would allow. He also wrote about being the subject of a training film.

The jump into Sicily was a notably significant combat jump by American paratroopers. The German paratroopers (Fallschirmjäger) had already jumped into Crete in 1941.[24] While the German invasion was not considered successful, experts say the German paratroopers proved their value. The Sicily jump had some major flaws but was successful enough to demonstrate the value of paratroopers to most naysayers. Sadly, friendly fire shot down many American planes filled with paratroopers. Over 400 paratroopers died on the way to the drop zones in Sicily.

On the other hand, the mis-dropped paratroopers were extraordinarily effective and caused havoc throughout the region. They cut power and communication lines, destroyed equipment, and attacked enemy outposts. It was discovered after the war that the Italians and Germans overestimated the number of paratroopers fighting against them. The Battle of Biazza Ridge was a significant success story proving the value of the paratroopers.

It is difficult to imagine what must be going through a paratrooper's mind as they board a plane for a combat jump, fly to the drop zone, and then jump out into an unknown combat situation against one of the fiercest enemies in history. While they are in the plane and lining up to jump, they have no idea what it looks like below until they exit the door. The following passage is from the book *The First Men In* by Ed Ruggero. (Ruggero, E. 2006. HarperCollins, New York p. 126) Paratrooper Ken Russell tells his story of jumping into France on D-Day. His gory tale is a good example of the terror that thousands of American paratroopers experienced in World War II...and they did this for us.

> *F Company troopers got the green light as they were approaching Ste. Mere Eglise. When Ken Russell got to the doorway, the first thing he saw was the beacon of the large fire. He had his first jolt of real fear when he realized that he might land in the burning building. Russell had an eerie view of the entire scene during the few seconds it took the parachute to descend. Charles Blankenship, the PFC from North Carolina, was drawn toward the fire by the drafts. He screamed once as he plunged into the two-story Inferno. Russell cringed as he looked down from 200 feet on the heads of the Germans, who are unshouldering their rifles and firing into the air. Ridiculous as it was, he tried to hide behind his reserve parachute, strapped across his belly. His friends Cadish, Tlapa, and Bryant got hung up*

on the telephone poles or on the tall Linden and Chestnut trees that line the square. Shot dead before they could react, they hung there as if crucified. Russell looked down past his feet and saw the church below him. He pulled on his risers, hoping to slip clear of the building, but hit hard on the steep slate roof and began rolling. He was a tangle of equipment and parachute as he rolled and could not stop himself. Finally, his chute caught the top of the roof, and he came to a stop right at the edge. (Ruggero, 2006)

CHAPTER SEVEN

JUMP SCHOOL IN FT. BENNING, GEORGIA

David arrived at Fort Benning around June 17, 1942 and wrote the following letter to his brother, Julius (Blackie or Jule):

Dear Blackie and Bonnie,

Here I am at Fort Benning Georgia after two miserable days and nights on a hot, dirty, slow train. It was a Pullman first class, but it surely wasn't enjoyable. There were three cars and a diner on our train. We sat around on sidings more than we moved. We heard a lot about the rough training here but we'll just have to find out for ourselves. And four weeks isn't very long to find out. This is a lot nicer country here than Texas, but just as hot. Right now it's good to look around and see tall pine trees instead of scrub oak. I'll let you know more about what's cooking down here in my next letter. Don't be afraid to ask me any questions. Good luck.

Yours
Dave

> *Here I am at Fort Benning Georgia after two miserable days and nights on a hot, dirty, slow train.*

Training at Ft. Benning was devoted first to learning how to be a parachutist. After a month of rigorous training—including using a 250 ft. tower—each paratrooper had to complete five jumps in five days to graduate from jump school and receive his paratrooper wings. Dave discussed this process in several letters, providing interesting details about qualifying for jump wings. He doesn't mention the wash-out rate during paratrooper training. Each string of a dozen or so paratroopers is called a "stick." It is critical that they go out the door as close together as possible so they land close together and can regroup on the ground. A few-second delay at the plane door can separate the men in the stick by a significant distance. If a paratrooper balks at the door during training, they can be washed out.

A thread throughout Dave's letters is Blackie's connection to the Hollywood movie industry. Blackie sent photos, candy, and other items to David to enjoy and share with his friends. The men appreciated unusual items sent from home.

July 23, 1942
Jule,

I sure am glad to receive your letter, but sorry to hear you're in a hospital. Hospitals are no fun. I hope you are a lot better by now. You'll have to take it easy and leave all the hard work to me, and boy, I sure get it. When they said the paratroops would be tough, they weren't kidding. All except this week when we make our five jumps to qualify. We jump in the morning and repack the chute in the evening after supper for the next jump.

> When they said the paratroops would be tough, they weren't kidding.

I was at Camp Wolters when the pictures for [Jane] Russell got there. He told me he was going to send you a letter of thanks. I left the next day so I don't know what happened. He might have lost your address, but I think he lost his gratitude after I left. That was a swell bunch of pictures too.

This stuff of jumping out of an airplane at 1500 ft is quite the stuff. The first one was the hardest for me. Nearly every one of us has one jump that takes all our nerve. It's usually either the first second or third jump. Sometimes the instructors here who have had lots of jumps will sweat one out.

Today one of the men sitting opposite me in the plane was having a tough time. He was tense and nervous, and the sweat was dripping off of his face. I was the last man out. There were twenty-four men in the plane and we made two mass jumps of 12 men each. There is no falling sensation when we leave the plane if our body position is okay. There is no jerk when the chute opens but when otherwise - wow! There are lots of stiff necks and strawberries on them. I got them too although not very bad.

Leaving the plane isn't as important as landing. The air here is bumpy, especially close to the ground where it is most dangerous. On my first jump I was coming down swell until I got close to the ground and suddenly, I got swinging back and forth under my chute and did I spread out on the ground. I should have tumbled but I hurt my knees last week and thought my best bet was to just spread out on the ground. My next three landings were easy. I came straight down and lit on my feet and as I was relaxed I just sat down on the ground. Some of the men try to make standing landings but I don't like that idea. That's what sprains ankles and breaks bones. Today one of the chutes didn't open right and the guy instead of using his reserve tried to make the main chute open all the way. It finally did about a hundred feet from the ground.

I will graduate Saturday, get my diploma and wings, then I will move to a new outfit. So I'll send my new address from there.

So long and good luck, Dave

On July 25, 1942, David graduated from jump school and received his wings.

July 25, 1942
Dear Jule,

I'm finally a qualified parachutist. I got my fifth jump off ok but I was more nervous than my three previous jumps. It was quite an affair. I was the fifth man in a 12-man mass, and when the jump-master said "go" the first man went okay but the second man stalled in the door, but not for long. A jump-master on each side of him just grabbed an arm and the seat of his pants and out he went. Then the rest of us followed OK, but the second or two the man stalled seemed like a whole lot longer. The fifth jump is the first time I remember putting my hands on my reserve but I must have done it before.

We were given diplomas and wings showing we are qualified parachutists. It doesn't seem possible that I have dropped a total of about 6000 ft through the air but I did! All I got out of it was a bruise on one elbow and a jar when I hit hard on my last jump. That doesn't include the training on the 250 ft. towers.

Did I tell you about the shock harness? Well on the second training tower ride we are raised up 150 ft from the ground. We are suspended in a parachute harness and are in a prone position with our heads about 2 ft lower than our feet. At the command "Go" we pull a ripcord drop 15 feet, count one-thousand, two-thousand, three-thousand, change the rip cord to the other hand all at the same time. It's quite a test. At a hundred and fifty feet the 4-foot by 6-foot mat on the ground looks like a handkerchief.

I am still here at Fort Benning, but I got a new address.

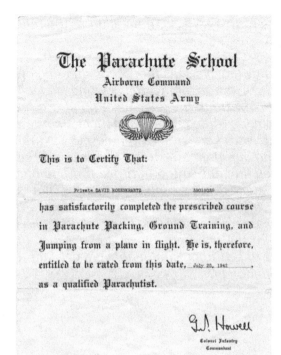

This is a combat outfit now and the fun is over. Now the real serious starts. We will get lots of combat training and rough too. From now on it's learn to kill or be killed. Sometimes I am sorry I grad-uated from high school.

Well, Jule, I hope you are home by now and feeling a lot better.

Write soon,
Dave

After parachute training, combat training began. Dave's next letter describes the physical aspects and weapons training. The paratroopers were given rigorous training all the way around.

August 8, 1942
Dear Jule,

I was glad to receive your letter but sorry as hell to hear about the divorce. I suppose that the Army sometimes is better than a bad marriage. I am glad you're back to work. You take it easy and I'll do the hard work.

Next Monday we start shooting on the rifle range with the M1 rifle—Garand to you. We shoot for record and the three highest scores in each Company rate a furlough. I am going to try like hell.

I got a letter today from Frieda. She is in Buffalo New York in case you didn't know. She says she can't get used to the weather and people out there. Everything is a lot different from LA.

I got a letter from home too, it seems that Ma is showing off some pictures I sent of our training towers and of men jumping from a plane. I think the folks are taking it a lot better than I expected. I didn't let them know about it though until the addresses here started giving me away. I bet you think jumping out of a plane is the toughest part of our training. Well we thought so too until we finished our jump training and started our combat training. That 3 miles of double time more or less every day sure is rough. Then after regular training we have two hours of athletics after supper or go to the training towers for practice in night jumps. We get to bed about midnight. We get half a day Saturday and Sunday off.

Jump Towers at Ft. Benning, Georgia

As far as I know, the folks haven't heard from Launie since last November. I write him a letter about every 3 or 4 weeks and tell him what I am doing. I hope he gets them okay. He was a radio operator the last time we heard. I imagine he's seen some excitement since the war started.

The war department is reducing the price of the theaters here in Camp from 20 to 15 cents. Tomorrow Abbott and Costello in Pardon My Sarong is playing. So you see we get pretty late pictures. The theater is actually the coolest place in camp. When you go inside the temp drops about 20 degrees. It's a nice theater too. Well that's about all I can think about now. More next time. So good luck and take it easy.

Dave

Dave mentioned three of his siblings in this letter: older brother Jule (Julius), younger sister, Frieda, and younger brother, Launie. No one mentioned Frieda's death in Buffalo, New York, around this time. Records show that her remains were returned to Los Angeles and interred at the Hope Cemetery on August 17, 1942. None of the 49 surviving letters refer to Frieda's death.

His next letter home was to his younger sister, Goldie (Janet), who was still recovering from some sort of illness. I was told many years ago that Goldie had a nervous breakdown sometime around the time of Frieda's death which could have been related to Frieda's death, alcohol use, or both. Dave's reference to Long Beach is probably to the Long Beach Pier and the associated recreational area called "The Pike." [25] His subtle sense of humor is evident even though he is going through rough training and many discomforts.

August 11, 1942
Goldie

How are you, you old-stay-in-the-bed-and-relax. Here I am out in the hot sun and the rain working myself to the bone (tailbone) and you are relaxing.

Well anyhow, today we fired the rifle on the range for record and I made expert. I tied for third highest score in our company. There were two 203's and two 199's. Mine was one of the 199's. Expert is 198 so I just made it. The highest possible score is 220. I guess I win about five bucks from different guys. Maybe I'll send you a geranium or something fancy like that.

This Saturday we are supposed to make a move to Alabama. Don't worry it is still in Fort Benning, about six or seven miles from here. We will have the same address I think-I hope.

I heard something about a furlough. I don't even know when. I hope I don't have to wait too long and I hope I have enough money to get home on.

Tomorrow is payday, this time we get 30 bucks. Maybe by the end of this month we'll get paid up in full, but until our records catch up to us we only get enough money to get along on. I'll have close to $150 coming to me about then. Wow! Just think of all the ice cream sodas I can buy.

There's nothing around the city near here that is any good. Too many damned soldiers. Someday I'm going to Atlanta to see what's cooking. It's about 100 miles from here and probably the same as Columbus, that's the city near here, but anyhow it'll be a nice trip. Well, Goldie, I hope you get out of the hospital pretty soon. I keep thinking of how nice Long Beach is now. Boy oh boy. It sure would be nice. Well maybe sometime maybe. So, Goldie, I'll close this letter you just unlax[26] and let me do the rest, and I mean rest.

> *Wow! Just think of all the ice cream sodas I can buy.*

Private Dopey,
Dave

On August 26, 1942, Dave wrote two letters, the first to Goldie and the second to Blackie. Goldie's letter may be of value in unraveling the mystery of how much Dave was told about Frieda's death in early summer, 1942. He mentions people not telling him much and even says, "I just have to guess about what's happening."

There were over 90 enlisted men in H Company so being one of the top four marksmen is commendable. When reading this letter, I remembered the clip in the series "Band of Brothers" where they were getting ready to jump and called out their number in line followed by saying "OK." Dave describes this also. His sense of humor about promotion gives a nod to the fact that at 26, he was a lot older than most of the other recruits. Perhaps his age had something to do with his cynicism and willingness to speak his mind.

Another interesting note is Dave's comment about Launie's lack of information. By now Launie had experienced some historical naval warfare, including the Battle of the Coral Sea, May 4-7, 1942. I wonder if two brothers in the military don't want to share anything negative or alarming about their situations to keep others from worrying about them. There are a few references to Launie in Dave's letters—but not many.

Dear Goldie,

I should write "Dear Gold Brick" when I start this letter. You sure must be taking life easy where you are! Are you really sick or did someone say you were going to have to go out and get a job?

What did Launie have to say in his letter? When Harry writes he doesn't say anything so I just have to guess about what's happening.

I hope you get to see your damned boyfriend out there pretty soon, then maybe you'll quit worrying about him so much.

I didn't tie for 3rd on the rifle, I tied for second, that's better than 3rd and even so it's plenty tough to be an expert on a rifle, or any kind of gun. I am private first class now, which doesn't mean much except six bucks a month more and one stripe on my sleeve. If I was in the regular infantry it would make me feel better, but in the parachutes, it just gets a little snicker now and then. I put some chevrons on my shirt, then tore them off a couple of days later. Maybe someday I'll be a corporal, but I have too much fun being a private, and even corporals are a dime a dozen around here. Most of the ratings go to section boys or old Army men. Us draftees don't stand much of a chance.

I made another plane jump last Saturday, it was the best yet. We were in the air less than 3 minutes. It happened so fast we didn't have time to worry. Usually we have to circle the field but that time we just took off and all of a sudden the lieutenant said "stand up." I wondered if we were going to ride standing but right away he says "hook up" so we hook the static line to the cable over our heads. Then we inspect all our equipment to make sure chute is hooked up right and everything is okay. Then we sound off starting with the last man. We had 12 that time so he says "12 okay" then the next guy says "11 okay" the rest of them go right down the line.

> I made another plane jump last Saturday, it was the best yet. We were in the air less than 3 minutes. It happened so fast we didn't have time to worry.

Still, I didn't think we were ready to jump but the officer was watching the field below through the door and says "stand in the door." Then he says that we are ready to jump so I changed my mind in hurry. The first man stands in the door and the rest of us are all set, and then it comes. "Go" and we do. 13 of us go out in 7 or 8 seconds, and that is plenty fast. This jump is actually the first time I remember actually going out the door. We left the plane at 800 feet so it only takes a few seconds. I think about 20 to get to the ground. We landed in a soft field. I landed as usual, I sat down on the ground, but it was easy. Maybe it's just an old habit. On this jump we carried a rifle boot and gas mask. Everything is strapped down so that we can hardly move, and that is just part of what we will eventually carry.

Well, now we are in our new camp in Alabama and I mean new. We are getting lights tonight, finally. Next week we should have a kitchen and good toilets.

So Goldie I think I'll close. Supper! You know how it is. So good luck and take it easy.

Dave

Dear Blackie,

I am glad to receive your letter, but in a way I'm not. I got four letters to answer today, and as I got yours this evening and the others at noon I'm answering yours last and I'm getting writer's fatigue, whatever that is. Anyhow there might be more mistakes than usual. Well, Jule, I hope you get all your troubles patched up at home. I don't know what it is all about so I'm not saying anything. Which I wouldn't do anyway. So much for that.

I am in our new camp in Alabama, and it is so new we have no kitchen or mess hall or toilets, so we eat out of mess kits and we use an 8-seater out in the back. Our shower room is an old shack and the hot water is always cold, so life isn't a bed of roses. In about a week though, everything should be in okay condition. We are able to listen to a radio for the first time in a week, and tonight we will have lights. Everything except a blond hostess soon, it seems. As far as the food is concerned, I doubt if it could be any better. There is plenty of it, and it is prepared as well as possible under the circumstances.

Those training towers have you a little bit worried, huh? Well, they are 250 feet high. The first time we go on them is a trip in the seat. Two men ride it. It goes to the top and is released and comes down guided by wires but no support but the chute. A tower with the wire guides is called the control tower. The other tower is the free tower. The only time we are lowered by cable is when we ride the shock harness. That is on the control tower too. The shock harness is the baby that made us sweat. Just imagine 150 feet from the ground, lying almost horizontal with your head lower than your feet. Then all you have to do is pull the ripcord with your right hand, change it over to the left hand, hold both arms out straight, count 1000, 2000 and 3000 and drop 15 ft all at one time. It is a nerve test I think! There is also the suspended harness on the control tower.

On that we are taken to the top and dropped to the ground. It is to get us used to the chute and to learn to handle the chute. Next is the free tower. That's the one you asked about. We are taken up to the top and released, from then on we are on our own. We get directions from the ground but they don't help much. That's the tower I got hurt on. I lost a week's training but I haven't hit nearly as hard on any of my plane jumps. We have more time to think on an 800-foot jump than a 200-foot jump.

I have been rated up to a private first class which doesn't mean a damn in the parachutes because there are so many other ratings given out. I think the only reason I got it is because I made expert on the rifle. The way I talk to the sergeants around here I doubt if I'll ever go any higher. But I don't care and they know it. I think we'll all admit there isn't much future to being in this war.

> *We have more time to think on an 800-foot jump than a 200-foot jump.*

Well as far as you being drafted, I don't know. If rumors out there are anything like we get they don't mean a thing. If I were you I wouldn't believe any till I were in the Army, then I would be a believer.

Anyhow, I wish you luck and more good health.

Dave

Having a brother in the Hollywood movie industry continues to be good for Dave. Blackie keeps sending him photos and other things to enjoy and share with the other paratroopers. Items from home that are unique or useful help improve morale and show that people care. His next letter home makes me realize that perhaps we don't realize how valuable simple gestures are. The letter to his parents mentions his visit to New Orleans and announces his upcoming move to Ft. Bragg, NC.

August 30, 1942
Dear Jule,

I've been showing off them pictures again you sent me, so a few of the fellows want some pictures. So if you find time sometime to get about a dozen pictures, that would be plenty, and send them to me, I can pass them out. Don't go to any unnecessary trouble, and don't get any autographs, because it won't be at all necessary either.

The poses that seemed to go over the best here are either bathing suit poses or full-length portraits. Action pictures don't seem to go over so big.

That's enough for pictures. Today is Sunday. We had a turkey dinner, and as we feed cafeteria-style, my plate got loaded up so much that I actually threw enough away to make a full meal. On Sunday there are so many men away from camp that a lot of food has to be thrown away to use up the day's rations. I ate enough jello to feed you for a week. It was good with peaches and ice cream.

Well kid that's all for now so I'll close, wishing you luck, and health and the rest, and take it easy.

Dave

September 22, 1942
Dear Folks,

I hope you are all okay and Goldie is feeling much better. By now she is probably going to dances. She can't sit still a minute, she can't.

I got here all right, but another day late because I missed the train in New Orleans by about 5 minutes, so I had to wait 12 hours for the next train. That gave me a good chance to see the old city here that I always heard about. It is worth looking at too. I got here yesterday afternoon, and they haven't said anything yet about being late, but they will, and it doesn't worry me a bit.

Tonight we are going out on a problem, so we will be out till about 12:00. It will be easy, and the moon is bright so I won't walk into any trees, I hope.

This is my last letter from here. We are moving to Fort Bragg, North Carolina next Sunday, so I will write to you from there. So don't answer this letter until I send my new address. So good luck to you all.

Yours,
Dave

CHAPTER EIGHT

PARATROOPER TRAINING IN FT. BRAGG, NORTH CAROLINA

The regiment moved to Ft. Bragg, North Carolina, on September 30, 1942. Today Ft. Bragg remains the home of the 82nd Airborne Division, is the largest military base in the world by population and covers 251 square miles.

Top: H Company photo probably at Fort Bragg. Bottom: Enlarged top left section showing Uncle David at top middle

September 30, 1942
Dear Blackie

We finally got situated here in North Carolina so I can write you a letter. We weren't allowed to write before we moved and we were too busy yesterday when we arrived and got situated, so this is really my first chance.

I received the pictures and they are plenty okay. Thanks a lot. Don't send anymore though, because I have all the boys supplied with all they can handle and they have a lot of fun with them.

We are living in barracks again with indoor toilets and showers, which is a big change for the better, and we have a real mess hall and kitchen again and eat out of dishes. Just think, dishes, after those mess kits that really is a morale boost.

World War II Army mess kit

There are two theaters close to us and a service club. That is something we never had before closer than 2 miles. There is an outdoor stage for shows here too. And two post exchanges where we can buy all we need to get along. This place really is a soldier's dream as far as conveniences go. But I haven't got any clean dress uniforms so I have to stay in at night and nearly everyone is going out tonight.

I finally saw some peach orchards but it was after I left Georgia. We are in cotton country down here. I have seen plenty of it.

Well, Blackie there isn't much to write about here yet, the trip was still and slow. Raleigh, North Carolina is about 40 miles from here. If I get a chance I'm going to see Duke University play football.

So I'll close, hoping you Bonnie and Donnie are all feeling fine and getting along okay.

Dave

In the following letter Dave introduces the topics of morale and the capability of non-coms (non-commissioned officers, primarily sergeants). This thread is interesting to follow through future letters as Dave himself eventually becomes a non-com.

November 1, 1942
Jule,

Glad to hear from you again. So you're thinking of joining the Navy. The outfit you mentioned are called the Seabees, aren't they? I read an article about them and it sounded pretty good, but don't do anything you'll be sorry for, but it would be more interesting than a regular fighting outfit, and just as exciting, if that's what you want.

We were out in the woods for a week getting some experience in tactics and problems and it all came back to the same thing. The noncoms are still lousy. In one problem they had the whole company killed off in about five minutes - not actually but it might have been and no one likes it. Even the officers know it and they are damn good officers, but there's that Army stuff of not raising hell with the noncoms because it ruins the morale of all the men which is low anyway. Maybe that guy you were talking to knows how the noncoms are picked, no one here does. If one gets broke a new man takes his place, and it's just as bad or worse. One of my friends here is sergeant, and a damn good soldier, and because he doesn't throw his voice all over the place trying to make a big impression, and uses his brain, the other sergeants don't think he's very good. Anyhow this sergeant got into the records and found out that only one of the rest of them had an IQ of over normal, by four points, and the rest of them were way down the list. And they wonder why the amount of AWOLs is so high in the paratroops. One more gripe - there is a rumor in our company that the two biggest rowdies and gold bricks are up for corporal. They have both been AWOL one time and have had more passes than most of the men. So, if they are promoted there is going to be several applications for transfer to the Air Corps and glider pilots and a lot more AWOL. Sometimes I wish I had joined the Navy.

We had a pretty good time on our tactics. They have a combat range where we use live ammunition against the man-sized targets that might pop-up anywhere in front

There is also a blitz course that we call Hogan's Alley.[27] The officer was giving our squad instructions when all of the sudden a machine gun started shooting live ammunition a few feet over our heads. We all hit the dirt, then some dynamite went off real close throwing dirt all over of us, then the officer yells for us to throw the hand grenades we have. It's lucky they are dummies because some of them only go a few feet and one of them hits a stump and bounces back and hits one of the men

...all of the sudden a machine gun started shooting live ammunition a few feet over our heads.

who throws it again. It's only a half minutes of excitement, but we learn a lot. Then one at a time we go through Hogan's alley. We walk along with eight rounds of live ammunition and fixed bayonets. We walk a certain course and look for targets that appear suddenly, and once in the middle of a barbed wire barricade, a bullet flies right close overhead. It isn't too close though. The course isn't very large, but it gives us a good idea of what to expect. A magazine writer would probably make it sound like we go through hell, because we always get a laugh out of the articles we read that make us sound like Supermen.

We had a couple of problems where one company attacked ours when we were dug in, in foxholes. We all had blanks, and captured prisoners when possible. It was fun, and in one afternoon we learned what we had been trying to learn for months. All the officers were killed, theoretically, and they said they sure needed the experience as much as anyone.

You should see the glider troops that we have to depend on after we land. A sloppier bunch of soldiers I never did see. After seeing them I don't wonder why some people call us suicide troops. I actually can't see how some of them got into the Army.

Well kid I guess I've cried long enough. Maybe my next letter will be a little happier. Anyway, I hope you are feeling ok and are getting along ok. If you hear any good stories let me know about them. The boys here are all easterners and like to hear about the studios. Tell Bonnie and Donnie I remembered them.

So Long

Dave

Dave's letters continue to reference his sister's illness and fail to acknowledge Frieda's death. I heard once that Dave was upset that they didn't tell him about her death right away and it will remain a mystery as to when he was notified. Wars can create a lot of unanticipated dilemmas. Dave's humor continues to shine through when he talks about his adventures and misfortunes...such as an unfortunate stream crossing.

November 22, 1942
Dear Folks,

The letter Goldie wrote on the 16th got here yesterday so I'm answering it now. I'm glad to hear the same old story that you are all fine. The same about me too.

We have the same old grind here. This last week we had a little problem. Everyone gets his fighting equipment on and out we go in the trucks, which are supposed to be planes. When we land, I mean jump out of the trucks, off we go in a hurry, and the first thing we know our platoon is lost from the rest of the company. So while the radios are trying to find out what is who, the general comes over and climbs up and down the lieutenants back a couple of times. In a few minutes we get organized and take off for our objective which is a hill about a mile away. We get about halfway there when we run into a couple of enemy scouts who fired blanks at us, but as I am in the rear with my little mortar all I do is wait until everything is clear before I advance. We are held up only a few minutes, then on we go again until we get to a little stream running through some swampy ground. It was a narrow stream,

> *I stepped in up to my neck. I only miss-judged the water about 5 feet.*

but we couldn't get a run to be able to jump over so everyone was crossing on a little log. But a few of us were braver. I decided to wade across. I picked a place where the water looked just deep enough to go over my shoes. So I stepped in up to my neck. I only miss-judged the water about 5 feet. But the war must go on. We set the mortar up in a position about 300 yards from the hill. We are attacking and I proceeded to blow it apart. I mean I go through all the motions. After the hill is softened up enough by the mortar, machine guns, and rifles, the men charged with the bayonets. We won of course. The general said that our company was the best in the 504th so we all came back happy.

Friday we had a little hike of only four miles, but it was tough. We had full field equipment which included two blankets and shelter-half which is half of a pup tent with a pole and five stakes, and underwear and toilet articles. I also carried a machine gun about halfway for a guy who was about to drop. That was a total of about 65 pounds.

What makes it so bad is the rate we walk. About 4 miles an hour which is twice as fast as the infantry walks. But after an hour we are all tired out so I don't know what we gain.

Anyhow after we get to our area where we are to stay, we set up our mortar just in case of an attack. It took us a little while to get set up though because the first place the sergeant showed us would have us firing at our own *troops. Finally, we got it right. Then comes the usual argument about what kind of holes to dig. I finally lose when the order comes out for slit-trenches. That is a small trench just large enough and deep enough to lay in. What really almost disrupted the whole situation out there was when I took my boots off when I went to bed. Everyone got excited except me of course, then comes another argument. The sergeant wants us to sleep in the trenches. That was a real argument. I lost again. About 3 in the morning we find the sergeant sleeping next to a big fire. So he loses this argument. We hiked back in the morning, ending up another week.*

This gives you a little idea of what we do around here once in a while. If it weren't for the glider boys in the 82nd division we would probably be across already, but the glider boys haven't enough training yet. In fact, they haven't even seen a glider yet.

If any of you have seen some soldiers in the newsreels adopting an eagle for their mascot that is the 101st Division. They are here with us getting their training. They are a little more advanced then we are.

Well, that's quite a lot of writing for me in one letter. Any how I'm not as lazy as Goldie. Somebody said we are going to jump again next week. It's been so long now since I've jumped that it'll be like my first jump again.

I'll close now wishing you all the best of everything. Love to Ma and Pa.

Dave

The next letter is to Launie who had joined the Navy before WWII and was a Radioman on the *USS Chicago*, a heavy cruiser in the Pacific theater. At the time of this letter, the *USS Chicago* was in Vallejo in the San Francisco area under repair from a Japanese torpedo hit incurred in the South Pacific. Launie went through many more battles later in the war and nearly lost his life several times. Dave's tone is light-hearted—probably not wanting to give his younger brother anything to worry about.

November 25, 1942
Dear Launie,

Sure glad to see you get home kid. If I was within a day or two of home I'd be there too, but here I am.

I got two of Goldie's letters the same time today and one of them told of you being home asleep. I hope it's not a habit. I do it myself once in awhile.

How's the Navy now? Got any ships to your credit yet? You have probably read my letters by now and see what kind of fighting I do. Today I was on a detail building a blitz course. One of those simulated one-man battles. Tomorrow if I'm not on guard duty I might have my picture taken going through the course. A real moving picture to be used in a training film. Who knows, I might end up in the movies.

Did you read how our outfits are doing in Africa? They seem to be doing okay. The only thing bad is that all the easy stuff will be knocked out by the time I get over.

The 82nd division glider troops have finally grown up. Sears Roebuck delivered their first gliders today. The boys will finally get to see one. They will be extremely happy and excited.

Well sonny boy, I will close up. Let me know how you are feeling. Enjoy your leave. Wish I were there.

Dave

As mentioned earlier, many of Dave's letters during training tell about his feelings toward his superiors. The letter below relates a story about arguments over what he considers trivial or unfair events. He often mentions how his argumentative nature will probably keep him from ever getting a promotion. The following letter includes one of these episodes plus an interesting description of acting in a training film.

December 20, 1942
Dear Jule,

Today I received your letter and the gun jacket. You couldn't have picked a better time to send the jacket either because the weather has turned cold and windy. Today we were out all morning and nearly froze. When the wind blows here it raises a lot of sand and dust.

I sure would have liked to been home when Launie was. Being 3000 miles away from home makes things pretty tough. I think I would be in line for another furlough in January but it would take 15 days and that is too long because all the furloughs have to be finished by January 15th. After that?

Being 3000 miles away from home makes things pretty tough.

We have been having a little bit of fun here this afternoon. A lot of us were restricted to camp last Saturday and Sunday because the major found us sitting around when we should have been cleaning rifles. I was the only one cleaning my rifle at the time and so I had a hell of an argument with the first sergeant. I lost as usual. So this afternoon we got caught again by the major. He raises hell with the lieutenant, the lieutenant passes it on to the sergeants, and then we get it. So just for the fun of it I start arguing with all of them. I said that us privates are too dumb to do anything on our own and that it is up to them to see that we know what to do because every time we do do something that is necessary they think it is wrong. In a couple of minutes I have them so mad that I think I have been turned in by now. We are restricted now so that we won't leave the barracks so that the lieutenant can talk to us later on. I expect the worst, but because I am a private I have nothing to lose. I still think I should have joined the Navy.

Well, I have had my fling of being an actor before a camera. The Army took some pictures of our Blitz course to make a training bulletin. I happened to be in the right place at the start so they took pictures of me going all the way through the course. I would walk along with a loaded rifle and when I came to a target I would fire as fast as I could from a kneeling position. They replace the camera behind the target, then I would use blanks. One of the targets was supposed to be a sniper up in a tree. There was a rifle right there that was fired by a string, but to make it more interesting for the film, an officer and cameraman got up in the tree and put a tracer bullet a couple of feet over my head and I shot back with a blank. It should look pretty good too.

At one time I had to go over some bailed wire and as soon as I got over a shot would go off on my left and a target spring up. This took more retakes than any other and one time I got caught by the wire and fell down. I cut my leg a little and just missed one of the steel stakes which holds the wire down. The stake is pointed and sticks up about 4 inches. It is pretty mean. I hope to see the picture when it is finished in a couple of months. They also took a picture of a group of us with machine gun traces passing about 4 ft over our heads. We hit the dirt, then one of the men throws a dummy grenade, and dynamite is set off. It should look pretty good too.

We were supposed to jump yesterday but it was foggy. We will jump tomorrow if it isn't foggy or too windy. Either way it'll be pretty cold. Well I guess I'll close. Tell Bonnie and Donnie hello. Be careful.

Dave

P.S. Can you get hold of a couple more gun jackets? The fellas get quite a kick out of it.

Gliders get very little attention in media coverage of World War II but in his December 13, 1942, letter Dave gives some details. Probably the best depiction of gliders on film is in the movie *A Bridge Too Far* as the C47s take off filled with paratroopers and towing gliders filled with glidermen. Dave also talks more about being a proficient mortarman. Dave concludes by encouraging Harry, to continue practicing the accordion.

December 13, 1942
Hiya Harry,

I got your little letter today and read it in about half a minute. You sure run out of things to say in a hurry.

I am on guard duty today and I'm in the guardhouse now sitting by a nice hot fire. There's a real cold wind outside that I'll have to walk in for 2 hours. It's no fun, especially the early morning shift of 2400 to 2 am. I'm going to freeze. A little while ago the officer of the guard put a 45 pistol bullet through his big toe. I was outside and thought it was a firecracker, but it wasn't. I think the lieutenant wished it was.

I haven't written anything about the glider demonstration we had last week. Well both the 82nd and the 101st divisions were there. First they took a glider up to about 6000 feet and let it go. The pilot did three loops on the way down and went through a lot of maneuvers. The glider can carry 15 men or a Jeep or 3700 lb of supplies. The plane they use is the Douglas C-17. The next time the glider went up and when it landed the pilot showed how to make the glider stop quick by putting on the brakes and making the glider ride up on the skids under the nose. It sure stops quick. The third time they used a glider with detachable landing gear that drops right after the glider takes off and has a parachute attached. This glider lands on skids alone, and makes a pretty nice landing too. I won't ride in a glider but the regular glider troops will. We parachutists always make fun of the glider troops when they are around. We act like we are gliders and stick out our arms like wings. They don't like us very much but in combat we are the ones who they depend on to get them a safe landing field so they don't say very much.

Yesterday we had a divisional review. That is where all the men in the division parade in front of the general or whoever is there at the time. The parade looked pretty good. Naturally the parachutists look the best with their boots. The glider and Airborne men wear leggings which don't look so hot. There was also a flock of jeeps too, which are carried in planes and gliders. There were three major generals and one brigadier general watching us.

I am a pretty good mortar man now. We have mortar drill almost every day. The mortar is all folded up and laid on the ground. The man lays next to it and when the timer says "action" a mortar is set up as fast as possible and aimed at "zero" which just centers it. When a target is used, then the mortar is set so many degrees from "zero" as necessary to drop the shell on the target. Anyhow the fastest time was 27 seconds, and I did it in 28, so I'm still pretty good. 40 seconds is expert.

Well kid, I guess I've told you enough. You just keep on practicing and taking care of yourself. Have a good time this Christmas. Are you going to play any caroles? You should be able to play Silent Night by now, huh? Give my best regards to everybody.

Your brother, Dave

Dave displays some maturity in appreciating good leadership when he sees it.

December 20, 1942
Dear Jule and the rest of the family,

Received your letter and the gun jackets. Thanks a lot.

Well, Christmas is almost here, and I think we might have that white one we've been hearing so much about. We had snow for a few days last week, and just got some more today, and expect more, especially as we have a three-day problem coming up. 25 miles out and emergency rations is what we are to expect.

I just got a pint of Calvert's Special for Christmas. The bootleg price is $4 which is pretty stiff price, but rationing is in effect here and it's the best we can do. Here's looking at you! One of the boys was supposed to bring me some stuff when he came back from furlough but he drank it on *the train expecting to buy more here but the rationing spoiled that.*

Our training keeps getting tougher. We have a new company commander starting yesterday and he is 100% Army. He was second in command before and we expect the worst because we have seen him in action a few times already. He is a real soldier though and a good man to lead us in combat.

Our division has set up some physical tests we are supposed to pass, one of them is 35 push-ups which is going to be passed by very few. And another one is to walk 4 miles in 50 minutes which we can do easily. There are several more that I can scrape through, but if the glider infantry have to take the same test here there will be a lot of failures because they have some awful looking specimens.

Well I guess that's taking in about all that's new around here along with the rest of the routine. Other than shooting in the wrong direction on our problems, and getting lost, we are improving. Have a Happy New Year.

Dave

Dave shares details about some of the weapons and training. In the next letter he is now in charge of a mortar squad and takes it seriously. By now he knows he is going to be in some very serious combat. His humorous writing is probably intended to help the family relax and not worry about him too much.

December 22nd 1942
Dear Goldie and Harry and the rest,

I got both of your letters today so I'll answer both of them at the same time. You can understand why I will do such a thing. You know me. Efficiency and all that stuff.

Harry, if I see any t-shirts in town I'll buy you a couple, but it's been so cold here lately I don't think there have been any ordered since we got here. There might be some from the 503rd who left here a while ago. We think they are in Africa.

As far as Goldie losing a link out of the medals, well I guess she'll have to have someone fix it for her. I can't get any more here. We have three days off this weekend, but I haven't enough money to go anywhere so I guess I'll have to stay in and do K.P. That sure sounds good, doesn't it?

> *I finally got to fire the mortar!*

I finally got to fire the mortar! We had a problem yesterday morning and 10 rounds to shoot away. See the drawing of the shell. The assistant gunner holds his thumb on the safety button, in his left hand, pulls the pin out with his right hand and drops the shell into the mortar. While the button is in, the Shell will not explode but when the button flies out after the shell leaves the tube, it will explode if the contact touches the slightest thing. There are four increments in the fins, but the assistant gunner pulls out as many as necessary, according to a chart, to shoot the required distance. The gunner aims the gun, from orders from the observer.

I had charge of the mortar squad, so that made me observer, but I fired the first round to show how it was done. We did okay even if we were slow. Everybody was kibitzing, even the lieutenant which made it harder for us to hit the target, but we did.

When we came back in last night we walked 9 miles in 2 hours with full field packs on. It was a tough walk. We only stopped once for 5 minutes which isn't very much. It was raining too, which made it that much harder. Tomorrow we are supposed to go on a 15 to 20 mile hike, but we won't carry any packs, which makes it a little easier.

If Harry wants to know what I had the shovel for it's because we all carry either a pick or shovel or hand-axe, to dig foxholes or trenches, or just about anything like that.

Christmas Day we are going to have a big dinner, with wine too. It is going to have all the trimmings. From what the cooks say it will be plenty good. I hope we have lots of cranberry sauce. It seems like they don't use it much around here.

Did I tell you we had some snow here last week, well anyway I took a couple of pictures which I will send home. I also took a portrait in town but it won't be finished till January 15th, or so. I'll send it home to, I guess unless it's real good, then I'll hang it up in the barracks here. It will help me go to sleep at night. If anything new happens around here I'll let you know about it. Anyway I'm glad Goldie liked it the present, but I didn't intend for Harry to give his money away. The dope!

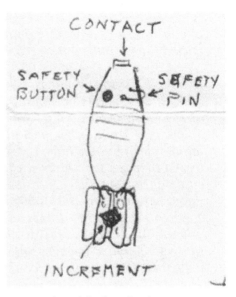

Dave's quick sketch of a mortar shell.

I'll close now. Think I'll go to the show tonight. The best to you all. Give my love to Ma and Pa.

Dave

Blackie continues to send Dave items whenever he can. This letter talks about a delicious fruitcake. My cousin, Doni, known as Donnie in Dave's letters, still has the family recipe for the fruitcake.[28] Also, there is speculation about where the paratroopers will go after they leave Ft. Bragg. The end of the letter mentions Launie.

January 6, 1943
Dear Jule and Bonnie,

I got your fruit cake yesterday but couldn't eat it till tonight because I was on guard, but it sure was worth waiting for. Well, it was all you said it would be. I really didn't know what to expect when you said it was the best, but you were right. Haven't got an extra piece laying around, have you? If you notice a crackling sound it's because I'm eating a pocket full of nuts while I'm writing this letter.

If you think the Army is better than income tax, you're nuts, and I know what I'm talking about. Sunday afternoon at 1:00 I went on a guard for 30 hours - 2 hours on and 4 hours off. Monday night I thought I would get a good night's sleep but we have to mop the barracks before we go to bed then get up 1 hour early at 4:30 and go for a 3-mile run before breakfast. That was because the barracks were dirty, mostly in the non-coms rooms. Then Tuesday evening - last night - I have to go out on a 24-hour guard - 4 hours on, 8 hours off - at the post waterworks. It's hard to sleep on guard because of the shift changing and because we have to sleep with our clothes on.

The rumors are flying thick and fast about where and when we move from here. They range from Indiantown Gap, Pennsylvania (embarkation point) to March Field, California, and a few points in between. March Field sure sounds good.

That package you sent the cake in had me a little worried for a minute, with the whiskey label on it, but I was relieved when I found it wasn't. Ordinarily I don't like whiskey, but the Army changed me a little.

I got a letter from Launie from Vallejo. They found more damage to the ship so they have to stay longer, which is a break.

Thanks again for the swell cake.

Dave

Dave's next letter talks about a 22-mile hike and how their pace compares to regular infantry. The airborne troops were conditioned more rigorously than the regular Army infantry. You can see Dave's attitude showing a lot of places and even joking about being a paratrooper.

January 15, 1943
Dear Jule,

I received your letter yesterday but waited to answer because we were to go on a little hike - 22 miles - last night, and I wanted to tell you about it.

Well we did it okay, in 6 1/2 hours which is really stepping. We had an 8-hour schedule but it went with the wind. So did we! On any Army march there is a 10-minute break every hour, so you can see we actually walked the 22 mi in 5 1/2 hours walking time, which is about four miles per hour, and that is going, when the infantry pace is under three miles per hour, for comparison.

I was ready more than once to turn around and slap him with a rifle butt.

I can well remember back in Texas when I first learned I was one of the lucky boys to go to parachute school. I said to the luckier ones who didn't make it that when they saw us flying by in a plane they would be sorry because we would be having the life of Riley, but it turned out that we are walking and they are riding by in trucks.
For the most part the walk was on hard gravel road except for a three-mile stretch of sand at about the middle mark that really took a lot out of us, and we didn't slow down any either. What really helped to make it all worse was one of those men just behind me, that kept complaining and criticizing anything and everything, all which got on everyone's nerves, and I was ready more than once to turn around and slap him with a rifle butt.

The man in front of me had flat feet, and the first mile they started to bother him, and he should have dropped out, but he didn't. Lots of guts, but it wasn't worth it. Lots of the time he was in a shuffling run, like a Chinaman. He covered miles that way. I don't think he will stay in the outfit. Bad feet are showing up all over the place, but not mine, damn the luck! Maybe if they would go out I would sign up for aerial gunnery, but that's the only way out of here, and I'm too healthy.

And our schedule today! One is close order drill marching and then walk to the packing sheds and check out chutes for a jump Sunday, which will be about a five-mile jog. Easy on tired feet, but we do have several hours rest with nothing to do except a little blackjack. I run about even all the time. I don't play much - two or three bucks, but I have seen men walk away with two or three hundred, even more.

The latest rumor around here is that we will be here for three more months. That is because the glider troops have just gotten a lot of rookies and we have to wait til they get their training.

The number one trick of the month here was pulled off last week by one of the local talents. We call him "Mickey the Mole." For a time it was "Mickey Mouse," but he degenerated. Anyhow he had a 13-day furlough and three months back pay coming at the same time, but a few days before they were due he is chalked up AWOL. Two days later the commanding officer receives a telegram from New Jersey requesting the furlough he sent to him. He got orders to come back immediately. Now he is under arrest to the barracks, awaiting trial. It is a nice trick if it works.

Since I started writing this letter we've done what we were scheduled to do. Our drill was turned into a lecture and bawling out to pep us up for a review tomorrow to honor one of our generals, who is leaving to form a new division. That was easy enough. Then we were taken back to our company and went over the jump and our positions on the plane Sunday. I will be the ninth man of a 16-man mass jump. After that we went over and checked out the chutes and adjusted the harness to fit.

Your fruitcake should be here in about three days, it travels as fast as a letter. I'll be glad when it's here, hope it's as good as the last one. Hope you saw the pictures of jump school I sent home. They are pretty good. Just like I tried to take, but couldn't at the time.

Looks like I've reached the end of the page. Tell Bonnie and Donnie hello for me. Good luck.

Dave

Dave was finally promoted to corporal, which is interesting in light of his previous comments about arguing with his superiors. His comments indicate growing maturity in learning and taking responsibility. Perhaps being in charge of a mortar squad brought out his leadership qualities. He also gives additional information about fighting exercises and their weapons: The 60 mm mortar and the Tommy gun (Thompson Submachine Gun).

February 10, 1943
Hello Bud,

Have you quit worrying yet about the Army? If they're going to get you there isn't much to do about it. It really doesn't matter much because there's a saying in the Army that the best outfit is the one you just left or the one you're going to. It is true too because no one is ever satisfied. I guess the same goes for Marines and sailors too.

We didn't get to make that last jump. From what I hear jumps are going to be mighty scarce. Well I'm still not mad, as long as we keep getting our $50 jump pay.

Last week we were shown how effective our protection in the air is. A flight of P-51's gave a demonstration of ground strafing. They use tracers and it doesn't seem possible that a plane could throw so much lead. They kept flying around here all the time when it isn't cloudy, which is very seldom.

Maybe you've noticed that Corp. In front of my name. Well, it finally arrived. I'm squad leader now of a 60 mm mortar Squad - 5 men besides myself. Maybe by the time you get my next letter it will be Sergeant Rosenkrantz. My lieutenant calls me Sergeant now, but it isn't official yet. January 29th was my one-year anniversary as a soldier of Uncle Sammy. I have learned a little about fighting, and it is pretty interesting if you're not too lazy.

> *January 29th was my one-year anniversary as a soldier of Uncle Sammy. I have learned a little about fighting, and it is pretty interesting if you're not too lazy.*

It's hard to teach anyone here if they don't want to learn, even if it is to save their own lives. It's going to be hard being a sergeant especially when it's with men you've been training with for six months.

We had another close shave Saturday night. We were on one of our problems, firing live ammunition, mostly tracers, because it was dark. We had foxholes and slit trenches dug and were worrying about a machine gun to our left because it was firing a little too close. We can tell by the sound of the bullet just about how far away it is.

Suddenly a tracer comes from the right, not over 10 feet from us. That's a little too close, so we make ourselves scarce in the bottom of our holes. Then another one goes right behind us closer yet. Somebody is very much off the beam because orders were to fire directly south, away from our line, and these bullets were going east, over everyone's heads.

Friday all the mortar squads were given a test on how long it took them to hit a target. We were given five shells each. The testing officer pointed out the target to me then started timing. I had to line the gun up, that is, give the gunner instructions, give him the range and fire order. The gunner can't see the target because he is behind a small hill. I am the only one who sees the target. My second shot was an effective shot, close enough to be called a hit. In any case, if you don't know it that is pretty good. The Army allows three shots to hit a target, so I did it a little better than they expect us to do. My time was good too, so the officer said, although I don't know how long it was, about 4 minutes, more or less. I was too nervous to notice the time much.

Since I have been rated, I now am the possessor of a Tommy gun. I don't like them much, but they are damned good for what they were designed for, close fighting. We have new carbines too. They fold right behind the pistol grip. The stock is a wireframe. They sure are easy to handle. The pistol grip is large enough for a good hold. When you hook the stock under your armpit the gun handles just like a pistol, but much better. I guess I have told you that it shoots 15 rounds as fast as the trigger can be pulled. The clips load easy and fast.

I guess I have written enough this time. If there is something special you would like to know, ask me. Tell Bonnie and Donnie hello for me. Take it easy.

Dave

Dave demonstrating how to shoot a Thompson Submachine Gun (Tommy gun)

In the letter below to Julius, Dave writes about finally getting a furlough and planning to spend time in New York City. He was frustrated that he wouldn't have time to make a trip home to Los Angeles. He acknowledges Launie's ship being sunk. Dave also talks about a tear gas attack, two jumps, and the rumors about leaving Ft. Bragg in three or four weeks.

February 20, 1943
Greetings,

Well, boy, I don't feel like writing a letter now, but I guess I'd better because I'll be on a furlough next week. I'm so damned mad because I can't get enough time to get home, so I'm going to spend my eight days in New York. I could leave in the morning but I've got to be Corporal of the Guard tonight and tomorrow so I won't be able to leave till tomorrow night, and it could have been arranged to let me go early, but it wasn't, so I've got reasons to be mad.

I guess you know about Launie's ship being sunk. I think he's okay because there was no news at home that he was hurt or missing. I guess it's quite an experience getting a ship shot out from under you.

> *I guess it's quite an experience getting a ship shot out from under you.*

We had a hike this morning of about five miles during which we were gassed by an airplane, an A-20A. We were marching along, I was the last man. I happened to look back and I saw the plane coming. It was about three or four hundred yards away, but looked like 30 or 40. I yelled "Air attack" and took off for the woods. I saw the plane spraying gas so I got my mask on in a hurry. Most of the others didn't have as much time as I did so they got a big whiff of it, tear gas was what they used and it was plenty strong. I could feel it burn the skin of my neck. The plane then simulated strafing us, but we all knew that if the plane had used live ammo we would have been in a bad way.

I have made two jumps since I wrote you last. We were very lucky that on the days we jumped the air was nice and still. Most of the time it has been windy and that's no time to be jumping. The first jump was just a plain practice jump, but the second one was a tactical jump with equipment. We made a 163-mile plane ride, hedge-hopping all the way. Some of the men got airsick from the ride, but I enjoyed it all the way. There were only twelve of us in the plane so we had lots of room. We were supposed to jump from about 600 feet but we're less than 400 when we left the plane. That doesn't give us much time to maneuver the chute before we land. Only 20 seconds isn't much time. I made easy landings on both jumps which made me happy.

Well, we might leave here in three or four weeks. Africa or South Seas, who knows?

I'm really sorry about the trouble you're having at home. Naturally the one who will eventually feel it most is the baby, as is usually the case. Don't worry about it too much. Things most often take care of themselves.
As for the Army, don't volunteer for anything, you won't get what you want anyway. Good luck.

Dave

PS We don't get paid for each jump. We get $50 a month extra whether we jump or not.

In the next letter Dave mentions that Launie was sent home on leave after his ship was sunk. He also gives great detail about his trip to New York City, where he was able to see his childhood friend, Irv Spector, who was stationed in New York City in the Army Signal Corps. Irv went on to become an accomplished animator in Hollywood after the war.

March 5, 1943
Dear Jule,

I was sure glad to get your letter and hear that Launie is home okay. It's the first I heard about it. I don't know why they didn't send me a letter right away from home, but you know how they are. I wrote a letter yesterday telling them to see the Red Cross to get in touch with Launie, but by the time the letter gets there he will have been home a week already. I sure would like to see him but I guess I won't till *the war is over. I bet he really had an interesting time for a while, enough to last a lifetime. If we keep knocking off the Japs like we have been the war won't last too long.*

I had a real vacation in New York for eight days. I was all over the place on the subways and Els. I went to all the theaters around Time Square and Rockefeller Center. If you remember Irv Spector, he's in the Army Signal Corps, and lives in a hotel across the street from Madison Square Garden. That's what I really call Army life, living in a hotel, eating in restaurants, and riding buses to work, all on the government. Seems too good to be true. They work in the old Paramount Studio on Long Island City and make training films for the Army.

New York is a nice place for a visit but I wouldn't like to stay here.

Anyhow, New York City was swell. I went to the top of the Empire State Building but it was so cloudy I couldn't see more than a half mile in any direction. The subways really are something too. The people go nuts when they get near one and get a terrific urge to crowd and push, and enjoy it. I always stayed away from them, waited for the next train if there was much of a mob. Radio City Music Hall was quite a show. A good picture plus a symphony orchestra and a stage show featuring The Rockettes, the best chorus I've ever seen, and all for $0.27. That's all I had to pay for any show except two, and I saw more than 10. I paid $3.85 for a seat at the Olisen and Johnson Show, and it sure was worth it. And I paid $1.65 to see the ice show, produced by Sonja Henie, but it wasn't as good as the show I saw at the Pan Pacific Auditorium in Los Angeles.

I also went to all the best-known nightclubs in Manhattan. I didn't get drunk once though, but I did feel pretty good a couple of times. New York is a nice place for a visit but I wouldn't like to stay here. I like a more open city like Los Angeles.

We had a couple of tests here for all the noncoms in the battalion. And I came out second highest in our company on the first test and highest on the second test. I think I have the best average for both tests in the battalion, but I'm not sure. Makes me feel pretty good. Remember me telling about our dumb staff sergeant a while back? Well, his scores were the lowest on both tests. I hope they get rid of him soon.

I see by the newspapers that they aren't going to take married men for a while, so that should make you feel pretty good. In my opinion, I think the Army is big enough now to win, and that all the new men are just for a reserved - in case.

Some of the men in our company made a jump in Florida this morning after a four-hour ride. Wish I could have been there. Maybe next time.

Well, old kid. I guess I'll close now. Write soon as I may leave here soon.

Good luck.

Dave

There has always been a rivalry between special forces units in the various divisions of the military including within the branches. In WWII the Army had the Rangers and the Airborne. In the next letter, Dave takes some pride in the success of an Airborne vs. Rangers training exercise. This letter has historic value also as it describes how the paratroopers of the 504 were experimenting with jumping with their fighting equipment.

March 17, 1943
Dear Jule,

Life goes on as usual around here. We keep training, and although it gets monotonous at times, we always learn something new.

I can't remember if I told you about one of our companies making a jump in Florida, anyhow, they had a sham battle against American Rangers, and beat them all to hell, so I guess the Rangers aren't as hot as they're supposed to be. Last week our battalion made a mass jump. Over 500 men on the ground in less than a minute. It really was a beautiful sight. It was the first time I got air sick, it's really a terrible feeling, and I had my chute harness adjusted wrong so that I nearly choked on the way down, and my helmet was down over my eyes so that I can only see my feet. It was by far my worst jump of all.

We are supposed to make a jump in South Carolina about 150 miles from here. It will be a regiment jumping and capturing an airport. The men will jump on three different sides at once and each Company will have its own objective. Ours will be an ordinance plant near the airport. We are to land on a beach so the landing should be plenty soft in the sand.

We have been experimenting jumping with our equipment on us instead of in equipment chutes so that we can fight within a few minutes after we land and instead of running all over the place trying to find stuff that the enemy might be covering with fire. We would carry only enough to hold us till equipment shoots could be dropped right to us, with extra ammo and guns and rations.

We intend to do a lot better than the men who dropped in Africa. We know that they didn't do so hot. They jumped all right but so far from their objective that ground forces took it first or it surrendered with only a little fighting. They were plenty lucky then, I don't know how they're doing now.

Before I forget I'll brag a little bit. The noncoms in our company were the first ones to jump with equipment in the paratroops in the US. Now it has been adapted by our regiment and others as standard procedure. Our jump Saturday if it comes off will be the first regimental jump, and the jump in Florida was the longest ever made in the US. The longest was the one in Africa. The boys brought a mascot back from Florida. A small wild pig. Maybe someday you'll see a picture of it in a magazine.

I've been saying we are going to leave soon for the past 3 months. Well the officers have orders to be all packed and ready to move at a minute's notice after April 1st. So I guess we will go along with them. We'll probably get the same order in about a week. Africa here we come. We are almost positive that's where we'll go. No Japs for us.

The noncoms in our company were the first ones to jump with equipment in the paratroops in the US.

I did get a letter from Launie but as usual he didn't say much. You have told me most of what I know happened to him. Maybe he'll open up in his next letter. I hope so.
I guess I've covered just about all that's new and of interest. The papers might mention something of our Saturday jump. We hope they do. We are publicity hounds.

When you answer notice the new way to write my address. Regulations you know. Take it easy and answer soon. Let me know what's going on in sunny California. Wish I were there.

Good luck, Dave

PS Say hello to the family for me

The next two letters are extremely rich with colorful descriptions of several training jumps—including some historic ones where they jumped with fighting equipment. Dave mentions qualifying as Expert in both carbine and mortar gunner. His mortar squad performed very well in training exercises—best in the regiment. Based on ratings and test scores he was always at or near the top in H Company, the 3rd Battalion, or the 504 PIR.

The letter to his brother Max is significant, showing maturing over the year and a half of training before shipping overseas as he became a mortar squad leader and was placed in charge of training and leading his men. He takes his leadership responsibility seriously and mentions his upcoming promotion to sergeant.

Dave also predicts leaving Ft. Bragg soon for deployment somewhere. In the last letter he talks about contacting his three brothers also serving in the military: Launie (Navy), Jack (Army Air Forces) and Lawrence a.k.a. Larry (Merchant Marine).

April 2, 1943
Dear Jule,

It's been a couple of days since I got your letter and the mag with your picture in it. I used the picture to prove that there was someone in the family that was good looking.

I had the pleasure Wednesday night of making a jump. We all have to have at least one night jump, and this was mine. There was 17 of us in the plane, which would have been okay if there wasn't two large gas tanks in the cabin. They are extra tanks and take up lots of room - too much room for us. Anyhow the air was smooth, which was a relief after our last ride. We rode for about 10 minutes before we hooked up on the red light, but the pilot didn't give the green light to go, so we had to circle around to pass over the field again, another 10 minutes while we were still standing up ready to go. Again we passed the field and no green light. By this time we are getting pretty tired because we put the chute harness on tight and they make our backs ache if we stand very long.

On the third pass over the field we got the green light after the third man had gone out the red light came on again but it was too late. Once we start nothing can stop us. A sergeant who was in the plane when we jumped said that an officer tried to stop a couple of men but they didn't even notice him, in fact we were going out the door so fast that he could hardly count us. The plane was dark and we couldn't see anyone anyway so no wonder we couldn't be stopped. I was number 13 man but it didn't make any difference, in fact I had one of the easiest openings I've ever had, and easiest landing. There was a fair amount of breeze blowing, and the pilot having missed the field, let us land about a mile from where we were supposed to. I believe we were higher than we were supposed to be, 800 feet. I drifted over woods and swamp, and landed in the

Someday I'll remember the cuss words I say just before I hit the ground. They must be good because the landing is the worst part of a jump for me, although I've never been hurt.

middle of a dirt road. My chute caught on a tree just as I hit and broke my fall, preventing me from falling. What a break. Someday I'll remember the cuss words I say just before I hit the ground. They must be good because the landing is the worst part of a jump for me, although I've never been hurt.

The really tough part was yet to come. It was the walk back. Imagine going through woods, brush and a small swamp in the dark, carrying our chutes in bags on our backs.

I don't know why the pilot gave us the green light after we had passed the field, but I do know that he was plenty nervous because there was lots of air traffic, bombers, transport, and other planes over the jump field which was close to the Fort Bragg Airport. He refused to take any more men up that night. In case you don't know, and I don't think you do, the lights are right over the door so that the lead man can be gone as soon as the green light goes on.

I saw the picture Casablanca a few weeks ago and I agree with you that it was very good. We get to see some pictures here for $0.15 before they play the big cities. But on Friday nights we have a double feature that would hardly do credit to Watts. And I mean they stink. I also agree with you that the movies are morale builders. It isn't very often that you'll find a show that isn't well packed, around here.

I have been telling you for the past couple months that we will leave soon, well this time I think I am right. All furloughs and passes have been canceled. Today the furniture in our day room was sold. After the 8th (according to the latest orders close) we won't even be able to leave our area.

> *Orders change so fast around here   that no one can be sure about anything except that if he's wrong he'll catch hell...I made expert firing the carbine*

Today I had to turn in my Tommy gun. I just got it last week after turning in one the week before. Such is the life of a soldier. Orders change so fast around here that no one can be sure about anything except that if he's wrong he'll catch hell.

Did I tell you that I made expert firing the carbine, I think I did. Today I made expert on the mortar gunners test.

Tomorrow I go out with my squad and get scored on giving fire orders and speed of having my gun crew hit a target. I did okay on this same test before, so I'm not worried.

I'm running out of stuff to say. There is probably quite a bit you would like to know, but it's the same old stuff to me. If you see a newsreel of some big guns firing, at a training camp, it's from here. Fort Bragg is the largest artillery camp in the world, at least in the US.

Dave demonstrating the proper way to handle a rifle

Well Sonny Boy, tell Bonnie and Donnie that I remember them, and to be good girls. Take things easy and write right away.
Dave

April 6, 1943
Dear Max,

I guess I better answer your letter right away before you get mad. I guess there are quite a few things to write about if I can think of them now, instead of after I close the letter.

> *Before I got in the Army I would have called anyone a nut who said I would jump out of a plane.*

Nothing new has happened except for the night jump we made last week. I told them about it at home so maybe you've heard about it already. So now I've got a total of 12 jumps from a plane. Before I got in the Army I would have called anyone a nut who said I would jump out of a plane. I don't even think there would have been a fortune teller crazy enough to say it and have me believe it. But I do it, and don't know why. The experiments in our company jumping with equipment we're so good that the whole 504 does it now, so we feel pretty good. When I jumped with the mortar tube and ammo I had to go through the door sideways, but made a perfect jump. Two men jumped with the complete gun but one of them dropped his and his Tommy Gun too, damaging both of them. I would rather have the tube and ammo, which can be used instead of a whole mortar and no ammo. Then all I could do is throw rocks.

Next week I may finally get that sergeants rating I've been waiting for. I heard that it went in a few days ago, and it takes 10 days to be approved, so I won't know for another week. I think I should get one because I'm pretty sure I've got about the best squad in the regiment. Our tests show it.

My gunner got 92, I got 90, and three other men made better than 70. Only one man didn't make it and he was new. 70 points is expert and when a man makes expert he is doing pretty good, because these tests are hard to make. I trained all these guys myself and that's what makes me feel good. I had a test Friday on how good a squad leader I am. We got five shells and a target, just like the test I told you about before. It took me three shots to hit the target, which is the correct way, one over, one under, to get the right range, then blooie, right on it. The officer who is giving the test said we had the fastest team he had tested yet. I hope you don't mind me bragging but I think we're pretty good.

Next week I may finally get that sergeants rating I've been waiting for... I'm pretty sure I've got about the best squad in the regiment.

It won't be long now before we take off. Things are getting packed. After the eighth we won't be able to leave camp anymore and we will be expecting to leave any time and spend a lot of time waiting and screwing around. When we travel we will look just like any other soldiers. We won't wear any insignia or anything that will show that we are special troops. If it wasn't that our clothes fit good, and that we march good, anyone will think that we are rookies.

I do know that when we do fight it will be against seasoned troops, so we'll have to learn the hard way.

I got a letter from Launie and he said he would let me know his new address when he gets there. It'll probably take a year for me to get a letter to him from where I'm going. I think it will be England or Africa, but that's only a guess. It won't be long though till I find out. I do know that when we do fight it will be against seasoned troops, so we'll have to learn the hard way.

Jack is probably a soldier by now in a camp somewhere in California. I hope he gets into some kind of special service instead of being just an ordinary Road packer.

I haven't heard from Larry for quite a while. I guess he's pretty lazy when it comes to writing a letter.

Well, Max, this has turned into a longer letter than I thought and I've just about run out of things to write about. So I'll wish you and Julie lots of luck and clothes. Right soon and let me know how the old town is.

Dave

The April 15, 1943, letter to his parents was Dave's last one from Fort Bragg. He talks about security and traveling unidentified after they leave Ft. Bragg. He has officially earned the rank of sergeant and tries to reassure his parents he will be OK by discussing his weapons, training, and plans not to take any unnecessary chances.

April 15, 1943
Dear folks,

This is the last letter I'll be writing from Fort Bragg. It won't leave here until after I do which won't be later than Tuesday so that when this letter finally reaches you I will be on my way to some port of embarkation, on the East Coast here somewhere. You understand that the reason the letter is held is so that no information will leak out to the wrong people.

I don't know how long we'll stay in the port of embarkation, but while we're there we'll have inspections of all kind and check-ups, and when we leave we'll have everything we need to fight except ammunition, and that won't be very far away.

I got a letter from Goldie and Max today and a few days ago I got letters from Ben, Jule, and Jack but I haven't answered any of them because the mail isn't going out. So you let them know why I haven't written. You will get cards with my new address as soon as we leave so you will probably know what it is as soon as I do.

I lost a carbine somewhere so that I might have to pay for it. They cost around sixty bucks so I don't like the idea much. My lieutenant said he would pay for it but I don't want him to. It really wasn't my fault for losing the thing but I don't want anyone to pay my bills for me, especially when he didn't have anything to do with losing it.

I have bought a lot of V-mail so that it will get home quicker after I get across. You ought to do the same thing because you have lots of letters to send out too.

I'm glad to see that Jack got into the Air Corps. He will probably work into a nice soft job like I ought to have, but haven't.

I wish you could see me all ready to fight. I have my Tommy gun and a carbine and a machete.

Gee, why I forgot to mention it but now I got my other stripe. It's sergeant now. It took a long time but finally got here. It's better late than never.

You should see us when we leave here, we will be dressed just like rookies. We will have to cover up the Insignia on our arms and take the patches off our caps so that when we leave here no one will know we're special troops. Last Tuesday night when I was coming back from Florida I saw guards along the railroad tracks for over a hundred miles so you can see we are getting quite a bit of protection when we leave here. No one from the airborne section of the camp has been allowed to go to town and tell any secrets about when or where we're going, which we don't know ourselves.

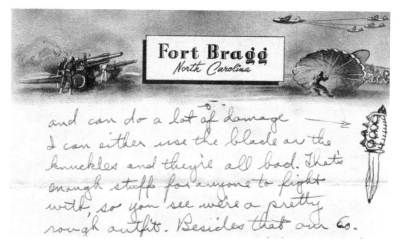

Dave's sketch of the trench knife on Fort Bragg stationery. Note the gliders in the upper right.

I wish you could see me all ready to fight. I have my Tommy gun and a carbine and a machete. The machete is a heavy knife about a foot-and-a-half long that I will use to clear brush out of the way so that I can fire my mortar, and it can be used for other things too. I also have a jump knife. It is a large pocket knife with a blade that jumps out when you press a button and the knife is kept in a secret pocket on the jumpsuit. We will also have a trench knife. It is a wicked weapon and can do a lot of damage. I can either use the blade or the knuckles, and they're all bad. That's enough stuff for anyone to fight with, so you see we're a pretty rough outfit. Besides that our company carries other weapons like a rocket launcher that shoots rockets at tanks and which causes a lot of damage and we also have rifles that shoot grenades which are also pretty wicked. We also carry twice as many machine guns as any other outfit.

This is probably the photograph Dave referred to in the letter.

Don't think we use all those guns at once though. Being parachuters means that we might fight anywhere or anything so that one time we might use only one kind of gun or another time some other kind. In any case we are prepared for anything and afraid of nothing.

Maybe one of these days you'll get a letter from me from Berlin or Tokyo and I hope it isn't too long away but I'm afraid it is.

There, now I've given you a lot of military information that you didn't know before but I want you to be sure that we will be able to take care of ourselves when the time comes which I don't expect to be for a couple of months yet. So I will close with love to Ma and Pa and the rest of you. Don't think about my future too much because this baby is taking no chances if he can

> *In any case we are prepared for anything and afraid of nothing... Don't think about my future too much because this baby is taking no chances if he can help it.*

help it. By the way, how do you like my picture? It was taken some time ago, but I didn't send it home. Well, be careful and don't catch any colds.

Dave

CHAPTER NINE

NORTH AFRICA, SICILY AND ITALY

North Africa May 10, 1943 – July 9, 1943

The 82nd Airborne left Ft. Bragg on April 18 and moved to Camp Edwards in Massachusetts. On April 29, 1943, they shipped out from the East Coast on the *USS George Washington* and sailed to North Africa. They arrived in Casablanca on May 10. From there, they marched eight miles south and set up an encampment. Then they were shipped in "40 and 8s" north to Oujda, Morocco, for several miserable months of training to prepare for the invasion of Sicily in July. They practiced in the desert heat and prepared as best they could. Dave wrote several letters from North Africa and was not too complimentary of the place at the time. He even made a few sketches to send home.

The letter below is the first to survive from North Africa and may well be the first one he wrote. Blackie was a stamp collector so Dave was always trying to help him out when he could. Dave gave kudos to the Red Cross. He has some unusual things to relate about the North African soldiers fighting the Germans in Tunisia alongside the American soldiers (these were probably the Moroccan Goumiers or Goums).[29] Dave seems to take the cutting off of German heads with a grain of salt.

May 3, 1943
Dear Jule,

I got your letter with all the stamps on it a couple of days ago but the reason I didn't answer right away is because we have been doing a lot of night work and it leaves me droopy all day. Sleep is no good because of the heat, so I waited till I felt pretty good to write. It's hard enough for me to make sense when I feel good.

I'm enclosing an envelope that I wrote to a friend of mine when I was in North Carolina. I don't know why he didn't receive it because he received later ones. Anyhow I thought you might be interested. It shows how the Army does try to get our mail to us.

The soldiers over here that collect stamps must be the ones who are more or less permanent, like MPs and N.Q. men and hospital attendants, or most anyone who has one of those nice non-combatant jobs we dream about. You know the kind of outfit I am in and how unstable we are.

I asked the censor officer in our company about the stamps on the envelope and he said it would be okay. I noticed that the foreign stamps on your letter weren't cancelled and I wonder if that is good or bad. Perhaps our post office doesn't cancel any foreign stamps at all, or does it?

I have been getting into town once in a while and find them pretty interesting. There is a mixture of the modern and ancient and the different dress of the different North African tribes. Each city has a district that hasn't changed for a thousand years. We aren't allowed to go in there because it is pretty dangerous, but some of the fellows have sneaked in and say it is quite an experience, just like stepping into a page from the Bible. The biggest nuisance though are the kids bumming for candy and gum, and will take anything they can get. The place is lousy with peddlers selling souvenirs. They start by asking ten times too much and end up by selling them by about five times too much. They do all right too, but the boys are gradually getting wise, or stocked up.

The food situation is really bad. There are no restaurants and where you can buy food there is no choice. You eat what you get, if you can stand the cooking. The best place to eat in any town is the Red Cross. They don't have too much to spare but what they have is American and good, and reasonable. No matter what anyone says, I think the Red Cross is doing a damn good job. Fountain pen went dry and I'm too lazy to go out and borrow some ink. As I was saying we were given the stationery I am writing on, more than a carton of cigarettes, playing cards, a pocket edition book each, candy, razor blades, pencils and other stuff, all to each man besides the usual coffee and donuts that really hit the spot. And besides that they provide recreational facilities or a soldier can relax or write, or see shows, and listen to a radio which has become a rarity.

No matter what anyone says, I think the Red Cross is doing a damn good job.

In town yesterday we saw a lot of the American soldiers who did the fighting in Tunisia. They were having a good time drinking and telling us about their experiences, and showing us a lot of the souvenirs they had. Their favorite seemed to be a small Italian bayonet. It is a nice weapon but in a fight I would rather have the longer and heavier American bayonet. One soldier told us about the black native troops who liked to sneak into a German camp where the men sleep three in a tent and would cut off the heads of the two outside men and then leave. He said that usually the man would go crazy in the morning when he woke up. Quite a sense of humor there. The native soldier also prefers the heavy knife to the bayonet because they have to stop to pull the bayonet out.

Well, philatelist, I guess I've covered the situation at hand. Naturally there are lots of things I would like to say but can't. I'm glad to see that the situation at home is coming along nicely. By the way, you couldn't stick Maria Montez in an envelope and send her over here. I doubt if she gets past a censor though. You could send me some candy - something that won't melt. Hard candy or caramels, or something similar.

Tell Bonnie and Donnie I remember them. Be a good boy.

Dave

Following sketches: first from Casablanca, next five from North Africa

COMING BACK FROM THE PARADE WHEN THE BAND
PLAYED "RETREAT"

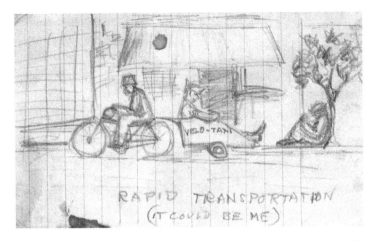

The next letter explains the sketches that were included with the original letter, but—sadly—not found in the surviving envelope. The envelope, postmarked October 27, 1943, was addressed to Dave's sister, Goldie, and the enclosed letter was dated June 1, 1943. So it was written prior to the invasion of Sicily, but not received at home until after he had been fighting for several months and was somewhere off the grid in the hills of Italy. The envelope also had a censor's stamp and was signed by E.J. Sims (Dave was later Lieutenant Edward J. Sims' Platoon Sergeant during Operation Market Garden).

The letter is light-hearted, whimsical, and self-deprecating. When writing home from the front soldiers knew the censors would not allow them to say much about what was going on. So to avoid alarming the folks at home they would write light-hearted letters free of any emotions and fears.[30] Dave's writing style seems to support that idea. A very amusing part of this letter involves a "big black beetle" that keeps invading his tent.

June 1, 1943
Dear folks,

I've been relaxing pretty much today so I got to fooling around with a pencil and thought I would send the results home.

That picture showing the pup tent shows how we spend most of our time — flat on our relaxations. The tents are so short that when I stretch out - which is how I sleep, that if it did rain I would have wet feet. Our barracks bags that we keep all our clothes in are out in the dust and our clothes that dry are just as dirty as when they were before they were washed.

Another picture is of a super-duper getting water out of a lister bag—that is where our drinking water is kept so that we won't run into any impure stuff. In this camp that bag is the only drinking water there is - pure or impure. It is brought in on trucks.

And then there is a picture of a guy when he starts the march and how he looks when he finishes. I don't think I've got enough droop on the guy in the back. Maybe hasn't got anything in his pack.

Then there is the row of chowhounds waiting to wash their mess kits, only actually the line is double and about three times as long. If you don't wash those mess kits good it means a lot of trips to the latrine - I know!

That picture of the pup tents again - those cans are C-ration cans that's what we eat when we don't have any kitchens set up -- or when we on the move. And that is a slit trench to the left of the tent - something to be used in case of an air raid.

If you don't wash those mess kits good it means a lot of trips to the latrine - I know!

I wrote a V-mail letter today too. Let me know which one gets home sooner. That V-mail is so small it doesn't allow a person to say much. Not that I say much anyway, but the principle is there.

I've just thrown a big black beetle out of the tent for the fifth time - one of us is going to get tired soon.

Two letters in one day is a new record for me, so I'll close before my chest expands too much. Boy I could sure go for some of that nice barracuda fried in butter. So long - good luck.

Love, Dave

I've just thrown a big black beetle out of the tent for the fifth time - one of us is going to get tired soon.

Dave began to send a lot of Vmail from now on. V-mail letters are one page long either typed or handwritten; reduced in size to take up less space and weight in the mailbag. Consequently, the letters are shorter than previous letters *(see the December 29, 1943, letter for an example).*

The paratroopers were training almost every day in North Africa to prepare for the invasion of Europe. This letter mentions TNT, mines, and booby traps.

June 27th, 1943
Dear Jule,

Today I received your letter of June 9th. I am answering right away as I have little time to spare today. We have been having quite a lot of training lately and there are lots of days when we don't have time to write, or don't feel like it. We train seven days a week and have sometimes we don't even know when Sunday comes around. It makes no difference either way, yesterday afternoon we got into town for a few hours. I saw the inside of a theater for the first time since we've been here. It was a nice place, pretty modern but even the screen was very dull and the sound was bad, and I think there was only one projector. The picture was a Republic production. I think the name was Ice Capades or something similar. Anyhow it was an American picture. French movies are shown sometimes but I hear they are not so good so I don't try to see them.

I had a lot of fun learning how to handle TNT and mines. We practiced setting up booby traps and there is no limit to the ways they can be set. Naturally, by making them we learn how to disarm and where to look for them. We got a kick out of a couple of Italian mines that have so many safety devices on them that they are unsafe and not to be monkeyed with. The wops are afraid of them too. Hope that water truck gets here pretty soon so that I can wash before supper. Wish I could help you with the stamps but you know how tough it is, especially in this outfit.

I had a lot of fun learning how to handle TNT and mines.

Comes the end again. Tell Bonnie and Donnie I remembered them and said hello. So long. Be a good boy.

Dave

PS notice the new address.

North African summers are sweltering, which seems to dominate the conversation. Not very many letters from North Africa have survived.

July 6, 1943
Dear Jule,

In that song Dear Mom the guy starts telling about the weather right away. Well, that's the way it is here. Nothing to talk about but the weather and all I can say is that it's plenty hot. Some nights we get cool enough to sleep. 125 degrees is pretty common here. I've got a tan that is better than I ever got at Long Beach. Even my bald head has a nice color. If you can find a way to send me one of those nice cool Tom Collins I sure appreciate it. We're going to have a surprise today. Nice cold American beer. Something I have not seen since before we came over. You should taste the stuff that's sold here. It's weak, diluted and has a sweetish taste. The wine is bad too, so the beer tonight should hit the bullseye.

Once in awhile here we hear that at home the newspapers have the war won already. Well, we're not so happy about the situation because we have to fight it yet.

> *If you hear anyone griping about the situation at home, tell him to see me after the war. I'll give him something to gripe about.*

I've been pretty busy today and writing a little bit of this letter whenever I can. That hot wind has come up again. Close to 130° now is my guess.

I guess everyone at your place is okay and getting along fine. Tell Bonnie and Donnie hello again for me. If you hear anyone griping about the situation at home, tell him to see me after the war. I'll give him something to gripe about. So long now.

Dave

Capturing 200 Italians in Sicily

The Allies decided to begin the invasion of Europe from the south and chose the island of Sicily as their first point of attack. The strategy was to attack from the south so that the Germans would eventually shift resources there and away from the northern coast of France. The Allies planned to invade from the northern side of Europe, so the attacks in Sicily and Italy intended to weaken the German forces in Northern Europe.

The initial drop of the 82nd Airborne was at night. The Third Battalion of the 504 (Companies G, H, & I) combined with the 505 Parachute Infantry Regiment for this initial drop, and David was in H Company. This drop was the first significant combat jump of American paratroopers. The pilots leading the flight formations were guided by compass bearing and travel time to judge distances with a near full moon to provide some limited assistance. Any small errors in bearing or timing would put them in the wrong place over Sicily to drop their sticks.

Consequently, most of the paratroopers were mis-dropped in Sicily. They were prepared for that possibility by having a plan for reorganizing on the ground. They also had a default plan for what to do if they could not find their unit.

Dave was mis-dropped. He and Corporal Lee Black, an H Company Medic from Tennessee, were captured by 200 Italians. In an interview by AP Reporter Clinton Green on July 15, David said the following:

"They captured us," said Rosenkrantz, "but then strange things began to happen. They held a conference and decided to turn themselves over to us for they heard that the Americans were only eight kilometers away. They presented us to the Chief of Police of the nearby town and he fed us, wined us, gave us good beds and declared on his honor that he was glad to see us. In fact, everyone was happy, including our prisoners. Around 4 that afternoon the Italians marched into Scicli, where they surrendered. They gave us their guns an hour before, so we let them go in alone. They were singing and just about raising hell, and a couple of them remarked that they hoped they would be sent to a prison camp in the United States."

This story became a big deal back in the United States and especially in Dave's hometown of Los Angeles. Americans were very anxious about when the invasion of Europe would begin and getting any news they could. Dave was an instant celebrity in the LA news which spilled over onto his mother. She was interviewed and

ANGELENO 'CAPTURES' CAPTORS---BY REQUEST

BY CLINTON GREEN

Representing the combined American Press. Distributed by the Associated Press

WITH AMERICAN TROOPS IN SICILY, July 15. — The toughest, roughest Yanks I have met since landing with American invasion forces in Sicily five days ago are our paratroops.

The easiest way of describing them is to say that they are always looking and spoiling for action.

THE WORLD'S WAR FRONTS

PACIFIC — MacArthur troops capture Mubo; 45 Jap planes shot down over Rendova, Jap counterattack at Munda beaten back. Page 1, Part I.

SICILY — United States troops drive inland in race toward Catania plain with British advancing up coast. Page 1, Part I.

RUSSIA — Red armies open offensives in Orel sector, recapturing 110 towns. Page 1, Part I.

KISKA — Fourth naval bombardment of Kiska in eight days indicates attempts to capture it near. Page 4, Part I.

They overcame all kinds of opposition and difficulties, which began when they were dropped some miles from their objective and rounded up hundreds of prisoners practically single-handed.

Along the dry, dust-covered highway outside the town of Comiso I found Sergt. David Rosenkrantz of Los Angeles and Corp. Lee Black of Jackson, Tenn., who captured more than 200 Italians and in turn were royally feted by the Chief of Police of the small town of Scicli.

When they hit the ground in the early morning darkness of July 10 Rosenkrantz sprained his ankle. He and Black hid out until daylight and shortly after they started walking. They marched right into a concentration of 200 Italian soldiers.

"They captured us," said Ros-

Turn to Page A, Column 1

Cont. on next page

honored for having four sons in the service. She was even in a parade in Los Angeles. The family was on a high knowing that Dave was safe after his first combat experience.

LOS ANGELES WARRIOR 'CAPTURES' HIS CAPTORS

Continued from First Page

enkrantz, "but then strange things began to happen. They held a conference and decided to turn themselves over to us, for they heard that the Americans were only eight kilometers away.

"They presented us to the Chief of Police of the nearby town and he fed us, wined us, gave us good beds and declared on his honor that he was glad to see us. In fact, everyone was happy, including our prisoners.

"Around 4 o'clock that afternoon the Italians marched into Schell, where they surrendered. They gave us their guns an hour before, so we let them go in alone. They were singing and just about raising hell and a couple of them remarked that they hoped they would be sent to a prison camp in the United States."

Six Close to Death

Private David F. Travis of Brawley, Cal., told me that eight of his fellow paratroops led by a Capt. Johnson of Texas waited in ambush and let an enemy half-track and German armored car go by. Then all eight let go with everything they had, said Travis.

One of the men told me that the captain shouted, "Hell, we mowed them," but that a split second later the vehicles just piled up.

Six paratroopers nearly met

death before they left their planes, Capt. Melvin W. Nitze of Los Angeles, along with Private Walter Cheney of Cumberland, Md.; Theodore Allegretto of Johnsonburg, Pa., and Corp. Randolph Wheeler of Deerbrook, Va., bailed out when they were caught by anti-aircraft fire. A wing and tail of their plane practically were shot away and the same mishap befell the plane in which Corp. Jesse Snow, Or-ange, Va., and Private Donald Giguere, Meriden, Ct., were riding. In the case of the latter pair their left wing was shot off and left motor on fire.

"But we're here, or what the hell," said Private Giguere.

Feted Paratrooper Went to Watts School

Sergt. David Rosenkrantz, 27-year-old American paratrooper, who captured a unit of 200 Italian soldiers in Sicily, joined the Army in February, 1942.

He is a Los Angeles boy, son of Mr. and Mrs. Hyman Rosenkrantz, of 1693 E. 92nd St., and attended Jordan High School in Watts.

The sergeant went overseas three months ago after receiving training for his aerial assignment at Ft. Bragg, N.C.

Three other brothers are serving their country, one with the Merchant Marine, one in the Air Forces, and one in the Navy.

His sister Goldie received her last communication from him on Wednesday—a brief note accompanying a handmade leather letter case picked up in North Africa.

Change Urged in Italian War Leaders

BERN, July 13. (P)—Roberto R. Farinacci in his Il Regime Fascista tonight demanded a change of military leaders in Sicily and assignment of Italy's best forces to defend the island.

In a violently phrased front-page editorial the former secretary of the Fascist party in Italy attacked useless elements in the Fascist hierarchy and demanded a "hierarchy of valore, a hier-archy that knows how to give the people a little sunshine after so many fiascos and so much bitterness."

Most outspoken of the Fascist editors, Farinacci declared that Italy is living in exceptional moments and it "is absurd and extremely dangerous to measure the choices of men and decisions with the military annual as a yardstick."

The Battle of Biazza Ridge

One of the most significant battles in the early part of the invasion of Sicily was the battle of Biazza Ridge. (Ruggero, Combat Jump, 2003) General Gavin discovered that there were several large forces of Germans heading towards the Allied beachhead. He believed that if the German troops could get past Biazza Ridge, they would have superior strength and could attack the beachhead before it was firmly entrenched. He decided the Allies needed to hold Biazza Ridge and keep the Germans separated and at bay. General Gavin collected paratroopers on his way there and ordered them to hold the ridge until the beachhead could be secured. With much sacrifice they bravely did just that, using small arms fire against German tanks. This was not only a significant battle; it was perhaps one of the most important in all of World War II regarding the use and deployment of paratroopers.

Critics of Sicily's airborne operation called it a SNAFU (Situation Normal, All Fouled Up). Gavin believed that it was the best executed SNAFU in the history of military operations and could be better termed a SAFU (Self-Adjusting Foul Up), but the true determination of success of any military operation can best be gauged by the enemy's evaluation. General Kurt Student was the foremost authority in the German Army on airborne operations and after the war stated:

The Allied airborne operation in Sicily was decisive despite widely scattered drops which must be expected in a night landing. It is my opinion that if it had not been for the Allied airborne forces blocking the Herman Goering Armored Division from reaching the beachhead, that division would have driven the initial seaborne forces back into the sea. I attribute the entire success of the Allied Sicilian operation to the delaying of German reserves until sufficient forces had been landed by sea to resist the counterattacks by our defending forces.

Gavin believed that it was the best executed SNAFU in the history of military operations...

I attribute the entire success of the Allied Sicilian operation to the delaying of German reserves until sufficient forces had been landed by sea to resist the counterattacks by our defending forces.

—General Kurt Student

The man who led the 505 RCT's drop onto Sicily should have the last word:

In the last analysis, the accomplishment of the mission is a tribute to the...fighting heart, individual skill, courage and initiative of the American Paratrooper.

General Eisenhower, Supreme Commander of the Allied Forces in Europe, questioned whether the use of paratroopers was a good idea. He was considering converting the airborne units back into infantry units. However, the Battle of Biazza Ridge and other substantial impacts that the paratroopers had in

Sicily caused him to change his mind and continue to support them. General Gavin is a fascinating military person to study.[31] He was promoted to general at age 37 and was the strategist behind the effective use of paratroopers.

I don't have any information about David's specific role at Biazza Ridge. It is hard to reconcile the date when he helped capture the 200 Italians with the date of the Battle of Biazza Ridge. He is in a photograph published in several places including the book *Combat Jump*.[32] The picture shows paratroopers with a German Tiger tank captured at the Battle of Biazza Ridge, he is standing at the forefront of the photo. On the turret of the tank with a rifle is his friend Sgt. Fred Thomas. I talked to Fred and his son Dave Thomas at the beginning of my journey to find out what happened to Uncle Dave. I wish I'd known about Biazza Ridge when we spoke so I could have asked for more details. Sadly, Fred is no longer with us. Incidentally,

German Tiger Tank Captured in Sicily supposedly at the Battle of Biazza Ridge. Sgt. David Rosenkrantz second from right. Sgt. Fred Thomas on the turret with a rifle.

Dave Thomas is named after my uncle Dave.

The following letter is the earliest from Sicily. Dave complains about the mail and a mistake that resulted in a delay in receiving his pay. He gives an interesting description of Casablanca that doesn't seem to align well with the movie of the same name.

August 1, 1943
Dear Jule,

I'll start this letter by complaining about the mail situation here. It's bad. We haven't received any mail since about July 6th. When we will get any no one knows. In my case the money situation is bad too. No pay for months. Someone spelled my name wrong somewhere. Hardly anything to buy here but who likes to be broke?

Most of the people are poor because of the war. New clothes are very rare.

When I was in Africa I got into Casablanca a couple of times. Not much like the city in the picture of the same name. The dirty Arabs and the smell of horse manure kind of detract from the glamour of all the African cities. Even when we saw a nice-looking French or Spanish girl she usually had sores on the calves of her legs that didn't look very pleasant. Here in Sicily everything is nicer, but the smell in the city still lingers. Most of the people are poor because of the war. New clothes are very rare. When we first arrived here the civilians were afraid of us because they were told we would rape and kill civilians. Since we have been here we have treated them very good and given them lots of our food and cigarettes. They were paying $0.50 for one cigarette. Now they get them free by asking. These V-mails sure are short. Send me those newspaper articles. News is very scarce here. Hello to Bonnie and Donnie.

Dave

The next letter was written from North Africa after the 504 was finished in Sicily and before going to Italy. This letter is significant because it talks about Dave's older brother Max having a serious accident. Max was working in a factory, and a piece of flying metal hit him in the eye and, sadly, he lost it. I can't help but reflect on my poor grandmother who had four sons in the military, lost her second daughter the year before, and now one of her sons at home lost his eye. Dave's sense of humor is captivating in how he talked to Max about the accident and the bad drinking water. Also in the second letter is a reference to Dave's younger brother, Launie, a Radioman in the Navy in the South Pacific. Launie had already been in many naval battles by this time, including one where his ship (*USS Chicago*) sunk and he was rescued from the ocean.

August 5, 1943
Dear Max and Julie,

Yesterday we got our first mail in over a month, and we were glad to see it come in. But today I got a letter from Goldie telling me about your accident and it wasn't good news. You know you should leave that kind of stuff for us guys over here that go out looking for accidents. Besides we can get a Purple Heart Medal to show for things like that. I suppose by now though that you are back at work, putting out the production.

I hope you saw those pictures in the newspapers about our jump. All the pictures and names of paratroopers are men in my platoon and good friends of mine. Those are the first pictures. I guess there are later pictures I haven't seen. They were printed July 12th.

Between now and the time I get home you better start stocking up on beer because it's going to take lots of it to get the taste of this chlorinated water we drink out of my mouth. Write soon and give me all the local news. Take it easy.

Dave

Back in North Africa (Kairouan)

After Sicily, the 504 shipped back to North Africa for a short time. Dave finally got some candy and a Hollywood studio magazine.

August 20th, 1943
Hello Blackie,

I received your candy and studio magazine yesterday. That really was swell candy and hit the spot. It's been several months now since I've had anything nearly so good. Thanks a lot.

That article in the magazine says you're thinking about joining the Marines. If you haven't already let me know when you do. I don't see where the Marines are such a hot outfit, but they get along OK, I guess.

We have moved out of Sicily back to North Africa near where we were before. This place has actually got some showers where we can get real clean again, but we are going to miss that shave-and-a-haircut in Sicily, all for $0.10. Shampoo is $0.05 extra. The first 3 or 4 weeks a girl in a house cost about 7 to 10 cents but after the Army took over the price went way up to $0.25 where we were. And other places the prices were a little more conservative, usually $0.20.

I understand we will have movies in this area. I sure hope so. Night before last, before we arrived, there was a French burlesque show at the Air Corps nearby. From what I hear it was pretty good. Take it easy. So long. Good luck.

Dave

Operation Avalanche: Sept. 9, 1943

On September 9, H Company joined with the 325 Glider Infantry Regiment and Rangers to land at Maori. They captured Chunzi Pass and the tunnel. In the meantime, 1st and 2nd Battalions jumped on the Salerno Beachhead the night of September 11. G and I Companies of the 3rd Battalion arrived at Salerno with a beach landing on September 13. The arrival of the 3rd Battalion helped repulse the Germans on September 18. The actions of the 504 during this time were highly praised by General Mark Clark.

Above: Tunnel near Maiori in 1943
Below: Tunnel today (photos courtesy of Dave Thomas)

Naples and Chunzi Pass Oct 1, 1943

The 504 entered Naples on October 1, 1943. After taking Naples, the 504 fought in the hills in terrible terrain against a determined German foe. We have very few of David's letters home from his time in Italy. Below is a V-mail letter written October 5. He refers to a movie that Blackie is working on with Maria Montez[33]. Maria was very popular, and movies were cranked out quickly during the war. Dave is unable to write about where he is or what he had been doing, although it turns out he had been in some very nasty fighting in the hills of Italy. His next two letters did not reveal much about their action, typical soldier's ploy to avoid alarming family.

October 5, 1943
Dear Blackie,

I guess you've been waiting quite a while for this letter, in fact I know you have. Anyhow, such as war, and we write when we can. I did receive those clippings you sent, and I'm expecting a package that you mentioned. If it's as good as the last one, it will be plenty okay.

It's hard to think of anything to write about because I can't say what I'm doing or where I am. When I can I know you'll be interested. The places are famous.

I suppose you're still working on the same pictures with Maria Montez. Wish I were there although I see some pretty nice looking girls around here, and they are awful friendly.

I hope you and Bonnie are still clicking and tell Donnie I remembered her. Be careful and lots of luck.

Dave

October 25, 1943
Dear Goldie,

I just received your package with the socks and handkerchiefs. When I first saw the package I thought if it was a cake, well, it wasn't anymore. A little early for a Christmas package but now is the time to get them.

I hope you like the bracelet in this letter, if it's still together. I'm taking a chance that it won't be broken. Anyhow, it's a little Christmas present from me to you.

I don't know how those short socks are going to work in the boots like we wear. I'll try them and let you know, and in case you ever send any more the size is 10 1/2. My feet are pretty dainty.

Sorry I don't feel like writing much today but I've got a headache - bad stomach or something - otherwise I'm still in good shape. I hope you and the rest of the family are all feeling fine and getting along well. Tell Ma and Pa I'm sending all my love as usual, and wish them the best.

Dave

Finally in his two letters dated November 29 he alludes to the action he saw. Conditions during his time in the hills were terrible. Again, we see that packages from home are greatly appreciated.

November 29, 1943
Dear Jule,

That box of candy I received from you yesterday really was a pleasant surprise. I wish it would have arrived here a couple of weeks ago when we were up in the mountains, tired cold and eating cold rations, but the mail is all held up til we have been in a rest camp for a week. Such is the Army especially our outfit that leaves everything behind except what we can carry. No kitchens or supplies or mail trucks keeping up with us. For three weeks all we had was what could be carried to us on mules, and even water was what I could catch in my canteen cup, dripping off my shelter-half for a couple of days. Right now my improvised camp isn't doing so good. This stable is a little drafty, but if the jackasses could stand it, I guess we can. So much for my troubles. Thanks again for the candy, which incidentally, is very good. Tell the family I remembered them. So long - good luck.

Dave

In his next letter from Italy to his brother, Dave talks about the poverty and conditions there during the war. What he sees in Italy here is contrasted later with his experiences in England.

Dear Jule,
December 2, 1943,

Well, today is starting out real nice. Just like at home. A little frost in the morning, then a bright clear sun, the rest of the day. At least we hope so. It rained about 26 days out of the last month. Not continual, but during some part of the day. This is sunny Italy all right, but the sun comes in such small bunches, and every time it rains the snow gets a little lower on the mountains. Might have a white Christmas yet.

We have been resting and eating pretty well. We have some fried chicken promised us from some people in the town here. We trade some stuff we

> *This stable is a little drafty, but if the jackasses could stand it, I guess we can.*

> *These people really are poor. They even put patches on the patches.*

would ordinarily throw away. These people really are poor. They even put patches on the patches. They won't take money because there is nothing to buy. The best shops in Naples wouldn't even be a close second in Watts. It's a nice-looking country, but looks don't count here.

As for me, I'm still okay and feeling pretty good now. Hope you are all the same. So long and good luck. Love to Ma and Pa and all the rest.

Dave

December 29, 1943
Dear Jule,

I received your Christmas cards about a week ago up on the top of a mountain. They got a little wet in the rain and beat up a bit, but got plenty of attention just the same. Yep they certainly were nice. We're in a rest camp now, so we can appreciate them a little better. Where we were, even the gals themselves wouldn't have taken our interest away from the Jerries's. You should have seen us. No shave or wash for over (censored) days. We really looked rugged, and felt it too. I'm getting to be an old man, in fact we all are. Our outfit has (censored) than any other as far as we know, here in Italy. It gets tougher as it goes along. I'll bet

> *I received your Christmas cards about a week ago up on the top of a mountain... I'm getting to be an old man, in fact we all are.... See you next Christmas - maybe - good luck.*

that our idea of when the war will be over here varies quite a bit with those analysts in the states. We don't have the armchairs. See you next Christmas - maybe - good luck. Hello to Bonnie and Donnie.

Dave

What makes the letter especially interesting is the censor stamp in the upper left corner and censored items in the letter. The censor was Lt. James "Maggie" Megellas. As of this writing, Maggie is 103 years old, and it has been my pleasure to talk or meet him several times over the last 19 years. In this letter, Dave alludes again to the terrible conditions they had while fighting in the hills.

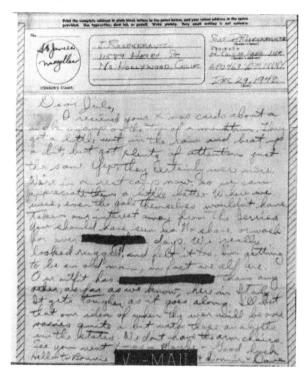

V-mail from Italy, December 29, 1943. Censored by Lt. James Megellas

Back to Naples (January 4, 1944)

The 3rd Battalion returned to Naples on January 4, 1944. In the next V-mail to my father, Harry, Dave continues to encourage him to play the accordion. He also continues to talk about the people in Italy. This letter was probably written in the hospital as according to the morning reports Dave went into the hospital on January 9 with a sinus infection. He returned to duty on January 22, the same day as Operation Shingle began. Dave mentions the hospital in his letters on January 21 and January 26.

January 19, 1944
Dear Rosy,

Yep, it's my nickname too. Some of the men think it's the only name I got - that is, when they're not in a bad mood. Makes me feel pretty good when my company commander calls me Rosy. Very seldom when a CO will call a sergeant by his nickname.

How is your accordion holding out? Must be pretty ragged by now. Goldie said something about it. Don't suppose it could be rebuilt, huh?

One restaurant in Naples has a duet, violin and guitar, one a vocalist, that wanders from table to table. If you ask for (what do you think) well-known Italian number, you get either South of the Border, Butcher Boy or Beer Barrel Polka. I think Butcher Boy is an old Italian number. This country sure isn't what we expected. They don't even have good spaghetti. As far as I'm concerned, everyone in town is a thief, and his brother's a pimp. All the good Italians are in the small mountain villages. Each village is different from the others - good - bad - or worse. Write soon.
Dave

January 21, 1944
Dear Jule,

I just received your letter of December 20th. Took quite a while to get here for some reason. I suppose that cut on Donnie's leg has just about disappeared by now. Over here she would have been listed as a casualty and received the Purple Heart just like a soldier. Probably you know by now that I ran into some sinus trouble and I'm in a hospital in (censored). We are well taken care of and get to see a couple of movies and stage shows during the week but these headaches I get are woozies and the treatments are killers. If the sinus doesn't kill me the treatments will. Right now my head feels like it is in a vice. (hope that nurse gets my pills soon) - tell Bonnie and Donnie I haven't forgotten them, hello, and regards. Be careful. I'd take the Navy.

Dave

Anzio – Operation Shingle (January 22 – March 23, 1943)

Anzio was a controversial campaign. Some felt that after landing at Anzio, there was a window of opportunity to head inland. Instead, the units held at the beachhead and were under attack for a long time. The Germans held a superior field position and bombarded them every day, resulting in heavy casualties.

Dave's next V-mail letter was typed, allowing him to fit more in, and dated soon after Operation Shingle[34] began. He mentions being out of the hospital.

Operation Shingle is the name given to an amphibious landing by the Allies in Italy during World War II. It took place on January 22, 1944, began on January 22, but it is unclear where Dave was on January 26. A Morning report shows Dave returning to "Light Duty" on January 22. However, the fourth sentence below hints that Dave was already out of the hospital a week before this was written on January 26. The fact that he is on a typewriter may hint of light duty—perhaps at the CP. The reference to recently attending a movie indicates he may not have been on the front on Jan 22. The letter after this one is dated March 7, 1944, so we are not sure when Dave rejoined his unit at Anzio.

January 26, 1944
Dear Jule,

I just received your letter of December 30 and about the most interesting thing I noticed was about Bonnie having her fortune told. If any chance she can find out when the war is going to be over please let me know. I'm very anxious to find out - - - - very anxious. When I was in the hospital last week I got into a slight argument with a medic when I told him that the further back from the front I got, the sooner the boys had the war won. He didn't like it a bit but it gets me the way the men who never were shot at have everything figured out. I tell them whenever I get a chance. Could I have some arguments back in the States, even a few practical demonstrations - - - you know what I mean.

Guess I'm not doing so bad with this typewriter so far but it is a lot slower than writing, for me anyway. It isn't every day that I have a chance to use one of these things. I can type as fast as I can pick the letters out, getting better by the hour. This is a wop machine and a couple of the letters are placed different than on an American so - - - well it's an excuse anyway.

Goldie sent me a subscription to the Los Angeles Daily News. The first papers are just getting here, only 2 months old. Did someone say better-late-than-never?

I got to see a new Deanna Durbin picture couple of days ago. Don't remember the name but it was with Pat O'Brien. Also saw Stage Door Canteen. Not bad pictures. Wish there were more.

Have you ever tried walking down a rocky mountain in the rain on a pitch-black night?

By the way next time you decide to send some pictures, how about the original instead? I'll pay the postage. Don't ask about the girls over here. I could write a whole letter about them - - - and none of it good.

Well so much for me. After the war when there are no censors I'll tell you more. By now you ought to be well into a picture. And I suppose you're still sweating the draft. Take the Navy - - - if you don't get seasick. There is a lot of difference between sleeping on the cold, wet ground and being in a warm ship. Have you ever tried walking down a rocky mountain in the rain on a pitch-black night? Well, I can finally see bottom. Longest letter I've written in a long

time. Take it easy and give my best to Bonnie and Donnie.
Good luck.

Dave

The 3rd Battalion was committed with elements of the British
1st Infantry Division in the heaviest combat. The paratrooper
companies, due to the severe fighting, were reduced in strength
to between 20 and 30 men. H Company drove forward to rescue
a captured British General and was cut off. They were rescued
by 16 paratroopers from I Company led by Lieutenant Roy
Hanna. It is unknown what role David may have had in that
battle.[35] For its outstanding performance from 8 to 12 February
1944, the 3rd Battalion, 504th was presented one of the first
Presidential Unit Citations awarded in the European Theater of
Operations (ETO).

For the remainder of their eight-week stay in the Anzio
beachhead, the men of the 504th found themselves fighting
defensive battles instead of the offensive operations for which
they were better suited and trained. For the first time, the men
were engaged in static trench warfare like that of World War I a

American parachutists...devils in baggy pants...are
less than 100 meters from my outpost line. I can't
sleep at night; they pop up from nowhere and we
never know when or how they will strike next.
Seems like the black-hearted devils are
everywhere...

—-Wehrmacht Officer at Anzio

generation before, with barbed wire entanglements and
minefields in front and between alternate positions.

Even though pinned down, the paratroopers would sneak out at
night across the German lines capturing and killing them as
they slept. Another paratrooper, Sgt. Fuller, who was with David
at Anzio was very sad to hear about his death and said David

was a very accomplished sniper there. He remembers David taking seven shots and making seven kills.

The name *Devils in Baggy Pants* stuck with the 504 Parachute Infantry Regiment and mainly to all paratroopers in the 82nd Airborne. It was taken from the following entry found in the diary of a Wehrmacht officer killed at Anzio:

> *"American parachutists...devils in baggy pants...are less than 100 meters from my outpost line. I can't sleep at night; they pop up from nowhere and we never know when or how they will strike next. Seems like the black-hearted devils are everywhere..."*[36]

The next three poignant V-Mail letters were from the Anzio Beachhead. An eye-opening excerpt of a proposed Presidential Unit Citation Award is included in the Appendix and gives a graphic description of the conditions they endured. Dave can't describe how bad it really is in the letters other than the few understated lines he snuck past the censors. In the March 15, 1944 letter, Dave also gives his opinion about the striking workers at home. Writing from a foxhole gives his opinion some credibility! In my opinion this letter should have been reprinted in the newspapers at home!

> *February 27, 1944*
> *Dear folks,*
>
> *Today is another one of those nice rainy days when you wish you were somewhere else. Usual Italian weather. My feet have been so wet and cold for days at a time that they ache nearly all the time now, even when I'm nice and dry. Spring should be here soon but I don't think that will stop the rain. I suppose you've guessed by now that we're on the Anzio beachhead. Where the fighting is the toughest, that's where I am. Not because I want to, but that is no reason. I'm not kidding when I say that I'm in for a good long rest if I ever get back from this war. Just going to sit back in front of that radio and eat and drink beer mostly.*
>
> *I hope that you are all in the best of health and taking care of yourselves. Be good and I'll do the same.*
> *Love, Dave*

Dave's next V-mail letter talks about sleeping in a hole and is probably a reference to the fox holes they slept in at Anzio. He also alludes to the possible adverse effects of his war experiences.

March 7, 1944
Dear Max and Julie,

Received a letter from you a couple of days ago. You told me about buying the place where you're living. It's getting pretty bad when you have to live in a house. I'll bet you don't even go outside for your toilet. Take me, for instance, I have a nice hole to sleep in and don't have to worry about windows to wash or lawn to mow. Just a little mud in the blankets is all I have to worry about, and believe it or not, I even shave once or twice a month. But I am glad that you're getting a home. Maybe I will someday too. Even get married, who knows? But by the time this war is over and I get home (I hope) I'll be so old and my nerves will be so bad, I won't be worth marrying anyway. All I'll be able to do is sit around and read dime comic magazines if they don't get too exciting.
So long now, be careful, good luck.

Dave

...by the time this war is over and I get home (I hope) I'll be so old and my nerves will be so bad, I won't be worth marrying anyway.

March 15, 1944
Dear Julie and Max,

Just received your letter of February 24th. That's good news about Launie getting a leave and being put on a shore station. It's a break he's deserved for a long time. At the rate of 1% a month going home from our outfit you can expect me in about a year. Remember that song. "I'll be home in a year" (I hope). We read about the strikes in the states and we would like to trade places with them, just for the duration of the strike. Let them dodge shells and sleep in a muddy hole, and sweat Jerry counter-attacks, and eat cold canned rations for a few days, besides going without a washing and changing socks for weeks at a time, and see how willing they would be to strike. Besides that doughboy is only getting 50 bucks a month and no place to spend it except on cheap wine and diseased women. This is a hell of a war here no matter what the newspapers say, and it's just starting. So long now.

Best of luck, Dave

On 23 March 1944, the 504th was pulled out of the beachhead by landing craft and returned to Naples. They were exhausted after eight weeks of nearly continuous fighting in Italy which cost the 504th dearly; just over 1,100 casualties were sustained. Almost 600 of these, or 25 percent, were suffered during the fighting at Anzio alone and two of three battalion commanders had become casualties.[37] On April 2, 1944, Dave wrote the following V-mail letter to his brother Max and his wife, Julia.

April 2, 1944
Dear Max and Julie,

Well, you're right when you say I want a long rest when I get home, but wrong about a pin dropping, waking me up. When I can sleep through an artillery barrage, I think it'll take something a little heavier than a pin to wake me up. I'm off the beach head now, in a rest area, and having a pretty soft time. In fact right now I don't feel so good because of eating too much. Have been getting a lot of champagne lately. Bootleg stuff I believe, but it sure goes down easy. I haven't drank enough of anything here yet to get drunk. Some of the brandy and cognac that is sold here actually is made with gasoline and other stuff, I don't touch any of it. Stick to wine which is real stuff most of the time. Pretty soon I won't know what water is, except that the

Army just won't let me forget. So long now. Be good. Best of everything.

Dave

CHAPTER TEN

RECUPERATING IN ENGLAND

On April 10, 1944, the 504 boarded the ship *RMMV Capetown Castle* and arrived in Liverpool, England, on April 22. He wrote the following letter home two days after arriving. He explains why he got his Purple Heart and mentions the Presidential Citation[38] the battalion received for its actions. Among the items returned home after Dave was MIA was a Presidential Citation Ribbon that had been worn. David also received a Bronze Star for action on February 22 at the beginning of Operation Shingle.

April 24, 1944
Dear Max and Julie,

Received your letter of April 12. Mail service is a little better to here. Didn't know I was in England, did you? Surprise! Can't say any more about it yet. I guess you've seen the Purple Heart I sent home. It's for the sprained ankle I got when we jumped in Sicily. Our Battalion got a citation for the fighting they did at Anzio. It is the

> *Our Battalion got a citation for the fighting they did at Anzio.*

second citation given to a battalion in the war over here, so we feel pretty good about it. I missed some of the action when I was in the hospital with my sinus, so I don't know whether I'll be able to wear the medal that comes with it.[39]

I'll let you know, though. So Tobias has to take his exam. I don't think he'll make it, but if he does, well, it's like we say here - tough sh--! Is he still married? I can't think of anything to write about. Everything that I would like to tell you wouldn't past the censor. So that's all for now. Keep sending your good letters. You say more than all the rest put together. So be good for now.

Dave

H Company of the 504 PIR was one of the last units to leave Italy before the invasion of Europe on D-Day, June 6, 1944. The 504 did not get back in time to rebuild their units with replacements and be at combat strength for D-Day. Twenty-five paratroopers from the 504 were, however, recruited to become Pathfinders for the June 6th invasion. The Pathfinders dropped behind enemy lines hours before the main attack so that they could set up signal flares for the Drop Zones. A lot of work has been done to document the 25 Pathfinders from the 504 by military historian Dave Berry. I had the privilege of meeting Bill Hannigan—one of the 504 pathfinders— at the 504 reunion in 2002 in Fond du Lac, Wisconsin. The gathering was also a book signing for Lt. James "Maggie" Megellas. Maggie's book, *All the Way to Berlin*, is a WWII classic in my opinion.

Dave's unit was in England for almost five months. During that time, they trained, and they drank. One of Dave's very best friends was Sgt. Albert Tarbell who told me about some of their exploits in England. Albert was also interviewed for the book, *Brave Men, Gentle Heroes*, by Michael Takiff (Takiff, 2007)—a fascinating book of interviews of fathers and sons. In each pair of father and son the father had served in WWII and the son had served in Vietnam. In his interview, Albert devoted 1 ½ pages to tell about his friend Rosy:

Right after D-Day a few of us rode our bikes up a long hill - there was an English pub there that we went to. We were sitting having this warm beer, and there was a bunch of locals. They kept looking at us, eyeing us.

Finally one of them says, "How come you guys are here enjoying yourself? We got all those people there in France.

They're sleeping on the cold ground, and they're not getting no beer. They're not enjoying themselves."

I told him, "Look, we saw action in Italy, and now we're trying to get enough men to go back into combat." I says, "Do you know this man sitting over here?" And I pointed to Rosy--his name was David Rosenkrantz; everyone just called him "Rosy." And Rosy's face starts getting all red. That's the kind of guy he was - he started to blush.

I said, "He's a hero."

The guy says, "What do you mean?"

Albert Tarbell is on the left
(Outridge, 2007)

"He captured 200 Italian prisoners." When he is was in Sicily before I joined the outfit he got captured by the Italians. He ended up coming back to camp two weeks later with two hundred prisoners - they all surrendered to him. We used to laugh about that.

My God, once I told them about Rosy, we couldn't drink enough beer. They were giving their rations of liquor to us.

We left there, and we had to go down that steep hill on our bicycles. I don't know how we made it that trick turn.

Rosy was quite a guy. I really love him. He was always kidding around. Rosy was a big, heavy man, and I understand that he was a very good shot. Sergeant Fuller told me one time that Rosy spotted some Germans and started picking them off. Every time they got up, he hit one man. He got seven shots off, and he killed seven guys.

Rosie was killed in the Den Heuvel Woods, in a German counterattack after we landed in Holland.

Rosie was killed in the Den Heuvel Woods, in a German counterattack after we landed in Holland. We took a shellacking there. We had to move that night, so we weren't able to bring out his body. Then, when some guys went to locate the body, they couldn't find it.

Dave wrote about England in the four letters below. He comments about difficulties training on English moors, reassignment to rifle squad leader, English girls, and being out of money. At one point he laments the fact he can't afford to go on furlough. Then, in a subsequent letter tells about borrowing money and having a good time. My favorite letter is where he describes the daily British routine in Blackpool. He was amused at how the beach would be vacated every day at 4:00 p.m. for tea time.

May 12, 1944,
Dear Max and Julie,

Did you hear about the bride who wore her clothes to bed because her husband said he was going to town that night? Joke finished! No I'm not a mortar squad leader anymore. It turned into an easier job, so someone else got it. I'm a plain rifle squad leader, which means I have to do all the different things that might come up, while the mortar sergeant sits back on his dead behind and waits for an order to fire. Made a jump a few days ago. First one since Sicily so we thought that being so long it might bother us, but it didn't. But on the way down some guy swings into my chute making me come down so hard I pulled some muscles in my back. For a while it felt like it was broken, but I'm tough! Was in London for two days. Tried to drink all the beer but couldn't. Wolf in me came out. Picked up a girl in a pub. A nice girl - damn it. Piccadilly is the part of the city where all the movies are and all the excitement is supposed to be but the town isn't alive like LA. So long now. Be good.

Dave

June 2, 1944,
Dear Jule,

Received your letter of May 23 today. Kind of spoiling me when you write such long ones. Might get so that I expect them all the time. I would have written you but I didn't know your address so what could I do? I've got lots of time to write now because we are getting restricted every other night. If more than two men miss bed check at 11 the whole company has to stay in the next night. Naturally the first night out again four or five men will be late so next night restriction again. It's hard to be in bed at 11 when it is still daylight outside, and when a guy has a girl out waiting for it to get dark so he can do her something he sure isn't going to worry about getting in on time. More than one girl has been given the works in a city park here in broad daylight, and people all around watching. That's why we keep getting more and more restrictions. Hey girls here are very nice. If a guy propositions one, she usually says to wait another night because she doesn't know you well enough the first night. Really though the girls are nice and good-looking. Easy to get along with, but they very rarely show up the second night. I got stood up three times now by three different ones so I don't mess with them very much anymore. Those Italian women were seldom nice looking, usually in need of a bath, and I wouldn't trust any of them. The more I saw them the less I liked them. Glad I'm away from there.

You explained some of the strikes at home. I know you're right but some are unnecessary now and could wait, but there is time to settle all this stuff when we get back, and settle it we intend to do. You asked me about this guy Russell Snow. I'll look around and see if I can find him. If you had sent me the company he's in, maybe you ought to, and if he isn't too far away I'll look him up. Meantime I'll see if I can bump into him.

As for coming home for a while we recommend one man a month which put me up in the first 10 or 12, but that has stopped now, and if it starts again I should be one of the first six, but there are politics in the Army too. There are at least four of us more eligible than the next man in line, but he's gotten his name submitted and we haven't, so as we say in the Army - It's just tough s***!

I wish I could tell you more of where I am and what I am doing, but everything here is hush-hush. Probably already said more than I should somewhere in this letter. But I'm still getting around, not as well as I used to but pretty well for an old man. Put on about 10 lb since we got here. Beer, you know. The weather really changes cold one day - hot the next. Never know what to expect.

Saw Ali Baba and the crooks in town last night. Old picture but still think Monty has got something.

So long for now. 8:20 now. Be getting dark in a couple of hours, can hardly wait. Be a good boy.

Dave

The following letter may be too much information (TMI) about VD in the paratroopers. At one reunion I was told by someone that after weeks and months of combat many of the paratroopers figured their days were numbered. Assuming they didn't have much time left they weren't too worried about a little more risky behavior.

July 19, 1944
Dear Jule,

Received your letter of July 4 a couple of days ago. Sorry about you and Bonnie. One of those things. We have a girlfriend? I've one or two or more over here. Getting so that I'm afraid to touch one anymore. Too much venereal disease. Same old story. She's too nice to have it then you find yourself in the clap ward. The paratroopers are the best and our outfit as always had the highest venereal rating. Another first! About this

Sad story two weeks to payday, five bucks in my pocket and five-day furlough coming up this week.

Russell Snow again. Sure it's H 504? There are other regiments with same APO and with H Company but not 504 or could be HQ Company. Sad story two weeks to payday, five bucks in my pocket and five-day furlough coming up this week. All very sudden so no one saved any money. Haven't even enough money to pay ordinary expenses. Everyone trying to borrow money - tough sh..! So long now. Write soon. Know any good stories to keep the boy's morale up? Be good.

Dave

The letter below has been published on Dave's website https://www.cpp.edu/~rosenkrantz/paratroop/sgtdave.htm for almost 20 years.[40] I received an email from a writer in England, Peter Outridge, who had seen my uncle's letter about his adventures in England. Peter was writing about the five-month period in England when the 504 PIR was between battles in Italy and Holland. He wanted permission to use the letter and also wondered if I could tell him anything else. I gave him Albert's phone number and told him he was a great resource for his book topic. I was surprised to see that Albert's picture ended up on the cover of the book. The book has a very appropriate title: *Baggy Pants & Warm Beer: 504 Parachute Regiment of the US 82nd Airborne Division in Leicestershire UK, 1944* I was able to meet Peter when we visited the Netherlands for the 65th Anniversary of Market Garden in September 2009.[41]

August 3, 1944
Dear Folks,

Well I guess you are all anxious to hear about where I went on my furlough. I went to a city in the Northwest part of England that is known as the "Coney Island" of England. It is a regular beach resort and has just about everything that a beach should have except good weather and Americans to give it the right atmosphere. It is funny as hell to see all the people leaving the beach at the same time to go home to eat lunch, exactly at 12, coming back all at the same time, then all leaving to go home to tea at the same time. You can just about tell what time it is by the way the people are going to or from the beach. The weather is no good for swimming,

> *It is funny as hell to see all the people leaving the beach at the same time to go home to eat lunch, exactly at 12, coming back all at the same time, then all leaving to go home to tea at the same time.*

too cold and foggy. Get about a couple of hours of sunshine in the afternoon about 9. I had a pretty good time though. Took life easy and really relaxed like I intended to. I want to thank Harry for sending the money to me. It didn't get here in time as I expected, but I managed to borrow the 50 bucks in the meantime so it didn't really matter too much but we would have all been in a pretty bad way if the Army hadn't arranged things so that the boys could write checks in a bank in town on the accounts that they had at home. Probably be a lot of rubber checks bouncing around here soon but I don't think anyone is really worried about them, least of all the guys that wrote them. I forgot to tell you the name of the beach - it's Blackpool, not what you'd expect the name of a beach to be, huh?

Received a letter from Goldie yesterday of July 22. Says she is taking a rest under doctor's orders. Well I hope that she is better now. She better take a nice long rest for me now. Last night we were out on one of those nasty night problems again. This time we were out on one of those English Moors that I have always read about but never saw. It is a part of the country that a heavy fog always hangs over so that the grass is always wet and the ground swampy. In a little while our feet and legs were soaking wet and cold. Go out of sight of everyone in the fog and you're lost and I do mean lost. If we didn't have compasses we'd walk around in circles. One fellow came back to the same place twice in 10 minutes and each time he thought he was going in a straight line. Really a fog!

That's all for now. All my love to Ma and Pa and all the rest. Goldie still like the Scotchman? So long now - be good.

Dave

CHAPTER ELEVEN

OPERATION MARKET GARDEN

After D-Day in June 1944, Field Marshal Montgomery from Great Britain came up with a plan for an operation intended to shorten the distance that troops would have to travel and fight to reach Berlin. The intention was to get to Berlin faster and reduce the length of the war. The operation was called Operation Market Garden—*market* referring to the air assault and *garden* referring to the ground plan. A British Tank Corps would head north through Belgium and Holland and then turn east into Germany heading for Berlin.

The plan was to use paratroopers to drop at or near three cities with critical bridges, Eindhoven, Nijmegen, and Arnhem...all in the Netherlands. The paratroopers would capture the bridges so that the tanks could head north through Belgium and the Netherlands and enter Germany. The 101st Airborne Division was tasked to drop at Eindhoven and capture the bridges there. The 82nd Airborne Division was to drop near Nijmegen and secure the bridges that crossed two lower branches of the Rhine River: the bridges in Grave crossing the Maas Canal and those in Nijmegen that crossed the Waal River. British Paratroopers and Polish Paratroopers were to capture the bridge at Arnhem on the upper branch of the Rhine River. The bridge at Arnhem later became known as a *Bridge Too Far*—the title of a famous book and movie by Cornelius Ryan. (Ryan, 1974) [42]

The whole operation was supposed to take only a few days and involved over 30,000 paratroopers and glidermen dropped in over two days to swiftly capture the bridges before they could be blown up by the Germans. Operation Market Garden was the largest airborne mission in history. It was risky for a myriad of reasons, but Montgomery ignored many of the concerns and convinced Eisenhower to proceed with it.

On September 17, 1944, Operation Market Garden began on a bright sunny Sunday. The 504 dropped into a drop zone near Overasselt just outside of Nijmegen. They quickly captured the bridge at Grave. However, the railroad bridge and the road bridge at Nijmegen were still tightly held by the Germans on both sides of the Waal River.

On September 20th, the 504 PIR was tasked with crossing the Waal River to capture the north ends of the railroad bridge and the road bridge. The 505 PIR was assigned to take the southern end of the road bridge that was securely held by the Germans. With the bridges at Eindhoven and at Grave secured and repaired the tanks were on their way. H and I companies from the 504 would be the first to cross the Waal River in small canvas-wooden rowboats provided by the British. The boats were delayed in arriving at the riverbank until almost 3:00 in the afternoon. The paratroopers would be crossing the Waal River (a.k.a. The Waalcrossing) in daylight instead of under cover of darkness. The need to ford the river was urgent. German Panzer divisions were devastating British paratroopers who had parachuted into Arnhem. The crossing of the Waal was necessary because both ends of the bridge were under German control and had to be captured simultaneously. The strategy was to use artillery fire across the river to create a smokescreen during the river crossing. However, it did not work as well as planned.

The British rowboats finally showed up; each one capable of holding about a dozen paratroopers plus three engineers. The 307 Engineers were tasked with manning the paddles and rowing the paratroopers across. The paratroopers mostly rowed with their rifle butts. When the boats started across the river, the German artillery and mortars opened up on them. Many of the rowboats did not make it across, and there were many casualties. However, a number of the boats succeeded, and those paratroopers then had to cross several hundred yards of open field to reach the bunkers, machine gun nests and hundreds of enemy soldiers. There was no other alternative. Remarkably, many of the outnumbered paratroopers made it across the open ground and took out the opposition. This action would turn out to be one of the most daring and heroic missions of the entire war. The paratroopers then moved upstream toward the first bridge—the railroad bridge. By the grace of God, Uncle Dave was one of those who made it across the river and to the railroad bridge.

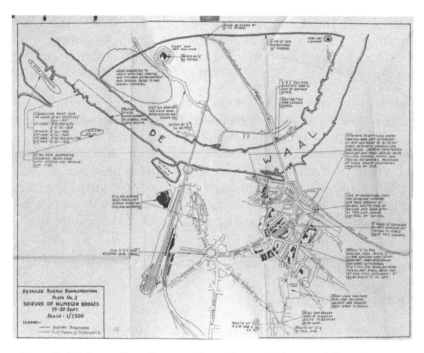

Detailed Seizure Supplement Plate No. 2 : Seizure of the Nijmegen Bridges

This is the only document I have seen that shows which companies crossed the Waal on each wave of boats. It also shows the times when each bridge was captured.

Uncle Dave was interviewed several days after the Waalcrossing battle by Times War Correspondent B.J. McQuaid. More detail about the article is mentioned in the next section, However, what happened next was a bloodbath as the Germans fought from the bridge and the Americans fought back and captured it.

The 504 paratroopers passed the railroad bridge along the Waal River and captured the north end of the road bridge. By then the 505 PIR had won the south end; British tanks arrived and were able to cross the bridge heading toward Arnhem. The 504 crossed the river at 1500 hours, captured the railroad bridge at 1700 hours and the road bridge at 2100 hours. The Germans tried unsuccessfully to blow the bridge with previously planted explosives, but the wires had been cut. There is some controversy as to who cut the wires, but it is commonly believed that a young Dutchman, Jan van Hoof, did it and was eventually captured by the Germans and executed. To this day he is considered a hero; his statue is located near the south end of the bridge.

The British tanks stopped at the end of the bridge and refused to move toward Arnhem. This upset the Americans who had just sacrificed half of H and I Companies by crossing in daylight, so the British tanks could head to Arnhem and rescue the beleaguered paratroopers. British paratroopers were also captured and killed in large numbers. The stopping of the tank corps is still a controversial action to this day. The Waalcrossing is considered one of the most heroic actions of World War II.

Newspaper Interview

A few days after the Waalcrossing David was interviewed by a *Times* war correspondent, B J McQuaid. The article was published in the *Indianapolis Times* and the *Chicago Daily News* on October 10, 1944.

SECOND SECTION	TUESDAY, OCTOBER 10, 1944

NAZIS DIED LIKE FLIES IN BATTLE OF NIJMEGEN BRIDGE—

Tougher—and Bloodier Than Salerno

War Correspondent Article by B.J. Quaid quoting S/Sgt David Rosenkrantz, October 10

David told about capturing the railroad bridge across the Waal or Rhine River. David was quoted in the newspaper as saying:

> *Several hundred yards downstream we saw the great Nijmegen railroad bridge which the paratroopers also*

captured intact. S.Sgt. David Rosenkrantz, Los Angeles, Cal., told us the story of the scene presented on that railroad bridge during the first hours after the assault boat crossing in which he was a participant.

Rosenkrantz, with a machine gun squad, was in position at the northern end of the bridge when suddenly a whole battalion of German infantry, unaware that the crossing had been made and intent on escaping back toward Germany, started across in marching formation, three abreast. The small band of paratroopers, outnumbered more than 10 to one, waited until the bridge was clogged with Germans from end to end and then, revealing their commanding position, called on the advance foe to surrender. Instead, the Germans began throwing hand grenades.

The Paratroopers sent forward a prisoner they had captured, who agreed to convey the surrender request to his countrymen. The Germans shot him dead as he

> *The small band of paratroopers, outnumbered more than 10 to one, waited until the bridge was clogged with Germans from end to end... At dawn the next day dead men hung from girders and blood dripped from steel beams.*

advanced. This was too much. The paratroopers opened up with machine guns, automatic rifles and bazookas. For the next few minutes the bridge presented a fantastic spectacle, with the Germans hopelessly trapped by withering fire but nonetheless trying to fight back. They took cover behind steel girders and even managed to wriggle up into the superstructure from which they fell like flies into the river.

At dawn the next day dead men hung from girders and blood dripped from steel beams. Paratroopers, walking out onto the bridge counted 267 and carried off scores of wounded. "It was typical of what went on during the battle of Nijmegen Bridge," Rosenkrantz said. "Nijmegen did not last as long as Sicily, Salerno and Anzio, but it was tougher, and bloodier while it lasted."[43]

Note that while this stretch of river is called the Waal River and is considered part of the Rhine River by the American paratroopers. They are clear that they were the first ones to cross the Rhine.

I have watched the nine-minute movie clip showing the Waalcrossing from the movie *A Bridge Too Far* many times. Each time I am amazed at the courage and sacrifices made by my uncle and the other men who crossed in those flimsy rowboats under direct enemy fire. I can't imagine what that would be like and am humbled to be associated with my Uncle Dave.

Arnhem: A Bridge Too Far

After the road bridge was captured and the British tanks crossed, they did not proceed to Arnhem, 12 km away. Consequently, the American paratroopers stopped here also. The British feared there was too much enemy resistance between them. British paratroopers were in deep trouble in Arnhem; they had dropped quite a distance from the bridge they intended to capture, and we're expected to make their way to the bridge and hold it long enough for the British tanks to arrive. The tanks never made it and the paratroopers had to surrender.

Operation Market Garden was considered a failure by most.

Everything that could go wrong for the British went wrong: their supplies were dropped to the Germans instead of them, their communications did not work, and their forward contingent of paratroopers was separated from the main group of ten thousand British paratroopers. Seven thousand paratroopers were either killed or captured. The Polish paratroopers who were supposed to help them were delayed several days by bad weather. From this standpoint, Operation Market Garden was considered a failure by most. There are compelling viewpoints that counter that opinion, but as far as getting to Berlin earlier it did not happen through Operation Market Garden. The Americans had liberated parts of Holland, and that was good. But sadly some follow-up bombings by the Germans in retaliation were bittersweet.

Zeldenrust or Maasmolen?

Several years ago someone sent me an image of my uncle reclining on the grass with some Dutch citizens and another paratrooper near a windmill. I eventually posted it on my website and some-time later received the following email from someone stating that the windmill in the picture was near the drop zone of the 504 PIR at Overasselt, Holland:

Hi, I am a citizen of Overasselt and read the story of your uncle, it makes me sad he has died! We Dutch are still

Dave with a Dutch family after the drop on September 17, 1944

grateful of thanks what the Americans did for our country! The picture with the mill at Overasselt was always a favorite of me. The mill broke down in 1972 in a storm in November. They rebuilt the mill in 1984 on a new place! The mill's name is Zeldenrust what means never at rest......If I can do anything for you please let me know. I hope you can read my English......the memorial is placed in 1985. I was in the Dutch Army then also as a para. I should have jumped with five veterans in September 1985 but the weather was bad so the dropping was canceled. If you want some pictures of something just let me know and I will send them to you.

Theo Fleuren, Overasselt

Judy and I visited the Netherlands in 2014 and wanted to find the restored windmill, which I had located using Google Earth before our trip. As we drove around the neighborhood A woman came out of her house and nicely asked if she could help us. She pointed it out nearby and Judy took my picture next to it. Seeing the windmill was more emotional than I expected. Standing next to it I realized that 70 years earlier Uncle Dave had stood next to the structure as well. The old drop zone is well-identified with monuments and every time we have visited there are memorial events.

...70 years earlier Uncle Dave had stood next to the structure

In September 2018 I wondered if there was any possibility of identifying the four women in the photograph. I reposted the photo on Facebook on a WWII related page. Amazingly—thanks to assistance from many Dutch people—I got some answers! Mirjam Maria Claus in the Netherlands contacted *The Gelderlander* newspaper. Staff member Ronald Peters contacted me and on September 29, 2018, published an article featuring the photo and asking readers for help in identifying the people. Almost immediately he got a response from Theo Ariëns who knew the answer and a lot more!! Theo said the following about the people in the photo [roughly translated],

"The wife is Jean van Haren-Dijkman, the wife of Lou van Haren, 'The mulder'. The girls are her daughters. The older girls are deceased, I do not know the youngest, but she does not live any more in the village."

But then Theo provided more to the fascinating story, *"We lived a short distance from the windmill, in a dike house. Father, mother and fourteen children. On the day of the landing James Megellas was... looking for Germans, but they were not there anymore... Megellas took (about 10 men) and moved into the house of the Ariëns family."*

Apparently, they slept in the barn. Theo goes on to say, *"But then and after the war the names of those soldiers regularly have [been discussed], including that of Rosenkrantz. My older brothers and sisters then talked about that."*

It is so amazing to find out such detailed information 74 years after it happened!

It is so amazing to find out such detailed information 74 years after it happened! We still hope that the young girl in the photo can be found.

Surprisingly, on March 1, 2019, I received the following information from Peter Pouwels about the photograph, the windmill, and the people in the photograph:

Nederasselt mill 17-18 September 1944, some US soldiers of the 82nd Airborne Division, with Sergeant David Rosenkrantz in the front right. The woman is Sjaan Dijkmans, the wife of Lau van Haren, "the mulder", the girls are her daughters; Miet 16 years old, Mien 11 years old and Truus 4 years old?

Peter included a photo of the de Maasmolen windmill in Nederasselt.[44]

The two contributors agree on the identity of the family in the photo, but not on the identity of the windmill. I am looking forward to resolving this issue someday.

Maasmolen Windmill 1965. (Image provided by Peter Pouwels)

That Fateful Day

Now we come to September 28, 1944, the sad day in history where our beloved Uncle Dave made the ultimate sacrifice. This part of the story takes place a week after the Waalcrossing when Dave's platoon was sent on patrol. H and I Companies were near the main line of resistance in Groesbeek near the Den Heuvel Estate. I Company was sent across the main line of resistance to Den Heuvel where they took the area back from the Germans and spent the night. First Platoon of H Company was sent across the main line of resistance to Heuvelhof, a small farm on the Den Heuvel Estate several hundred yards south of I Company, where they also spent the night. A large counterattack was being planned by the Germans. They attacked both companies at dawn after shelling the area for quite a while. The terrible attack against

The H Company retreat was not orderly, it was every-man-for-himself.

I Company involved hand to hand combat and heavy casualties. I Company troops at Den Heuvel and the H Company 1st Platoon were told to retreat as soon as they realized what was going on. The H Company retreat was not orderly, it was every-man-for-himself. The platoon members took cover, but Dave did not get the word. According to Sgt Ted Finkbeiner and PFC Larry Dunlop, David went running by them near the farmhouse where they had taken cover in their foxholes. Ted yelled at Dave to get down, but Dave stood up behind a tree, apparently to take aim at some Germans in the distance. Unfortunately, they were being attacked from behind also and he was killed by machine gun fire. Ted and Larry Dunlop said Dave lay there dead and they couldn't do anything about it because they couldn't leave their cover. At night they snuck out across the main line of resistance. When they returned later to get Dave's body, they could not find it.

MIA at Heuvelhof

The DPAA report summarizes the battle with additional details about the German forces involved and the action that took place:

> *The farmland east of Wylerbaan Road was the focal point for a more intense battle on 27-28 September 1944, involving soldiers of the 504th PIR. The 504th PIR had landed south of Nijmegen during the 17 September drops. They assisted in the capture of the Waal River bridge at Nijmegen and were then sent east of town to Groesbeek. On 27 September 1944, 3rd Battalion of the 504th PIR took positions along the Wylerbaan Road, running northward from Groesbeek, Netherlands. German soldiers of the 58th Replacement Infantry occupied a farmstead known as Den Heuvel. While mostly open ground, the German forces had dug into the orchard and wooded area in front of the farmhouse. With the help of British tanks, the paratroopers pushed the German troops back and occupied the orchard and woods.*

The 504th estimated that the German 58th Infantry had suffered a 75% casualty rate in trying to hold Den Heuvel. Nonetheless, the 504th PIR expected the Germans to counterattack at dawn. By the early morning hours of 28 September 1944, Company I, 504th PIR, held Den Heuvel farm itself. Company H occupied the Heuvelhof farm, approximately 400 yards south. Company G defended the northern flank of Den Heuvel. At five in the morning, the German 58th Infantry launched an intense artillery barrage upon the Americans. For the next half hour, approximately two thousand rounds of shells fell upon or exploded above a piece of ground one hundred square

...two thousand rounds of shells fell upon or exploded above a piece of ground one hundred square yards... German shells burst in the trees, raining shrapnel down upon them.

yards. Most of the Americans had dug themselves into slit trenches, but the German shells burst in the trees, raining shrapnel down upon them. When the artillery barrage ended at 5:30 AM, the Americans realized the German 58th Infantry had moved forward – perhaps supported by Waffen SS troops – and were soon swarming over their positions in irresistible numbers. Three German Mark IV tanks bore down upon the Americans, firing their 75 mm cannons and spraying machine-gun fire. The firefight involved thirty-three minutes of intense small arms fire and artillery before the 504th PIR soldiers received orders to withdraw. The surviving Americans fell back, firing upon the advancing Germans as they pulled back to their main line of resistance.[45]

Another version of what happened with additional detail about the situation at Heuvelhof is quoted from *The Battle of the Bridges* by Frank van Lunteren:

To the east, south of the Den Heuvel farm, Lt. Joseph Forestal's 1st Platoon became surrounded as the German attack progressed towards the Wylerbaan. The platoon

was dug-in around the farmhouse, where Lieutenant Forestal had set up his C.P. [Command Post]. S.Sgt. David Rosenkrantz, his platoon sergeant, effectively executed command because Forestal had just been transferred-in the previous day, and hardly knew his men. Having suffered casualties during the flight and Waal River Crossing, the platoon was understrength, functioning with about 20 enlisted men and very few non-commissioned officers.
A German tank hit the barn behind machine-gunner Pvt.

...four soldiers of the 504th PIR are still unaccounted for... Sergeant David Rosenkrantz was reportedly killed near the Heuvelhof farm...

Lawrence Dunlop, setting it on fire: "The lieutenant was frantically cranking on the field phone, but I was certain lines were cut or blown up. By now artillery was firing at the Germans and driving them back, along with troopers from G and I Company. I remember Finkbeiner saying, 'We'll try to get back to our own lines when it gets dark.'

"Just around four o'clock, I decided to try and get back to our lines. I crouched down low and started out [on] the path that we had originally come from the night before. I hadn't gone 100 yards and there staring at me 50 feet in front of me were two big Germans. I turned around and was gone in a flash before the two Germans could move. I made it back to the house and took cover, looking in the direction of the Germans."

Suddenly Staff Sergeant Rosenkrantz ran past Dunlop. Rosenkrantz crouched behind a tree about 15 yards from one of his squad leaders, Sergeant Finkbeiner. Unaware that they were already surrounded, Rosenkrantz stood up to shoot at Germans some distance east of him. Finkbeiner shouted a warning: "Rosy! Rosy! Get down!" Almost simultaneously, Dunlop cried out a similar warning; but Rosenkrantz seemed not to hear him. "I heard the burp of a

German Schmeisser machine pistol that got Rosie 50 feet in front of me. I could see him when he went down and I was pretty sure he was killed. If I tried to get anywhere near him I would be a goner too. Staff Sergeant Rosenkrantz was killed near a tree in front of the house, but apart from his dog tags, no remains were ever recovered. Pvt. John J. Baldassar was also killed. Sergeant Finkbeiner, now in command as platoon sergeant led the remnants of the platoon back to the H Company area after dark. (van Luntern, 2014)

Again referring to the DPAA Memorandum of Record:

By mid-morning, the enemy held Den Heuvel and the surrounding farms. ... four soldiers of the 504th PIR are still unaccounted for from the fighting on September 1944: Sergeant (Sgt) Robert Dew, Staff Sergeant (S Sgt) Leon Baldwin, and Corporal (Cpl) David Stanford of Company I; and Sgt David Rosenkrantz of Company H.

...Those three [I Company] soldiers were last seen killed within the woods and orchard of the Den Heuvel farm, a distinctive oval-shaped feature lined by a farm road, present on wartime and modern-day maps and aerial imagery.

Sergeant David Rosenkrantz was reportedly killed near the Heuvelhof farm, the farmstead held by members of Company H, 504th PIR, during the 28 September 1944 German attack.

It is rare and exciting when you have the opportunity to visit the site of a relatively intact battlefield where someone was KIA or MIA, guided by an expert along with a living veteran who was there at the time. Over the past 20 years, I have collected shelves of books related to World War II history, biographies of people who died during the war, and memoirs of veterans or relatives of veterans. Most of these do not have accounts accompanied by actual on-site visits.

I had such an experience. While we were at Heuvelhof on September 19, 2014, an interview was conducted by personnel of the DPMO as part of the Operation Market Garden 70th Anniversary Oral History Project, September 2014. The team consisted of Dr. Ian Spurgeon, Ms. Christine Cohn, Dr. Ed Burton, and Dr. Jeff Johnson. The interview took place along the tree-lined driveway up to the Heuvelhof farm, outside the main house. Several family members were present, including myself, S/Sgt David Rosenkrantz's nephew, and Bud Kaczor, Cpl David Stanford's nephew, who was killed at Den Heuvel. Also present was Capt (ret) Moffatt Burriss, who commanded I Company during Operation Market Garden.

Ben Overhand had been researching the events at Den Heuvel and Heuvelhof for about 30 years at the time of the tour. Ben and members of the DPMO (later the DPAA) had been trying to discover what happened to the MIAs from the fight on September 28, 1944 and bring them home. At that time the missing 504 PIR men unaccounted for were: Sergeant Robert G. Dew, Staff Sergeant Leon E. Baldwin, and Corporal David L. Stanford of Company I; and Sgt David Rosenkrantz of Company H.

Interview Key:

BO = Ben Overhand
EB = Ed Burton
MB: Moffat Burriss
PR: Phil Rosenkrantz

The first part of the interview discusses where S/Sgt David Rosenkrantz was actually killed. The map below gives an aerial view showing the basic layout of the area.

BO: That's the road. These are the trees he initially took cover behind. And he tried to run that way, and he was shot from somewhere where we got the cars. That's where he was shot from. So he had 100% vision.

EB: It might have been around the second or third.

BO: Yeah, he was killed right on this road, or a little to the right of here.

The morning of 28 September 1944 First Platoon of H Company was at the Heuvelhof farm. They had spent the night there and were heavily shelled in the early morning. A major counterattack came from the East. However, German soldiers were also approaching Heuvelhof from the Southwest. S/Sgt David Rosenkrantz stood up behind trees lining the access road from the street to the farmhouse. He was facing east when Germans approaching from the Southwest shot him.

MB: That's the panzer division that we faced on that ridge up ahead right there... live fire.

BO: Rosie ... Rosie was killed here. Initially, he was laid up here because that's where the firearm business that the American paratroopers were just lying there. And Baltazar was buried by the Germans, Rosie initially had a shallow field grave. This is a heavily shelled area because the Germans occupied it. So the 75s and 81s, they started really pounding the hell out of these Germans because they didn't want to have them advance through the fields. And then, Rosie's body in the field grave got hit again.

Then the discussion turned to the location of the remains and what happened to them over the next few months. The ferocity of the German attack did not allow for Dave's remains to be collected and taken back to the company command post. His body was on the ground for a while because it was too exposed for the Germans to move. He was eventually buried in a shallow field grave but was hit hard by artillery fire and dislodged. The farm owner was evacuated until 1945.

The ferocity of the German attack did not allow for Dave's remains to be collected and taken back...

> BO: *Now the story of the farmer, the old farmer, was that when they returned in '45. In 1945, there was a field grave there, and there were remnants of an American paratrooper in this area right there. And this is where in '51 the little parts were found. But he saw in 1945 half a body, decomposed, with jump boots, having been removed. And this is the body the report says, one on the soil – topsoil – and one in the field grave. Now that's the one that sort of disappears out of the reports like a month after.*
>
> EB: *Yeah ... so, that's, I guess ... that's a lower half, you said?*
>
> BO: *Yeah, the lower half. Because he saw the jump boots.*
>
> EB: *So that, and Baltazar were the two that were found.*
>
> BO: *And Baltazar was obviously found and identified because the Germans put him in a proper field grave. But if you look at the position you are in here already, this is like an open field because there wasn't any corn. You can look all the way up to the Wylerbaan Road. Because nobody in their right set of mind would even walk here, you know because that would call artillery.*

Photo taken 27th of September 1999... showing approximate position of the Germans. According to Larry Dunlop's account Rosie came running from the direction the picture was taken. The barn on the left, visible through the trees, is the site of the old farm. It is here and in the surrounding orchards that the platoon of HTC 504 took up their positions. The orchard used to be where the two clumps of trees are in the background. I've found the remnants of a .30 cal. machine gun position there. Maybe Larry's old position?   Rosie is not the only soldier missing near this farm. The other MIA is Gerald W. Kight. He may have been of D Co but is predominantly listed as H Co and went officially MIA on the 28th. (Thanks to Ben Overhand for providing this photo and description).

So everybody stayed behind the hedgerows, behind the farm, so that no movement could be seen during the day. So they never really gave Rosie a proper burial with a marking on it.

BO: Well, the Germans ... just did a full-on, head-on attack, after the artillery barrage they did a full-on attack and they were overwhelming them. And I mean there were these guys from H Company that actually didn't get the order to pull back and they played dead.   They put themselves on their parachute and behaved like a corpse like they were dead. And he [another private] got out in the middle of the night, because he'd never heard the retreat order. Sgt Ted Finkbeiner and PFC Larry Dunlop were there

...there were these guys from H Company that actually didn't get the order to pull back and they played dead.

and were witness to what happened. They have slightly different accounts, but were trying to warn Dave to get down because they were surrounded by Germans.

BO: *Well, they were next to each other, because there were two different accounts about who warned Rosie – because, either one of them – but anyways, someone called out to him "Rosie, Rosie, get down! Get down!" because they'd already seen German troops go behind him. And obviously due to the din of the fight he didn't hear them, because he kept walking out straight into the German submachine- or machine-gunner.*

BO: *These are two Italy combat vets, and once they say that they said he was dead immediately, I think that you can pretty much call them experts on whether someone is dead or not.*

BO: *So, as I said before, in 1945 they found pieces of remains that were removed. I might talk to the new owner and see whether we can do some digging... I don't expect much to be left anymore, but ....*

...we got the dog tags that were recovered here!

PR: *And ... we got the dog tags that were recovered here!*

BO: *Those were found in 1951.*

> *BO: They also found his fighting knife. He had an M3 fighting knife that was still with him, two sets of jump wings – one of plastic, one of metal – his dog tags, his watch, and that was about it.*

The location of the field grave was near some existing stumps. The conversation turned to the field grave and condition of the remains.

> *BO: That's where the lower body part was found ... because he had a shallow grave ... so the Germans ... when the farmer was evacuated at the end of September, he saw him lying there.* *They were evacuated out toward Germany.* *And they went out of the barn and saw the body lying there, by the barn. He had seen him. So the Germans must have put him in some sort of shallow grave for hygienic reasons, they stuck him underground because they occupied this area.*

> *BO: And after that, after that initial H Company fight took place here, this area was shelled the hell out of. I mean, we found sixty pound Typhoon rockets standing right in the German trenches. None exploded, and one exploded. And we found parts in the whole German trench: left, right, up, but, everywhere. So they really blasted the hell out of them, and then in '45 again, when the Canadians and the British went into the Reichswald forest to invade Germany from here – from this place, or basically from the Wylerbaan – well ... it was like Verdun. There were four thousand guns firing just on this area.*

The question was asked: How many H Company got out of here?

> *BO: Everyone except those two.*
> *Voice: Oh. And they got out and moved where? Just Den Heuvel?*

> *BO: Just get the hell out. To the Wylerbaan Road and get the hell out. They were being swarmed. They saw tanks left and right. They saw tanks go right by. They needed to go. We found, literally hundreds of ammunition parts. Shells. Mortar shells. Rocket bombs. Still live, but it gives*

you a good indication of what they all put down on this farm.

It is no surprise that Dave's body was dislodged from his shallow grave, since thousands of artillery shells hit the area after he was killed. The shell also knocked his dog tags off his body. Had the tags remained with him, the identification of his remains would have been more routine. The book *Soldier Dead* explains that while finding dog tags on the body of a deceased soldier is helpful in identification, it may not be enough to ensure certainty. There are many historical examples where wrong dog tags were present for some reason and led to misidentification. Consequently, mortuary personnel encourage searching for confirming evidence. In the case of the Defense POW-MIA Accounting Agency (DPAA), historical, dental, DNA, and other means of corroboration are used to confirm proper identification. (Sledge, 2005)

Dave's boot size (7EEE) and dental records would have supported the identification. The proximity of the remains relative to the historically known location where he was killed would also support identification. Because there was nothing found on the remains to provide identification, the time frame for bringing him home changed from a few years to over 73.

PART THREE

THE 73 YEAR JOURNEY TO FIND UNCLE DAVE

CHAPTER TWELVE

WHY SEARCH?

The book, *Soldier Dead* (Sledge, 2005, pp. 8-29) discusses these reasons in depth, following is a compelling summary:

Forensic – It is essential to know how soldiers died to study the tactics, type of weapons, and armament that was most lethal in battle. This information can be used to prepare for future conflicts. For example, if poisonous gas was the cause of death, then some sort of gas masks should be available. Another reason is to verify if war crimes had been committed according to Geneva Conventions[46] related to the humane treatment of prisoners. For example, forensic analysis can determine if a soldier died in combat or was executed.

Morale – The esprit de corps developed between fellow soldiers is hard to describe. Soldiers feel honor bound to take care of the bodies of their dead buddies. It is demoralizing to see the bodies of fellow soldiers in the hands of the enemy or left behind.

Family – *"...without strong proof of death, families almost never give up believing that maybe their missing and presumed dead soldier is still alive."* (Sledge, 2005, p. 50) A funeral helps the living with the mourning process by confirming the reality of death. It expresses respect for the dead and gives people a chance to share their sorrow and grieve. This missing part of the grieving process was certainly true for our family. My grandmother died still believing her precious son was still alive somewhere. The funeral service in 2018 did help our family bring closure even though only two family members present at the funeral had any recollection of Uncle Dave.

Politics – A soldier's body is a physical representation of his or her nation. When in possession of the enemy there is a sense the enemy has some power over the battlefield. When the enemy displays footage of captured and dead soldiers, it horrifies those back home. When this happens, the tremendous political pressure to eventually bring our fallen soldiers home can affect controversial military decisions.

A soldier's body is a physical representation of his or her nation.

Morality – *"The cause for which they are sent to fight must be a just and vital one. Recovering the remains of our fallen measures the political and human costs of that cause, creating a ledger against which accounts must be balanced."* (Sledge, 2005, p. 27)

While fighting against the expansion of Nazism in WWII would be considered by most to be a just cause, one of the best examples acknowledging the value of the sacrifice took place at the National Cemetery at Gettysburg on October 19, 1863. The *Gettysburg Address* is a classic narrative about the value and purpose of sacrifices. Abraham Lincoln demonstrates the morality aspect behind honoring our fallen:

> *Four score and seven years ago our fathers brought forth on this continent, a new nation, conceived in Liberty, and dedicated to the proposition that all men are created equal.*

> *Now we are engaged in a great civil war, testing whether that nation, or any nation so conceived and so dedicated, can long endure. We are met on a great battle-field of that war. We have come to dedicate a portion of that field, as a final resting place for those who here gave their lives that that nation might live. It is altogether fitting and proper that we should do this.*

But, in a larger sense, we can not dedicate—we can not consecrate—we can not hallow—this ground. The brave men, living and dead, who struggled here, have consecrated it, far above our poor power to add or detract. The world will little note, nor long remember what we say here, but it can never forget what they did here. It is for us

The brave men, living and dead, who struggled here, have consecrated it, far above our poor power to add or detract. The world will little note, nor long remember what we say here, but it can never forget what they did here.

—Gettysburg Address

the living, rather, to be dedicated here to the unfinished work which they who fought here have thus far so nobly advanced. It is rather for us to be here dedicated to the great task remaining before us—that from these honored dead we take increased devotion to that cause for which they gave the last full measure of devotion—that we here highly resolve that these dead shall not have died in vain—that this nation, under God, shall have a new birth of freedom—and that government of the people, by the people, for the people, shall not perish from the earth.[47]

Uncle Dave *gave his last full measure of devotion* on 28 September 1944. His remains were not identified until early in 2018. That is over a 73-year journey.

CHAPTER THIRTEEN

THE JOURNEY BEGINS

Medals on the Mantle

I was born in 1949. While growing up in the 50s, I was often over at my grandmother's house. A framed plaque displayed on the mantle contained a picture of Uncle Dave with some of his medals. Every once in a while, someone would mention that he was a war hero, but there were never any conversations. Every once in a while, I would ask what happened to him and got a different answer depending on who I asked. One relative told me he died in France. Another said he died crossing the Rhine River. When I was about seven years old, one day my grandmother told me that everyone thinks that David is dead but that she knew that he was still alive somewhere. She believed that someday he would find his way home.

My grandmother passed away in 1960 without having any closure. The tragedies she experienced accumulated and took a toll on her. So, when she was told David was missing in action but presumed dead, she couldn't handle it and hung on to the MIA status as a way to cope with her emotions.

His loss was incredibly tragic for her. In the ten years I knew her, she never really smiled or laughed much. I can also look back at little signs that my father was still grieving the loss of his older brother as well. I speculate that my father threw the mantle plaque out because of the painful reminders.

When I finally found out what happened to Uncle Dave, I called my dad on the phone and asked him if he would like to know. He said he wasn't sure he wanted to. I did end up telling him, and he didn't have any comment. Dave was more than just an older brother to him—Dave was like his father. He was the one who took him to accordion practice, encouraged him and—even when he was away in the Army— wrote letters to my dad urging him to do the right things. Looking back, based on observations and conversations with my cousins about the impact on their families, I can see that there was grieving going on underneath the

...there was grieving going on underneath the surface of our family. Some of the joy was gone.

surface of our family. Some of the joy was gone. War can do that. Multiply this by the hundreds of thousands of families affected by the war in various ways, and you can see there is an impact on our country for generations after a major war.

Saving Private Ryan

Around 1997, I saw the movie *Saving Private Ryan,* starring Tom Hanks and Matt Damon. The story involves an Army squad sent into the countryside of France after D-Day to look for Private Ryan. Ryan, portrayed by Matt Damon, was a paratrooper dropped into France on D-Day. Unknown to him, his three brothers had been killed in various WWII battles about the same time. Upon realizing this tragic coincidence, the Army decided to find Private Ryan, pull him out of combat in France, and send him home. While this movie was fictional, the storyline is based on true stories where entire sets of brothers were killed in WWII, leaving bereaving families without a surviving son. Probably the most famous set of brothers from WWII were the five Sullivan brothers. They were sailors serving together on the *USS Juneau* and were all killed in action on its sinking around November 13, 1942.

In the movie, Tom Hanks plays Captain Miller, who led the squad on their search for Private Ryan. One of the squad members was the Jewish character Stanley Mellish. In the movie, they captured a German soldier and Mellish got very emotional and flaunted his dog tags at him, pointing out the embossed H, which stood for Hebrew-or Jew. Stanley used the German word for Jews: *Juden*. History would show that Hitler's *Final Solution*[48] for ridding Germany—and the rest of the world—of the Jews was to exterminate them in labor and death camps. Hundreds of concentration camps were constructed in

Hundreds of concentration camps were constructed in Germany and Poland for what is now known as the Holocaust resulting in the killing of over 6 million Jews and millions of others as well.

Germany and Poland for what is now known as the Holocaust resulting in the killing of over 6 million Jews and millions of others as well.

This part of the movie hit home to me because Uncle Dave was Jewish[49]. I later found out two things related to his faith. In 2012 we received his recovered dog tags, which had the letter "J" embossed on them indicating Jewish. Many—if not most—of the Jewish dog tags had an "H" on them. My understanding is that it was up to the commanding officers to decide what was embossed on the dog tags to indicate a soldier's faith. An interest of both the family and Dave himself was what would happen if he was ever captured by the Germans? If Dave was a POW, how would he be treated since he was Jewish? That fear and lack of closure haunted the family the remaining years of the MIA status until we learned of the events surrounding his death in 1999.

A final observation about the movie was that Private Ryan and my Uncle Dave each had three brothers serving during WWII. Those families with multiple sons serving in combat experienced the stark reality that the chances of having all come home safe was not high.

Dominic Biello and the 504 Website

When I began online research using search engines and keywords, I stumbled across Dominic Biello's 82nd Airborne website[50] containing casualty lists for the 504 PIR. Uncle Dave's name was listed, and he was MIA on 28 September 1944. It also had a link saying he was memorialized on the Wall of the Missing at the Netherlands American Cemetery. Now there was finally something to dig into.

With the date established, research could be done to find out what was going on with H Company and the 504 to narrow down where and maybe how he was killed. At this point, the September 28th date was a confusing because I knew the Waalcrossing was September 20th. I wondered if possibly he had been lost during the crossing of the river and on the 28th they declared him MIA. So in my research, I found that on the 27th and 28th the 3rd Battalion was near the Den Heuvel Woods. I contacted a researcher from the Liberation Museum in Groesbeek and they did their best to narrow down where the battalion was on those days. However, they really did not have any specific information about Uncle Dave. Interestingly, the Liberation Museum is very close to the spot where Uncle Dave was killed. You can stand where he died and see the top of the museum's parachute canopy roof rising above the trees.

The next part of the story sent chills up my spine, and again, you just can't make this stuff up.

The next part of the story sent chills up my spine, and again, you just can't make this stuff up. I sent an email to Dominic and asked him if he had any email addresses of anyone who might know about my uncle. Dominic's family story in World War II has some parallels to my family's story—an immigrant family with multiple brothers serving in World War II and one being killed. He was kind enough to send me 10 email addresses that were a mixture of veterans, relatives, and researchers. I got some quick bounce-backs from obsolete emails and received several responses saying they didn't know anything about my Uncle Dave. Finally, about three weeks later I got a reply from Dave Thomas. He was Sgt. Fred Thomas's son, and he said he had been looking for a relative of my uncle's for five years. He asked me to call him! I talked with both he and his father, Fred, who had been good friends and served with my Uncle Dave. Fred had been wounded in Italy, ending his time in the war. He went home to recuperate. However, they had the phone number of Ted Finkbeiner in Louisiana, who had been an eyewitness to Uncle Dave's death. One of my favorite photos was sent by Dave Thomas and shows Fred Thomas, Ted Finkbeiner, and my Uncle Dave along with Louis Holt and one other paratrooper posing in Pompei. It is bizarre to have a photo with Fred, Ted and David together who are so integral to the story events.

Keep in mind this contact happened during the early days of search engines, so it was considered a surprising find. Looking back I feel it was very fortunate that Dave Thomas had been reaching out and Dominic was kind enough to respond to my

request and connect us. This connection was just one of many amazing incidents over the past 20 years.

Paratroopers in Pompei: L-R Standing: Sgt. Ted Finkbeiner, Sgt. Fred Thomas, Sgt. David Rosenkrantz. L-R Kneeling: Unknown, Pvt. Louis Holt

CHAPTER FOURTEEN

HUMBLE VETERANS

One of the richest parts of the journey to learn about my uncle was meeting and getting to know some of the veterans he served with in the 3rd Battalion. They represent a generation that grew up in the Great Depression and then sacrificed a part of their lives to serve their country.

SGT Ted Finkbeiner

When I received Ted Finkbeiner's phone number, I called and first talked to his wife. Later, I called back and spoke to him for a while on the phone. Ted was very gracious and was surprised that the family had never heard what happened to David. He had been interviewed by Cornelius Ryan's people way back when Ryan was working on the book *A Bridge Too Far*. (Ryan, 1974)

In reality, other than the telephone and radio, there was no electronic technology back in the 1940s for communicating and sharing information. Also, trying to find somebody through phone books without knowing where they lived was very difficult. Ted confirmed that they were on the Den Heuvel Estate at Heuvelhof and had spent the night at the farmhouse. He described the events of the German attack and Dave's death as mentioned earlier, witnessed from his fox hole. Larry Dunlop, the paratrooper who created the hand-drawn map for Ben Overhand, related a similar story. Ted sent me some black and white photographs that he had taken of David, including several that were taken at Heuvelhof the day before he was killed. He also provided a few phone numbers of other H Company paratroopers who probably knew David very well.

1SG Albert Tarbell

Albert Tarbell was one of Dave's fellow paratroopers and now lived in New York. I called him and we had a marvelous, long conversation. He was probably Uncle Dave's best friend in the platoon and told stories about things they did when they were in England before Operation Market Garden. Albert was Mohawk and also Catholic. He related an amusing story about attending chapel service while in the 504. Since most of the paratroopers were Protestant, the chapel services were Protestant. Albert and Dave were Catholic and Jewish respectively. They would stand in the back and tell each other since they were the minorities they were going to stick together. I think that says a lot about them.

> *They would stand in the back and tell each other since they were the minorities they were going to stick together.*

Albert also told a story about the night before David was killed. The Heuvelhof farmhouse was across the main line of resistance. Albert was a communications specialist, and they had run a radio communications line about a thousand yards to the house. Sometime during the day, something cut the phone wire. Broken wires were not uncommon with artillery shells and other objects flying around. So in the dark Albert followed the line until he could find the break and fix it. As he approached the farmhouse, he realized that he didn't have a password or signal so that the guys in the farmhouse wouldn't shoot first and ask questions later. While he was standing in the dark trying to figure out how to approach, Dave yelled from the farmhouse for Albert to come in. Albert never did know how Dave knew it was him out there. He credits David with probably saving his life at that point.

After learning what happened to Uncle Dave I planned to call my aunt Janet (Goldie) and my father and tell them how Dave died. They would then at least have closure on that. I called Aunt Janet and told her that I had found out where Uncle Dave had died in the Netherlands and how it happened. She commented that Dave had never been

I had the pleasure to meet him in person a couple of years after that at an H Company reunion...

to the Netherlands. I described what really happened so that she would no longer wonder whether he had suffered, was a prisoner of war, tortured, or anything that caused prolonged suffering. I mentioned that I had talked to one of Dave's very

Harry Rosenkrantz and Albert Tarbell talking at the 504 Reunion in Fond du Lac, Wisconsin in 2003

best friends, Albert Tarbell and that he was interested and willing to talk to her. At first, she refused his phone number, saying that she probably would be too emotional to talk on the phone. I said that if she ever changed her mind, she could give me a call back. A few hours later Aunt Janet called me and asked for Albert's phone number. The details of her conversation with Albert are provided in Chapter 24. I had the pleasure to meet him in person a couple of years after that at an H Company reunion in Fond du Lac, Wisconsin.

1LT James "Maggie" Megellas & the 504 Reunion in Fond du Lac, Wisconsin 2003

In 2003 First Lieutenant James "Maggie" Megellas completed his book about H Company of the 504 in World War II titled *All the Way to Berlin: A paratrooper at war in Europe.* (Megellas, 2003) He held a reunion and book signing in Fond du Lac, Wisconsin in May 2003 and was kind enough to invite my father and me to attend. It was a thrill meeting many of the paratroopers who had served with Uncle Dave. Several knew him very well. The reunion lasted three days, so we had a chance

L-R: James "Maggie" Megellas (H Company), Judy Rosenkrantz, Francis Keefe (I Company) during the Waalcrossing reenactment at the 60th anniversary of Operation Market Garden, September 20, 2004

to meet and talk to a lot of the veterans who had been through Operation Market Garden. Of the 17 World War II paratroopers who attended only a couple of them are still living as of this writing.[51]

I spoke at length with Maggie who told me a lot about what he did after the war as a civilian working for the government. His book *All the Way to Berlin* stands out to me because he seems to relate more about what he and his fellow paratroopers were thinking along the way—not just what happened. In these enjoyable conversations Maggie didn't pull any punches in stating the honest truths about what goes on during wartime. I have heard him speak several times since then and he never hesitates to say what he thinks even if it may ruffle a few feathers.

Of particular importance at this reunion was the ability to speak at length with Ted Finkbeiner and Albert Tarbell. One aspect of the trip was especially enlightening in view of my goal to hear any stories about Uncle Dave and what happened to him. When we arrived the first couple veterans we met who knew my uncle said that their memory was foggy and they couldn't remember anything specific. After that we backed off from asking specifically about Uncle Dave. Then a funny thing happened. First, Albert Tarbell asked us to meet with him in his room so he could talk to us. He had begun remembering details about Uncle Dave that he had mentioned previously on the phone and was kind enough to repeat them with more detail. The same thing happened with Ted Finkbeiner. He also approached us later and said he wanted to talk privately because he had remembered details about Uncle Dave. We sat down, and on a scrap of paper Ted drew out what had happened, similar to what he had related on the phone and to what Larry Dunlop had drawn on his map. He described the story in a very emotional and respectful way with more detail.

What we realized from these two incidents was that all during the war these guys were losing their buddies. To cope and be able to keep functioning at a high level they would repress many memories. They had to move on to stay alert and stay alive. Those memories sometimes stayed repressed for many years. Figuring this out was a revelation.

I learned a lot about my uncle by learning what these men were like!

However, a more meaningful revelation was right in front of me: I was trying to learn what my uncle was like since I never knew him. The reality was that he was like these veterans that I was meeting. I learned a lot about my uncle by learning what these men were like! They were humble and very respectful. They did not brag about what they did—in fact, most downplayed their actions. They were all kind and very gracious to my father and me.

We also met Chaplain Captain Delbert Keuhl. While he did not personally know my uncle, he was familiar with the name from his days in the 504 PIR. As chaplain of the 504 he had 1800 men to try and keep track of and serve. Delbert wrote a short book about his time in the 504 PIR and how he went on to become a missionary in Japan for many years.

PFC Larry Dunlop

PFC Larry Dunlop was one of the H Company paratroopers who was in the unit from the beginning to the end of the war. In the early 90s he provided a hand-drawn map to Ben Overhand explaining how Heuvelhof was overrun by the Germans and my uncle was killed. The map showed what happened at the Heuvelhof farmhouse that stood there at the time and included a narrative of what happened. Larry's explanation differs slightly from Ted Finkbeiner's description, but I think they are easily reconciled. At the 504 H Company reunion in 2003 he repeated to me what he had described on the map. I later sent him a hard copy of my website pages and he graciously annotated it with lots of narrative about other aspects of the events at Heuvelhof. I was fortunate to meet him while he was still alive.

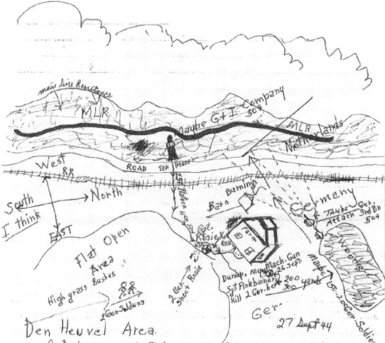

I, Dunlop, H company, 1st Platoon, 504 Run from the house and about 25 yards and 2 Ger. Soldiers are standing looking at me. I turn around fast and go back to the house. The Ger. and myself were very surprised. No shots fired. 5 minutes later Rosie goes the same way I go. I tried to warn him. Rosie doesn't hear me. He keeps going. Then, Brrp Brrp, the Ger. shoot a Schmeizer. They kill him. Only 150 feet from me. I see him, but I know he is dead. I can see him lying there. I cannot help him. I will too be killed

Map of the battle at Heuvelhof 28 September 1944
by Larry Dunlop

Lieutenant Roy Hanna, DSC—A 504 Legend

L-R: Captain Roy Hanna, Author Frank van Lunteren, Captain T Moffatt Burriss at a reunion during the 65th Anniversary of Operation Market Garden in 2009.

To fully appreciate the bravery and fortitude of our military forces both in WWII and now, more needs to be said about Captain Roy Hanna, an 82nd Airborne legend. We have had the pleasure of meeting him and his family several times over the years at reunions and trips to the Netherlands. I consider myself fortunate to know him and others like him, who served with my uncle. Through him, I have vicariously learned something about the uncle I never knew.

During the fighting at Anzio, at one point all the officers in Roy's platoon in I Company had been killed or wounded except him. He was ordered to reorganize the platoon and rescue some H Company paratroopers that were surrounded by Germans. H Company had just rescued a British general, but in the process had gotten in trouble. Roy reorganized his men and led the attack to save the paratroopers. While driving the attack, Roy was

Every time he fell he got up and continued leading his men until the victory was theirs.

shot through the chest. The bullet went through his lung and out his back. Every time he fell he got up and continued leading his men until the victory was theirs.

Remarkably, Roy got up and continued to lead his troops! After the battle was over, he spent a month recuperating and then rejoined his unit for the rest of the war. Roy received a Distinguished Service Cross for his actions at Anzio. Because of his legendary bravery, he is revered throughout the 82nd Airborne. When Judy and I attended a 504 reunion at Ft. Bragg in 2017, Roy was there. Amazingly, when I introduced my self in 2017, Roy remembered me from our brief encounter in the Netherlands in September 2009!

At the 504 reunion in 2017, the 82nd Airborne dedicated and named their 504 Regimental Meeting Room after Roy. One of the most heartwarming aspects of that trip was watching the respect and reverence the current 504 paratroopers have for him. Like all the other 504 veterans I have met, he is humble and proud to be one of those Devils in Baggy Pants.

Captain T. Moffatt Burriss

I've had the pleasure of meeting Moffatt many times over the years at reunions and Operation Market Garden celebrations. The first time was at Fond du Lac. Every time I've seen him since, he has impressed me by remembering me and showing great kindness.

He knew my uncle and occasionally even called me Rosie. He was an extraordinary person both during and after the war.

L-R: Battlefield expert Ben Overhand, Captain Moffatt Burriss, and Moffatt's son, Francis, at the 1944 Liberation Museum in Groesbeek reception in 2014 during the 70th Anniversary of Operation Market Garden.

Moffatt led I Company through many major campaigns. His action filled memoir, *Strike and Hold: A Memoir of the 82nd Airborne in World War II*, is a great read and full of first-hand descriptions. (Burriss, 2000) After World War II he spent many years as a legislator in South Carolina, leaving a solid mark on both the battlefield and in the state.

CHAPTER FIFTEEN

AMAZING RESEARCHERS

This book would not exist—and chances are my uncle's remains would still be lost somewhere—without the tremendous assistance of special people from the Netherlands and several government agencies. Besides Ben Overhand and Frank van Lunteren mentioned below, I received a lot of information from Jan Bos, people at the National Liberation Museum in Groesbeek, and many others. [52]

L-R: Ben Overhand and Frank van Lunteren at a 504 Reunion in Nijmegen, September 2009

Ben Overhand

A significant person in our story is Dutchman Ben Overhand. Soon after creating a website containing basic information about Uncle Dave, I received a surprising email message from Ben. He had just gone online the day before and found Uncle Dave's website. He asked for my phone number and we later spoke for three hours. I hate to think what his phone bill was for that international call.

As a young boy, Ben often heard from his parents and grandparents about the sacrifice that thousands of American soldiers had made to liberate Holland and defeat the Nazis. They also lamented that there were a lot of American MIA soldiers, and unfortunately, people were not searching for them as they should be. They said there seemed to be a lot more interest in finding MIAs in other places—such as Vietnam—

As a young boy, Ben often heard from his parents and grandparents about the sacrifice that thousands of American soldiers had made to liberate Holland and defeat the Nazis.

while there were still Americans missing in the Netherlands. Ben decided he wanted to do something about that situation. After doing some research, he learned the locations of some battles that resulted in American MIAs. The Den Heuvel estate was one of these and included a farmhouse called Heuvelhof. Ben would take the train from his home in Rotterdam along with his metal detector and search for MIAs at Den Heuvel and Heuvelhof.

In talking to veterans and others, one of the names they kept coming up as MIA was Staff Sergeant David "Rosie" Rosenkrantz. Veterans told Ben that if there were one MIA they wished he could find it would be Sergeant Rosenkrantz. He had searched for two years with his metal detector but never could find David. However, he did locate one American: Pvt. Victor J. Willson, Jr. He also recovered 12 German MIAs. He suspected that David had been buried in a field grave by the Germans and even guessed the field grave's location but never could find any evidence of his remains. He did find some paratrooper wings that could have been David's.

Ben was able to talk to a resident of the estate who was 15 years old at the time of the battle at Heuvelhof. His family owned the estate, and he lived there during the war. He remembered seeing a body on the ground at Heuvelhof sometime after the battle and said that the Dutch Graves Ministry came and took away. Ben found a log record that showed the Dutch Graves Ministry removed an unidentified American Soldier from Heuvelhof. There were several MIAs there so he couldn't be entirely sure if it was Dave they found. But over the years—by process of elimination—Ben concluded that that the remains were most likely Dave's. He wanted the Dutch and the Americans to look at interred remains of unidentified soldiers that they had at other locations and start checking them to see if one could be Dave. For various reasons that did not happen for many years and Ben continued trying to convince the authorities to look for and examine unidentified remains in their possession.

In 2015, as a final action, the Dutch went to Heuvelhof and dug up the area of the field grave just to make sure there were no remains there. Ben watched the dig—which did not produce any remains. Unidentified remains that Ben helped locate were finally exhumed in 2017.

I have had the pleasure of meeting Ben every time we went to the Netherlands for the five-year anniversary celebrations of Operation Market Garden.[53] He was genuinely devoted to bringing our soldiers home and giving them the recognition they deserve. Our family cannot thank him enough for his efforts on our behalf. I consider him to be a good friend and one of the finest people I know. I am very touched by his devotion to unselfishly search for our missing fallen.

Frank van Lunteren and Disneyland

Soon after I started Uncle Dave's website, I connected with one of the 504 A Company veterans who lived in the Los Angeles area. His name was Fred Baldino, but his friends called him Baldy. In October 2003, Baldy contacted me and said a young Dutchman that he had become friends with online—Frank van Lunteren—was coming over to the US to visit him in California. Baldy was going to show him around sites in California and wondered if I could help. I offered to take Frank to Disneyland. On the assigned day, Baldy and Frank showed up at my house. Frank was only 21 at the time and we went to Disneyland along with my daughter, Debi. He entered as the guest of one of my former industrial engineering students, Kim Kinda Chirco, who worked at Disneyland. We had a lovely day going on rides and watching parades and shows. Then at the end of the evening, I drove Frank back to Baldy's home in Burbank.

Neither Frank nor I realized at the beginning that either one was interested in Operation Market Garden. We quickly made the connection and had a great time talking about what happened in 1944. Even at the young age of 21, Frank was already a leading expert about Operation Market Garden. He was

Frank has become the premier historian about Operation Market Garden and the 504 Parachute Infantry Regiment.

able to learn more about it from our family's point of view. That was the beginning of a long friendship. In 2004, when Judy and I visited the Netherlands for the 60th anniversary of Operation Market Garden, we had the pleasure of spending a lot of time with Frank, his parents, Wim and Meike, his sister, Esther, and brother Paul.

Frank has become the premier historian about Operation Market Garden and the 504 Parachute Infantry Regiment. He has written a series of five books, chronicling them from their inception to the end of the war. Three of the books are published, and—as of this writing—the other two are in the process of being published. He has also written a book specifically about the history of A Company of the 504 in World War II. Frank is Historian and Honorary Member of the 504th Parachute Infantry Regiment, the 504th PIR Association, the

Colonel Reuben Tucker Chapter of the 82nd Airborne Division Association and the (closed down) South Devon Branch of the Normandy Veterans Association.

Our family owes Frank a debt of gratitude for his friendship, support, knowledge, and other contributions that eventually helped in locating and identifying Uncle Dave.

CHAPTER SIXTEEN

IN HIS FOOTSTEPS

Europe 2004

In September of 2004, Judy and I made our first trip to Europe and the Netherlands. This was the first of many visits to the Netherlands that would continue to add deep meaning and significance to our lives in many ways. The main purpose of our initial tour was to see where Uncle Dave had fought and died. However, we were enriched by many historical highlights on this journey, in London and other locations. I want to encourage younger readers to study history and take it seriously. This will give you more joy and understanding throughout your life— especially when you travel. (Welch, 1973)

Upon arrival in Amsterdam we rented a car and drove to Nijmegen. The roads were very good and the Netherlands is a beautiful country with glorious window boxes adorning almost every home. Trying to follow the signs was the tough part. We stayed at a conference center in Berg en Dal that had been reserved for veterans and relatives attending the 60th-anniversary events for Operation Market Garden.

Our trip was rich in building relationships and gaining a depth of understanding about WWII events. Highlights included making friends with some of the other relatives. We spent a lot of time with Ray and Kathleen Buttke. Kathleen's uncle, Pvt. Walter J. Muszynski, had been killed during the Waalcrossing and received the Distinguished Service Cross posthumously. Ray and Kathleen had already researched the lives of the men who died in the Waalcrossing and were continuing their efforts. We also spent time with Bud and Elaine Kaczor. Bud's uncle,

Cpl David S. Stanford of I Company was killed the same day as Uncle Dave a few hundred yards north at Den Heuvel. Corporal Stanford is still MIA to this day. We caravanned together to attend various events. We also spent significant time with two of the 504 paratroopers who had participated in Operation Market Garden: Francis Keefe of I Company and Albert Clark of A Company. It was a valuable experience visiting with two humble veterans who had been there 60 years earlier. We met other paratroopers who had been there as well such as Moffatt Burriss and Walter Hughes. I had previously met Lt. James "Maggie" Megellas and was able to see him briefly as well.

We stood where Uncle Dave was killed and could visualize much of what happened on the 28th of September 1944.

Prior to our visit, Frank van Lunteren and Ben Overhand were instrumental in helping us understand what happened in the Netherlands. Ben gave us a first-hand tour of Heuvelhof and Den Heuvel. We stood where Uncle Dave was killed and could visualize much of what happened on the 28th of September 1944. The experience was more emotional than I anticipated.

Our first visit to Heuvelhof with Ben Overhand was September 2004. By this time Ben had been re-searching and searching for MIAs at Heuvelhof for almost 20 years.

Another moving event was participating in a commemorative reenactment of the Waalcrossing with other soldiers' relatives. There were several restored amphibious vehicles called Ducks (DUKW)[54] The passage ended on the north side of the river at the memorial dedicated to the 48 soldiers who died crossing the river and capturing the bridges.

At Frank van Lunteren's invitation, we attended the British commemorative events at the British Cemetery in Osterbeek near Arnhem. We were privileged to spend time with his entire family. Jammed in with a crowd of about 20,000 people near the back of the cemetery, we could see that there were very few Americans present. We stood next to some British paratroopers who were hilarious. They had perfected joking around to a new level that made Saturday Night Live look boring. I eventually had a brief, but rich conversation with them and asked what Operation Market Garden meant to them—after all the British paratroopers in Arnhem were decimated by the Germans. They told me that Operation Market Garden defined them and was their heritage.

The best part of the trip to the British Cemetery was yet to come. Queen Beatrix of the Netherlands and Prince Charles from England were there and made a grand entrance. They entered through the rear of the crowd as guards yelled: "Make way." The crowd parted like the Red Sea at Moses' command. The Queen and Prince passed about 70 feet from us. They made their way to the front of the cemetery for the wreath-laying ceremonies. After the celebrations were over, they walked back through the crowd to exit, heading straight toward us! As

Operation Market Garden defined them and was their heritage.

Prince Charles approached, I had to quickly decide if I wanted to take his picture or shake his hand. I opted for taking a picture. He looked at me from about four feet away and I took his picture. It was an unexpected thrill to visit the Netherlands and have a close encounter with English and Dutch royalty.

Prince Charles at the British Cemetery near Arnhem

Europe 2009 The Wall of the Missing at Margraten

At the Wall of the Missing in Margraten standing below Uncle Dave's name. R-L: Russ & Gina Buehler. Phil, Julia, Judy, Sarah, David Rosenkrantz, Adam Paradis

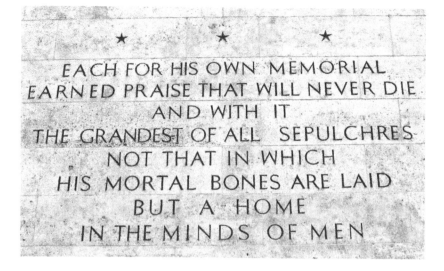

★ ★ ★

EACH FOR HIS OWN MEMORIAL
EARNED PRAISE THAT WILL NEVER DIE
AND WITH IT
THE GRANDEST OF ALL SEPULCHRES
NOT THAT IN WHICH
HIS MORTAL BONES ARE LAID
BUT A HOME
IN THE MINDS OF MEN

Poignant tribute on the kiosk at the Wall of the Missing.

Our 2009 trip for the 65th anniversary of Operation Market Garden was also remarkable, but in other ways. Our son David, daughter Julia, daughter Sarah and her husband Adam, and my sister Gina and her husband Russ joined us for the trip. After arriving in Amsterdam we began a week-long trip around the Netherlands visiting Den Haag, Bruges and Brussels, ending up at the Netherlands American Cemetery in Margraten. There we saw Uncle Dave's name on the Wall of the Missing. The cemetery was immaculate and deeply honored the dead and missing. We did not realize until many years later that there were 105 markers for unknown soldiers at the cemetery—one belonging to Uncle Dave. I did see one of the grave markers and took the photo shown here. There is a small probability[55] that the grave marker in the photo belonged to him.

Grave marker at Margraten

An American veteran visiting the cemetery was wearing his old Army uniform. He said he was a glider pilot during Operation Market Garden. He joked that he decided to be a glider pilot thinking it was safer than being a parachutist. We learned that he lived only a few miles from us in California.

We then drove to the Bastion Hotel in Nijmegen, where we stayed for the rest of the trip. Additional highlights included commemorative parachute jumps at both of the significant drop zones: Overasselt and Groesbeek. At Overasselt we watched drops that included two of the paratroopers who had jumped in 1944,

Glider Pilot Bob Meyer at Margraten

now near 90 years old: Francis Keefe and Moffatt Burriss. Unfortunately, Francis injured himself when he didn't land properly. I was standing near him after the jump when Moffatt walked up to him while Francis was still on the ground. Moffatt's sense of humor was still intact. He said, "Francis I told you not to land like that, but you never listen!" These guys never lost their sense of humor.

"Francis I told you not to land like that, but you never listen!" These guys never lost their sense of humor.

The reenactors who had jumped had gathered their equipment and were walking to their waiting cars and trucks. One of them was our Dutch friend, Anton van Ensbergen. He suggested we attend the drop at Heuvelhof

(Groesbeek) because reenactors were dedicating that jump to Uncle Dave! We hadn't known this, so changed our plans and had one of the best days ever. We arrived early for the 4:00 drop and drove into Groesbeek to walk around. We went into one of the most awesome cheese shops we had ever seen and bought many delicious things for a tailgate picnic before driving back to Heuvelhof. We Americans don't know what a good cheese shop is. They are all over Europe in villages everywhere.

While waiting for the jump, we observed people driving by in restored WWII jeeps and wearing reenactment regalia and enjoyed talking to them. Thankfully, most of the Dutch people we encountered throughout our trip spoke fluent English.

Eventually, people started gathering for the commemorative jump, and it began. One of the first ones down was their leader When I introduced myself as David Rosenkrantz' nephew, he was astonished. He did not realize anyone would be present from David's family and asked if we would participate in the ceremony after the jump. We agreed of course! He asked us to wait a couple of hundred yards away at Heuvelhof. They had already put a wreath on the fence dedicated to Uncle Dave.

After the reenactors finished, they marched in formation to where we were waiting by the wreath. The wreath even had David's picture in the center. The leader gave a thoughtful explanation of what happened with Uncle Dave and how he went missing. Then, every one of the participants, about 40, shook hands with all of our family members and thanked us. They also gave us booklets that had pictures and information about Uncle Dave and 504 PIR. We were overwhelmed by the dedication and felt fortunate to be there. This experience was the highlight of the 2009 trip for me.

At Heuvelhof by the wreath laid by the Dutch parachutists. Uncle Dave was killed near the large trees shown on the left side of the background. His field grave was just behind the trees. L-R: Phil Rosenkrantz, Gina Buehler, Judy Rosenkrantz, Russ Buehler, Julia Rosenkrantz, David Rosenkrantz

We did lots of networking; the week of commemorative events included many gatherings with other 504 relatives, veterans and Dutch friends. Besides seeing Ben Overhand, Frank van Lunteren and Ray and Kathleen Buttke again, we met other 504 relatives. There were major events at the Waalcrossing Memorial, including speeches by General Petraeus from the United States and Timothy Broas, Ambassador to the Netherlands. General Gavin's daughter, Barbara, was also there.

Europe 2014

The 2014 Netherlands trip was also filled with exciting events plus more in-depth relationship building. Judy and I started with a Viking river cruise from Nuremberg to Budapest. We learned valuable European history that provided context for our future European trips as well as some aspects of World War II. Nuremberg was the birthplace of the Holy Roman Empire, which lasted for 700 years. In World War II Hitler centered many of his propaganda events from Nuremberg because of the symbolic connection to the Holy Roman Emperor.

After the cruise, we traveled to Nijmegen. Highlights included seeing the new road bridge constructed over the Waal River, built at the location of the 1944 Waalcrossing. The Dutch call the bridge *de Oversteek* in memory of the crossing and the 48 paratroopers who lost their lives in the battle.[56] A nearby elementary school is also named *de Oversteek* in commemoration. The original crossing memorial was relocated a short distance away in order to construct the bridge in the

Each night at sunset forty-eight pairs of streetlamps on the bridge are lit in sequence every 13 seconds from the south side to north side, commemorating the 48 lives that were lost.

desired location. A thoughtful design feature of the new bridge is the built-in memorial experience called the Sunset March.[57] Each night at sunset forty-eight pairs of streetlamps on the bridge are lit in sequence every 13 seconds in the same direction the paratroopers had crossed the river, commemorating the 48 lives that were lost.[58] People can visit the bridge and join the walk across at sunset. This daily event is just one example of the many ways that the Dutch people remember the Americans who helped liberate them.

We visited Heuvelhof and Den Heuvel again with Ben Overhand, Drs. Ed Burton and Ian Spurgeon from the DPMO, Moffatt Burriss and Moffatt's children and grandchildren. Ben served as guide, providing graphic summaries of what happened. Moffatt gave detailed accounts of how I Company was overrun by the Germans while we were standing on the exact spots that paratroopers were killed. With us also was Bud Kaczor and Beverly Cooper Miese, whose uncles also died that day. I Company was outnumbered about three to one and engaged in hand to hand combat. Moffatt described what happened to their uncles in great detail, filling in details Bud and Cooper had never known before.

L-R: Phil & Judy Rosenkrantz, Catherine Metropoulos, Kathleen & Ray Buttke 504 KIA and MIA relatives at the Grave Bridge during the 70th Anniversary of Operation Market Garden

Heuvelhof: Ben Overhand showing Drs. Ed Burton and Ian Spurgeon from the DPMO the location where Uncle Dave may have been when killed. The field grave where he was buried by the Germans was located between the tree stumps in front of the house (Note: During WWII a barn was located where the house is today).

We were able to spend more time with Ben Overhand and Frank van Lunteren on this trip. Frank had finished his book about the Battle of the Bridges and had a book signing at the Liberation Museum in Groesbeek. On this trip, one of the commemorative jumps was conducted by the 82nd Airborne Division; we met many of the paratroopers and their officers.

Viking River Cruise 2015

Phil Rosenkrantz-Presentation about Uncle Dave and the Waalcrossing on the Viking Eir, August 20, 2015

In August 2015, Judy and I took a Viking River Cruise from Basel, Switzerland to Amsterdam on the Viking Eir.[59] Via satellite tracking of a Viking cruise a few weeks prior, I determined that our ship would pass through Nijmegen around 9:30 a.m. on Thursday, August 20. I spoke with Social Director, Ryan Cofrancesco, and offered to tell Uncle Dave's story as the ship passed under the Nijmegen bridges. He was familiar with Operation Market Garden and got permission from the captain to allow the presentation.

About an hour before arriving in Nijmegen, we began the presentation from the bow of the ship. I was expecting a dozen or two people to show up and listen. Ryan must have done a pretty good job selling the presentation because about 100 people were gathered on the bow, in the lounge, and on the top deck to listen and watch. The presentation went well as I went back and forth between Uncle Dave's personal and family stories and the fascinating history of the Waalcrossing and Operation Market Garden. It was no surprise that there were some World War II buffs on board, and several approached me afterward and were very complimentary. This experience was the highlight of the trip for me and reconfirmed the value of the journey to find Uncle Dave and bring him home.

Ft. Bragg 2017

In February 2017, Judy and I flew to North Carolina for a 504 Reunion and Change-of-Command ceremony at Fort Bragg, another location where Uncle Dave had walked and served. There were five veterans in attendance from the 3rd Battalion: Capt (R) Moffatt Burriss, Col. (R) James Kiernan and Capt. (R) Roy Hanna, Francis Keefe, and Robert Devinney. Frank van Lunteren flew in from the Netherlands as a featured speaker. There were over 100 participants affiliated with the 504 either as veterans, current members, relatives, historians or friends. It was a great chance to renew acquaintances and celebrate awards. Frank van Lunteren was still working on his five-part book series about the 504 PIR. He was also well along in creating a database of all 504 paratroopers indexed by company.

Europe 2019

This trip to the Netherlands for the 75th Anniversary of Operation Market Garden was special in many ways. Our son, David, and his wife, Elizabeth (Liz), were able to join us. Catherine Metropoulos (niece of PFC John Rigapoulos who was killed during Operation Market Garden) joined our family in renting a lovely four-bedroom house in Leuth. Leuth is a small village four miles outside of Nijmegen and not far from Heuvelhof.

The main event for our family was the Rosette Ceremony at the Netherlands American Cemetery. We were able to dine many times with other 504 relatives we'd gotten to know and love. We met General Gavin's daughter, Chloe and her son, James. We participated in many events alongside 82nd Airborne paratroopers, Dutch friends, members of FAN (Friendship

Albany Nijmegen), members of the American Consulate, and Dutch citizens from all walks of life.

A major joy was spending time with Ben Overhand and Frank van Lunteren again; they had been part of the searching journey with us from the beginning. We enjoyed a superb dinner joining all three of our families together...a truly wonderful time.

David and Phil at Heuvelhof where Uncle Dave was killed. The cross is a memorial to Uncle David left after a commemorative parachute jump in 2015.

Celebratory dinner with the Overhand, van Lunteren, and Rosenkrantz families at Restaurant de Thornsche Molen near Leuth, a truly fun evening.

David, Liz, and Phil in front of de Oversteek Bridge prior to the Sunset March on September 19

Liz, David and other 504 relatives talking with US Ambassador to the Netherlands Peter Hoekstra at a reception at the Nijmegen City Hall.

Neuengamme and Vught Concentration Camps

One of my favorite mini-series of all time is *Band of Brothers*. Episode 9 is titled *Why We Fight*. [60] In the episode, some men from Easy Company are on patrol and discover an abandoned labor camp near Landsburg, Germany. They are horrified by the dead and barely living prisoners in the camp. The men are witnessing firsthand the effects of Hitler's Final Solution—the extermination of all Jews. It is one thing to hear about the Holocaust, but it is another to see the facilities and visualize the horrors the prisoners faced.

We took a half-day trip to the nearby Vught Concentration Camp in the Netherlands.[61] Judy and I visited the Neuengamme Concentration Camp near Hamburg, Germany, the previous year. The visits to Vught and Neuengamme were sobering. At Neuengamme, I was most affected by the remaining foundation of the small building where they exterminated inmates by hanging.[62] I will never get that out of my head. At Vught, the most sorrowful sight was the monument dedicated to over 1000 children who were sent away along with an accompanying parent under the pretext of going to another camp with better facilities for children. In reality, they were all transported to extermination camps.

Like so many others, I have trouble comprehending all this. Since then, I have wondered more about any second or third cousins of mine who may have died in the Holocaust. At both camps I looked on available lists of victims and did not see any with the last name Rosenkrantz. However, a search of the Rosenkrantz name on an online list of Holocaust victims listed many Polish Rosenkrantz's who died in the Holocaust.[63]

It is difficult to understand much of what is going on in our world today if you do not understand the causes, results, and aftereffects of World War II.

I highly recommend that younger generations who are somewhat distant from World War II take the time to study it in some depth (I advise watching the documentary *Paper Clips*).[64] It is difficult to understand much of what is going on in our world today if you do not understand the causes, results, and aftereffects of World War II. Had Americans—including my Uncle Dave—not gone over to fight and sacrifice to defeat the Nazis, their evil empire would have spread over all of Europe and probably most of Asia. Concentration camps would have multiplied and millions more people been exterminated. I am humbled and proud of my uncle and the millions like him who served in World War II and the wars since to preserve freedom.

CHAPTER SEVENTEEN

THE DEFENSE POW-MIA OFFICE (DPMO)

A few years after beginning the journey with Uncle Dave's story, we connected with the Defense POW-MIA Office or DPMO. They sent a report about what they had, but the document didn't have much additional information that we didn't already know. At that time, they did not seem to be too interested in researching remains of unidentified soldiers.

In 2011 seven members of our immediate family attended a family meeting in Scottsdale, Arizona. These meetings are held around the country every year to allow families of POWs and MIA's to meet with the government representatives that are working on their cases. The meetings provide both general and specific information. Families can make an appointment to talk to someone about their missing loved one's case. We met with Heather Harris who was very familiar with my uncle's situation and had been to the Netherlands. However, the follow-up report we received later didn't have anything new—which was disappointing.

On January 12, 2013, I attended another family meeting by myself in San Diego. I wanted to talk with them about the information that we did not have in 2011. I met with Dr. Stephen Johnson and discussed information about the dog tags and details from Ben Overhand that the DPMO seemed not to have grasped. There were compelling reasons to look for unidentified remains in possession of the Dutch or the Americans somewhere other than Heuvelhof, exhume them, and check for DNA. Dr. Johnson seemed fairly enthusiastic, but several months later I received a report which was the same as the previous one. There was no acknowledgment of what I said or of any effort to do anything different. I now know that the DPMO was taking action on my information, but I believe that somehow an old report was sent to me that did not acknowledge the new information. Dr. Johnson and others continued to work on our behalf in researching what happened and where the missing remains could have been relocated.

In 2015 the DPMO combined with the Joint POW-MIA Accounting Command (JPAC) to form the Defense POW-MIA Accounting Agency (DPAA). About a year later I got a letter from the DPAA saying they were going to start exhuming remains that had some favorable potential for being Uncle Dave. I waited about a year-and-a-half and checked back to find out what was going on. I discovered that they were doing something, but I didn't know exactly what.

CHAPTER EIGHTEEN

DAVE'S DOGTAGS FOUND

In March 2012 I received a contact from the DPMO that Uncle Dave's dog tags had been found. After finishing processing these and the accompanying 1952 report, they sent the dog tags and a copy of the documents to me. The report provided information on David's death and burial discussed earlier in this book and included evidence of trees that had been destroyed by artillery fire next to the site of the suspected field grave location. The Dutch Graves Ministry had been summoned to recover the remains, but they did not spot the dog tags. They recorded that they had recovered an unidentified American Soldier. Sometime later the farmer saw the dog tags on the ground and called the local magistrate. Dutch authorities then collected the dog tags and a few other artifacts.

In 1952 the Dutch returned the dog tags to the Americans, who investigated the site where they were found. The report accompanying the tags said they found a few bone fragments, part of an entrenching knife, and a watch. They sketched out a map of the area; according to the sketch this spot was the same place Ben Overhand had suspected was the location of the field grave.

By 1952 they had gathered letters from nearby magistrates saying that they did not have any unidentified remains in their possession, so the Army finally concluded that his remains were unrecoverable. Then for some reason, the report and the dog tags were misplaced until about 2012 when they were found and matched up with David's case.

I never heard an explanation of why the bone fragments and the dog tags were misplaced.

Supposedly, the records were stored somewhere in a mausoleum in Greisham, Germany. When I sent a copy of the report to Ben Overhand, he could see how it all made sense. His speculations about the remains' location was backed up by the report.

I remember the day the dog tags arrived in the mail. Up to that point in time, it was the most emotional moment for me regarding my uncle. I

1952 map showing where the dog tags were found at Heuvelhof in 1951. Bone fragments were found at the spot of the suspected field grave.

stood there holding the dog tags he had worn throughout his time in the Army. They had somehow miraculously returned to the family 68 years later. Ironically, the dog tags look like they still have bloodstains on them.

> *Ironically, the dog tags look like they still have bloodstains on them.*

In 2014, at the 70th Anniversary of Operation Market Garden, I had the dog tags with me the day we visited Heuvelhof. Some of Moffatt's grandchildren were there and listened to Ben's description of what happened to my uncle. I pulled out the dog tags and the children asked if it would be possible to hold them. Of course, I said yes. It was apparent that touching the dog tags of a soldier who had died right where they were standing was impactful.

A notable feature about the dog tags is what is embossed along with David's name and serial number. In addition to that information were stamped his mother's name and address in Los Angeles and the letter "J", for Jewish. I had been under the impression that the letter stamped on his dog tags was an "H" for Hebrew (as in the movie *Saving Private Ryan*).

Dave's dog tags. His mother's name and address are on the bottom three lines. Note the letter "J" stamped on the lower right denoting that he was Jewish.

CHAPTER NINETEEN

SOLVING THE MYSTERY

DNA

At the DPMO family meeting in Scottsdale in 2011, I provided a DNA sample they could use for identifying Uncle Dave's remains. Several years later we got another DNA sample from David's surviving sister Janet (Goldie). For matching purposes, DNA from a mother or sister is very desirable and the DPAA said that they like to have three DNA samples. Janet passed away a few months later. We asked David's nephew, Bill Clabaugh, (mother-Frieda) to also provide a DNA sample.

Final DPAA Reports

So what did happen to Uncle Dave's remains over those 73 years? One of the most compelling aspects of this adventure are the parallel stories of the search for his remains and the actual journey of his remains and dog tags. Based on final reports from the DPAA we can reconstruct the journey. To tell the story cohesively, we will start with what happened to his remains now that we have 20-20 hindsight. Then, we will concentrate on the efforts to find them and finish where the two-tracks converge.

On April 14, 2018, William "Shorty" Cox, Senior Mortuary Affairs Specialist-Identification Case Manager, Past Conflict Repatriations Branch (PCRB) and an Army Casualty Assistance Officer visited our family at my home in California to explain the journey of Uncle Dave's remains. Twenty-five family members were in attendance as well as two *Los Angeles Times* Reporters and representatives from Risher Mortuary.

As already explained, the Dutch Graves Ministry responded to contact by the farmer who owned the Heuvelhof land. We have a record of them picking up an unidentified American soldier from the farm as mentioned in the 1952 report:

> *The undersigned declares herewith that on the list which was transmitted on 2 November 1945 to Lt. Col. Dr. A van Anrooy, Identification Service in Berging, Carel van Byiandiaan of s'Gravenhage , it was listed that an American body was buried near Lamers, Lagewaid, the subject deceased having been recovered in 1945 by the mentioned service.[65] (signed: Groesbeek, 20 February 1953, The Burgermeister of Groesbeek, The Chief of IIIe afdeling)*

Here's what happened after that:

On June 22, 1945, the Dutch transferred Uncle Dave's unidentified remains to the Second Canadian Graves Registration unit. The Canadians gave them the number X-1234 and noted they were found in the vicinity of Heuvelhof. They took the remains because the Canadian National Cemetery is located only 1.5 miles from Heuvelhof. The Canadians were willing to hold on to the remains and transfer them to the Americans in the future. On July 28, 1945, the Canadians transferred the remains to the American Graves Registration Commission (AGRC), who interred them at the new Netherlands American Cemetery in Margraten, located in the southern end of the Netherlands about 90 miles away.

On April 1, 1947, the AGRC reprocessed the unidentified remains—including the boots that he wore—and buried them in plot LL Row 11 Grave 274. On April 24, 1948, they disinterred the remains and on September 20, 1948 transferred them to Belgium. In the summer of 1950, the AGRC investigated Den Heuvel and Heuvelhof and then interred the remains again at the Netherlands American Cemetery at Margraten in Plot O Row 22 Grave 16. It is not clear what they were doing in the Den Heuvel area that related to the unidentified remains X-1234.

While all this was going on some other things were occurring as well. Unfortunately, the AGRC was not able to connect the dots.

According to a DPAA report, in 1945 the Netherlands Identification Service found the dog tags, bone fragments, paratrooper insignia and a wristband at the location of the field grave but for some reason, they did not turn them over to the AGRC until 1952. The AGRC investigated the spot and found some ammo and part of an entrenching knife that they suspected belong to Uncle Dave. They evaluated the bone fragments and other things they saw and eventually declared that the remains were unrecoverable. As mentioned previously, the report about the dog tags along with the tags was misplaced at a mausoleum in Germany until 2012. So, for 73 years there was no connection between the dog tags and the unidentified remains.

The AGRC investigated the spot and found some ammo and part of an entrenching knife that they suspected belong to Uncle Dave.

At the 70th anniversary of Operation Market Garden, Dr. Ed Burton, Dr. Ian Spurgeon and several other members of the DPMO visited Heuvelhof with Ben Overhand and me. Afterward, they recommended a formal analysis of the site.

In February 2015, Ben Overhand met with the BIDKL (Dutch Grave Registration Service) and the council of Groesbeek and convinced them to conduct an official dig on March 17th for the possible remains of Uncle Dave on the location of his former suggested gravesite. I believe the purpose of this dig was to remove all doubt that the remains were not there and, therefore, had been relocated. A digger was used to dig to the depth of two meters (7ft.) to the original undisturbed soil over a square of 5 x 5 meters. Unfortunately, they did not find anything in context with Uncle Dave or the grave. Except for a few pieces of shrapnel nothing else was found. Although very disappointing, it was still further evidence the remains were removed. The conclusion we shared at that point was that the former gravesite was either destroyed in 1952 by building the house, that the body was either disintegrated by the shell or, as the eyewitness farmer Lamers stated—some remains were relocated in 1945.

Ben Overhand (Standing Left) at Heuvelhof observing the excavation of the believed site of Dave's field grave.

The DPAA Summary Report provided to the family on April 14, 2018, dated January 3, 2018, explains what happened next:

In November 2015, the same team of historians from DPMO and JPAC—which in January 2015 had combined to become DPAA—returned to Groesbeek as part of an official investigation team. They again met with Mr. Overhand and Mr. Van Lunteren regarding S Sgt Rosenkrantz's case, as well as other missing soldiers of the 504th Parachute Infantry Regiment. During that investigation, the DPAA team learned that the Netherlands Recovery and Identification Unit (RIU) had conducted an excavation in early 2015 at Heuvelhof for the remains of S Sgt Rosenkrantz. Unfortunately, no remains or artifacts had been found during the effort.

The small portion of remains recovered with S Sgt Rosenkrantz's identification tag in the 1940s were cremated by the AGRC. However, several other sets of unidentified remains currently buried in American Battle Monuments Commission (ABMC) cemeteries in Europe likely came from the battlefields north of Groesbeek. The DPAA team then worked with Mr. Overhand to analyze the

AGRC documents and maps from the files (also known as X-files) of these unidentified remains, to determine the recovery locations and most likely candidates for association. During this effort, the historians and Mr. Overhand noted a few unknown remains that may have been recovered from area around Heuvelhof. Upon completion of the investigation, and additional historical study of combat and losses around Groesbeek, DPAA historian Dr. Jeffrey Johnson recommended X-1234 Margraten (X-1234) for disinterment and scientific reanalysis.

The remains designated X-1234 had originally been recovered by the 2nd Canadian Graves Registration Unit, reportedly east of Groesbeek, and buried at the Canadian Military Cemetery on 22 June 1945. A Canadian "burial return," dated 22 June 1945, notes that the remains were those of a U.S. soldier and lists the coordinates where they were recovered as "768565." This corresponds to QE768565 on the Nord de Guerre Zone grid coordinate system that was used by the Allies in parts of Europe during World War II. This coordinate is about one mile northeast of Groesbeek, in the vicinity of Heuvelhof.

The DPAA Summary Report also stated:

With this information, the DPAA historian recommended the disinterment and analysis of X-1234. Because several American soldiers are missing from combat north of Groesbeek, and since information within the AGRC documentation did not directly associate the remains to an individual or unit—other than indicating that the soldier was a paratrooper—the DPAA historian included a list of 17 soldiers who could possibly associate to the remains. Staff Sergeant Rosenkrantz was among the top candidates on this list.

On February 17th, 2016 the DPAA responded in a letter that possible remains were going to be exhumed and examined. Historians at the DPAA had decided to look at known remains of MIAs of unidentified American soldiers with encouragement from Ben Overhand, Frank van Lunteren, and the family.

On June 14, 2017, the remains were exhumed by the DPAA and the ABMC. They were transferred to the DPAA Lab at Offutt Air Force Base on July 13, 2017. They conducted historical and skeletal analysis. Historical reports indicated that based on location the remains could belong to S/Sgt David Rosenkrantz and transferred the body for DNA testing in January 2018. The DNA analysis at Offutt AFB confirmed that the remains belonged to David. The DNA sample used was the one collected from David's Sister, Janet (Goldie) Norman only a couple of months before she passed away.

> *The DNA analysis at Offutt AFB confirmed that the remains belonged to David.*

A Remarkable Story

The story of what happened to Uncle Dave's remains during and after the war is remarkable. The mystery revolves around the question of what happened to his remains starting from September 28th, 1944, when he was killed, up until January of 2018 when the DNA test confirmed what happened to him. There is also the parallel story of what happened to his dog tags and the remnants of his body found at the location where he was killed and buried in a field grave. Then begins the 35-year journey of Ben Overhand and others to discover what happened to David's remains. Intersecting all of that are the communications of the family with the Army, DPMO, DPAA, and Dutch experts. Within the DPMO and the DPAA, there were a multitude of other dynamics because of the various offices involved and the handing off of the case to many different handlers over the decades. None of these threads of this bizarre mystery even touch on what the family was going through during those years after David was reported missing – including my 20-year journey in search of closure. The following pages discuss the family's search for resolution.

PART FOUR

GRIEF, CLOSURE, AND AMBIGUOUS LOSS

This section is about family closure and examines three different types. The first type of closure is discovering what happened to Uncle Dave. The second type is learning what he was like as a soldier. Finally, the third type of closure is finding his remains and bringing him home.

CHAPTER TWENTY

THE WAR AFTER THE WAR

One surprising aspect of the 73-year journey was beginning to understand the impact on the family of David's loss and the lingering effects of the war. The topic of closure expanded in importance as Uncle Dave's story unfolded over the last few years. I taught classes and lessons on grief at our church several times over the years. In those classes we discussed the classic stages of grief often found in contemporary literature based on the book of Job in the Hebrew Scriptures.[66] Five or six stages of grief match what many grief experts talk about. I didn't find the six stages of grief quite as helpful in coping with closure in the case where the person is MIA. Research about grief and pain in this type of situation led to the discovery of some fascinating things.

In his book, *Soldier Dead*, Michael Sledge states,

> *The process of grieving is highly cultural specific and in the United States there is a general consensus about the steps required to work toward resolution of death of a loved one. The first is the acceptance of the reality of death. Obviously, the presence of a properly identified set of remains is final proof. J W Warden, quoted in Beyond the Body says, "Seeing the body of the deceased helps to bring home the finality and reality of death." (Elizabeth Hallum, et al, 1999) For those who have lost family members in military service, the recovery and return of the body confirm the death of their loved one. Sergeant Lemuel Herbert of Scranton Pennsylvania was taken prisoner during World War II and according to witnesses executed. Based on this information, the Army reclassified his status from missing*

in action MIA to KIA. In 1988, a farmer near Kommerscheid, Germany was plowing a field and disinterred Herbert's remains. After discovery and subsequent identification, the remains were buried at Arlington National Cemetery. A niece Mae Miller said, "My grandmother was always hoping and praying that he would be found. Even though he was listed as being killed, without his remains we were always hoping." That Herbert's relatives held out hope of his being alive for decades after he was declared KIA is evidence that, without strong proof, families almost never give up believing that maybe their missing and presumed dead soldier is still alive. (Sledge, 2005, pp. 23-24)

The professional term used for this type of grieving situation is called *ambiguous loss* and refers to cases where the person is gone physically or psychologically. The circumstances for physical loss could be the person is MIA during a war or could be missing due to a kidnapping or unexplained disappearance.

Ambiguous loss is a loss that occurs without closure or understanding. This kind of loss leaves a person searching for answers, and thus complicates and delays the process of grieving, and often results in unresolved grief. Some examples are infertility, termination of pregnancy, disappearance of a family member, death of an ex-spouse, a family member being physically alive but in a state of cognitive decline due to Alzheimer's disease or dementia, etc. An ambiguous loss can be categorized into two types of loss, physical or psychological. Physical loss and psychological loss differ in terms of what is being grieved for, the loss of the physical body, or the psychological mind. Experiencing an ambiguous loss can lead to personal questions, such as, "Am I still married to my missing spouse?" or "Am I still a child to a parent who no longer remembers me?" Since the grief process in an ambiguous loss is halted, it is harder to cope or move on to acceptance from the type of loss experienced. There are various types of grief that can occur due to the type of ambiguity experienced and corresponding therapy techniques to address certain types of grief. The overall goal of therapy to cope with ambiguous loss is to overcome the trauma associated with it and restoring resilience.

A physical ambiguous loss means that the body of a loved one is no longer around, such as a missing person or unrecovered body from war, but is still remembered psychologically due to the chance of coming back, for example in missing person cases. A physical ambiguous loss can occur across generations, such as the families of victims of the holocaust, and can cause traumatic distress as Posttraumatic stress disorder.[67]

The point here is that these situations are different because those left behind don't know what happened or even if the loved one is dead. The fact that ambiguous loss can occur across generations and can cause PTSD is enlightening.

The recommended treatment or therapy for those experiencing an ambiguous loss is not the same as for normal grief. With the ambiguous loss the mental anguish is different, and you are not experiencing any closure. Typically, when a loved one dies those left behind to grieve receive counseling on an individual basis. Even if loved ones attend some group therapy sessions, they are trying to cope primarily with personal grief. With the ambiguous loss, the counseling methods used are more along the lines of helping a family or related group go through the process together. Effective treatment is more of a group support model. As far as I can tell, no counseling ever happened in our family. It appears that ambiguous loss was what my grandparents, aunts, and uncles suffered through for the rest of their lives.

Because of David's loss, our family suffered through many issues over the past 73 years. Probably the overarching question was closure. For the sake of discussion, closure includes dealing with grief and loss. Here's how the three types of closure mentioned earlier weave through the 73-year story. The first concerns not knowing what happened to Uncle Dave. The family always wondered about his fate. Did he become a POW? Is he dead, and, if so, how did he die? Did he suffer? Where are his remains? Will he ever be found?

The second type of closure concern is knowing what he was like as a soldier. Was he highly respected? Was he brave? Did he have many relationships? These are things that you don't learn during the war because communications to the family at home are limited and cryptic. While this may not seem like an important consideration, it turns out that many who were close to David wondered about these aspects of his life during his years of service.

The third type is knowing what happened to his body, where his remains are located, and can we ever bring him home and put him to rest. This did not happen until 2018. Our family had no closure on any of these issues until around 1999 when we finally discovered what happened to him. At that time we were also able to learn what he was like as a person and a soldier. The rest of this section is devoted to closure.

The best way to describe these 73 years is to divide them into three different eras that explain what was going on in the minds and hearts of the family. The first was from 1944 to 1960 when Dave's mother was still alive. We will call these the Denial Years. The period from 1960 until around 1997 or 98 were the Silent Years when hardly anything was discussed or learned regarding Uncle Dave's status within the family. From 1998 or until 2018 we call the Searching Years where we finally received some closure and were able to bring Uncle Dave's body home to rest.

The Denial Years (1944-1960)

In the remaining 15 years of her life, my grandmother refused to believe that her son David was dead. She held on to the hope that somehow, he was still alive. She was holding out because he was officially Missing-In-Action (MIA) on most lists and not Killed-In-Action (KIA). The early denial years were very traumatic because she was actively looking for him. She would implore some of her children to help her by searching for him in downtown Los Angeles and writing letters to the Army. The Denial Years were filled with pain, grief, frustration, and silence.

The Silent Years (1960-1998)

From my grandmother's death in 1960 until I started searching for information about him around 1998, nothing happened from the family standpoint; conversations about Uncle Dave were infrequent. Behind the scenes, the Army had made several attempts to find his remains at Heuvelhof between 1945 and

1952. Ben Overhand was actively looking for David at Heuvelhof starting around the mid-1980s. News of these efforts never reached the family.

The Searching Years (1998 to 2018)

During these 20 years, I and others began to question what happened, learn what Dave was like, and realistically hoped that his remains could be located. The Searching Years have turned out to be extremely interesting and rewarding. Even if we had never found Uncle Dave's remains, we discovered a lot of new friends and developed great relationships. One group of new friends are the other 504 PIR relatives—those who had fathers, brothers, or uncles who fought alongside Dave or died along the way. A bond has also developed with the still living 504 veterans and others in the 82nd Airborne. The reunions and commemorative events we've attended have been quite rewarding and allowed us to witness this bond first-hand.

A bond has also developed with the still living 504 veterans and others in the 82nd Airborne.

The Dutch people are another group of new friends. They have been very gracious and appreciative of the sacrifices that Americans made to help liberate the Netherlands and all of Europe. They continue to teach the history of World War II to future generations. There are monuments throughout the Netherlands dedicated to various individuals and battles. These monuments are adopted by local schools, and the children regularly tend to them and hold commemoration ceremonies.

Finally, the Dutch researchers—especially Ben Overhand and Frank van Lunteren—who we have come to know like family, are very inspirational and important to us. Their devotion, passion, and kindness are significant and appreciated. I have made friends with many other Dutch people who were either re-enactors at events or who reached out by email, even meeting with several when they were visiting California.

One of the goals of this book is that younger generations in the United States and other countries will more fully appreciate what happened in World War II and the long-term effects of war. I believe that Korea, Vietnam, and now the Middle Eastern Wars are repeating the cycles of human loss experienced in World War II. We need to discover ways to avoid and deal with the effects of war better than we have in the past.

CHAPTER TWENTY-ONE

LACK OF CLOSURE DURING THE DENIAL YEARS

Sadly, Eva Rosa never did get closure about Dave. Lack of closure affected her and the rest of the family for many years. From September 1944 until 1960 what happened in the family dynamics were dominated by her denial that David was dead. Everyone, of course, loved her and did not want her to suffer more than she already had. I mentioned earlier that Grandma lost two daughters already and also experienced her son, Max, suffering through several serious injuries. She also suffered through her son, Launie's, terrible experiences in the South Pacific while in the Navy. I believe that during the denial years that her children kept information from her that referred to David's status as being killed in action.

I believe that during the denial years that her children kept information from her that referred to David's status as being killed in action.

When a loved one is killed or missing while serving their country the impact of the loss is devastating for the family. The toll taken by imagined scenarios also have a demoralizing effect.

When I was around seven years old, I remember being at my grandmother's house and having a one-on-one conversation with her. I always remember her accent. She spoke English, but her native languages were Yiddish and Russian. She would call me her little darling, but with her accent, she would pronounce it "darlink." One day while standing near Uncle Dave's plaque she said that even though everybody thought that David was dead, she knew that he was still alive. She knew that someday he would figure out where he was and come home. I did not know what to say to her. I found out later more about what she had been going through. Looking back on those visits I can recognize there was a dark cloud over the family. Everyone loved each other, but there was very little laughter and joy. Everything seemed serious and routine.

Regarding Grandma's house in Santa Fe Springs, Uncle Launie owned the house and supported Grandma. Two of David's other brothers also lived there: Jack and Lawrence. These three brothers, who had also served during World War II perhaps made a choice, either conscious or unconscious, to stick together while Grandma was still alive.

Searching for David

Eva Rosa's belief that David was still alive was more than wishful thinking. She would wake up at night with a vision that he was still living and had somehow found his way back to Los Angeles. In her dream, he could not remember where his home was and was wandering around the streets. She would make my Aunt Janet or Uncle Max drive her into Los Angeles so they could cruise around the streets looking for Uncle Dave. I can't imagine what

She would make my Aunt Janet or Uncle Max drive her into Los Angeles so they could cruise around the streets looking for Uncle Dave.

Janet and Max went through during those times. The impact of lack of this type of closure can be monstrous.

Cover-up: Four amazing artifacts

While growing up, I occasionally asked my parents, aunt or uncles, what happened to Uncle Dave. I would get a quick comment that he died in France or died crossing the Rhine River or something like that; no one ever mentioned Holland or the Netherlands. Some people even told me he died during D-Day in June 1944. As I started to gather information, there was evidence that my aunts and uncles really did know more of the truth in those early years. I believe the two reasons discussed earlier, Grandma's denial and the family's general grief, are the reasons why his death never became common knowledge. As a result, no one talked about the facts, and eventually the facts were blurred.

The first evidence was two letters the Army sent to my grandparents soon after Dave was killed both stating that he died in Holland on 28 September 1944. It would seem that even with Grandma's state of denial, among Dave's siblings this would be common knowledge.

AG 201 Rosenkrants, David
PO-N ETO 236

3 November 1944

Mr and Mrs. Hyman Rosenkrantz
1633 East 92nd Street
Los Angeles, California

Dear Mr. and Mrs. Rosenkrantz:

It is with regret that I am writing to confirm the recent telegram informing you of the death of your son, Staff Sergeant David Rosenkrantz, 39,018,039, Infantry, who was killed in action on 28 September 1944 in Holland.

I fully understand your desire to learn as much as possible regarding the circumstances leading to his death and I wish that there were more information available to give you. Unfortunately, reports of this nature contain only the briefest details as they are prepared under battle conditions and the means of transmission are limited.

I know the sorrow this message has brought you and it is my hope that in time the knowledge of his heroic service to his country, even unto death, may be of sustaining comfort to you.

I extend to you my deepest sympathy.

Sincerely yours,

J. A. ULIO
Major General
The Adjutant General.

COPY

The next piece of evidence for this conclusion is the book given to me by my cousin, Doni, titled *The Devils in Baggy Pants* (82nd Airborne Division), published right after the war (not to be confused with the book *Those Devils in Baggy Pants* written by Ross Carter from C Company of the 504 PIR). The book was sent to the family soon after the war and contained photographs from throughout the war and narratives of all the battles of the 504 Parachute Infantry Regiment. It also listed each action along with the names POWs, MIAs, KIAs and those who died of wounds (DOW). In the section on Holland, my Uncle Dave is listed as KIA (Killed In Action) rather than MIA (Missing In Action). I believe this is because the Army was sure of what had happened. Interestingly, the book's cover is worn, and the pages frayed from being handled dozens—if not hundreds—of times. Based on all the statements, the family knew at one time that he died or was missing in Holland, yet no one ever mentioned Holland when I asked.

Another interesting story about the book, *The Devils in Baggy Pants* occurred in 2006 while we were visiting Spokane, Washington for a family event. I had mentioned this trip to Frank van Lunteren and he informed me that a 504 paratrooper lived in Spokane—Herman Littman.

Harry Rosenkrantz, Phil Rosenkrantz, and Gina Rosenkrantz Buehler visiting Herman Littman and his wife in Spokane, Washington.

When we arrived, I called Herman and asked if we could visit. My father, son David, sister Gina, and I visited Herman and his wife. He was delighted to see us and loved talking about World War II. Herman had been captured by the Germans in Italy and spent the rest of the war as a POW. He told us colorful stories about how he escaped several times—but each time was recaptured. After the war, Herman continued a career in the Army and spent time serving with Captain Carl Kappel. Captain Kappel served in the Netherlands and Italy with Uncle Dave. They swapped stories about my uncle many times and kept his memory alive.

Herman showed us a fascinating photograph in the book, *The Devils in Baggy Pants.* There on page 7 was a picture of paratroopers marching in North Africa. The photo was taken from the rear, but several of the men had turned around to look back for some reason. One of them was Uncle Dave. He was looking back directly toward the camera. Herman said everybody thought that

One of them was Uncle Dave. He was looking back directly toward the camera.

that was pretty funny and that the photo reflected Uncle Dave's personality.

Photo from "The Devils in Baggy Pants" page 7 showing Dave (center of the picture) looking back at the camera.

More evidence that the family knew more than they let on is a letter from the Army dated 1947 and addressed to my Aunt Janet (Goldie). The Army was apparently responding to a letter she wrote them asking about the possibility that David could still be missing—perhaps having amnesia or being a POW somewhere. My grandmother's beliefs most likely motivated the original letter to the Army that David was still alive. A thoughtful reply was sent back to my aunt addressing each of those concerns. The letter stated very clearly that although they didn't have the details, they did have further confirmation that Uncle Dave died in Holland on 28 September 1944.

AGRS-DC 201 Rosenkrantz, David
(6 Aug 47)   6 October 1947

Mrs. Goldie Woods
c/o Social Service, Veterans Administration
1031 South Broadway
Los Angeles 15, California

Dear Mrs Woods:

     Reference is made to your letter requesting additional information regarding the death of your brother.

     I realize how much it would mean to you to know a possibility existed that your brother, Staff Sergeant David Rosenkrantz, Army Serial Number 39,018,039, Parachute Infantry, might be alive, but I am sorry that on the basis of official information received concerning him, I can offer you no hope that he has survived. Military authorities in theaters of operation were specifically instructed to submit reports of death only in cases where conclusive evidence of death existed. The casualty message received from the Commanding General of the European Theater of Operations stated only that he was killed in action on 28 September 1944 in Holland. Additional information has now been received which confirms this report but unfortunately no further details were given. The conditions of warfare have denied many families complete knowledge of the circumstances surrounding the death of their loved ones and I am sure you will appreciate the difficulty involved in obtaining information concerning casualties of this nature.

     With reference to your statements, nothing has been found of record to show that your brother was a prisoner of war. In the event your brother had been suffering from amnesia and could not have been immediately identified, his fingerprints would have been checked with the files in Washington 25, D. C., and his identity conclusively established.

     The Quartermaster General of the Army, Washington 25, D. C., has jurisdiction over matters pertaining to the burial of our military personnel who dies overseas and a copy of your letter has accordingly been forwarded to that official for necessary action.

                          C O P Y

But the most surprising piece of evidence that the family knew what happened to Uncle Dave was a letter that came to light about 2017 while I was visiting my cousin Alan's house. Alan is my Uncle Max's son and several times invited cousins over to his home just to socialize. I usually take advantage of these gatherings to give the family an update about the search for Uncle Dave's remains. However, this time he had found a photo album with photos from the 30s and 40s. It had pictures from before, during and after the war, including photos of Uncle Dave from Fort Bragg and other places. Remarkably, stuck in

between the pages of the album was a half-page letter from the Army. It was the second page of a letter the Army had written to my grandparents telling about what happened to Uncle Dave. I don't know where the first page is. The first thing that astounded me was that the letter was signed by 1LT James "Maggie" Megellas! Here was a letter from someone that I knew personally and had visited many times. Now—over 70 years later—I was holding a letter he wrote to our family. The letter talked about my uncle being killed in Holland at Den Heuvel or

Remarkably, stuck in between the pages of the album was a half-page letter from the Army. It was the second page of a letter the Army had written to my grandparents telling about what happened to Uncle Dave.

Heuvelhof and why his remains were not recovered. The worn fold of the letter destroyed one line of text which may have been crucial, but now that we know what happened to my uncle it probably doesn't matter. The letter included the address they could use to write to First Lieutenant Joseph Forestal to get more information. The page was falling apart from having been read and handled so much— a half page was all that was left. This letter gave great detail about what happened to Uncle Dave and yet it was not part of family knowledge or family lore when I came along in the 50s.

These are incidences of discovering artifacts containing accurate information that was obviously handled many times by family members. Yet, because of my grandmother's denial, they were not discussed openly and eventually that black cloud of denial just smothered everything.

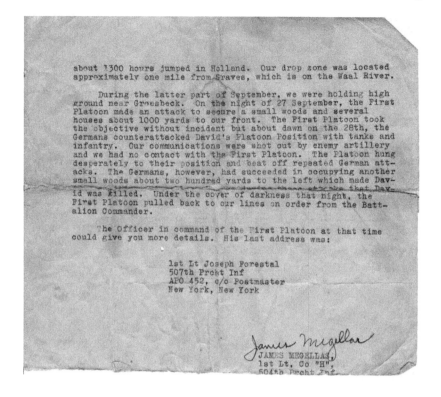

about 1300 hours jumped in Holland. Our drop zone was located approximately one mile from Graves, which is on the Waal River.

During the latter part of September, we were holding high ground near Groesbeck. On the night of 27 September, the First Platoon made an attack to secure a small woods and several houses about 1000 yards to our front. The First Platoon took the objective without incident but about dawn on the 28th, the Germans counterattacked David's Platoon Position with tanks and infantry. Our communications were shot out by enemy artillery and we had no contact with the First Platoon. The Platoon hung desperately to their position and beat off repeated German attacks. The Germans, however, had succeeded in occupying another small woods about two hundred yards to the left which made David was killed. Under the cover of darkness that night, the First Platoon pulled back to our lines on order from the Battalion Commander.

The Officer in command of the First Platoon at that time could give you more details. His last address was:

1st Lt Joseph Forestal
507th Prcht Inf
APO 452, c/o Postmaster
New York, New York

JAMES MEGELLAS,
1st Lt, Co "H"
504th Prcht Inf.

Letter from 1LT James "Maggie" Megellas explaining how Dave died.

The Impact on my Father

My father, Harry, was the youngest of the 11 children and as mentioned in Part 1, David was the closest thing he had to a real father. Dave was kind of the spark plug of the family and had strong relationships with all his siblings.

The plaque with Uncle Dave's photo and medals was at my grandmother's house during the '50s. When my Uncle Launie moved and took Grandma to Canoga Park, we bought the house from him and the plaque ended up on a shelf in our garage. I believe that when we sold that house in 1967, my dad threw the plaque away because he just couldn't stand the pain of keeping it. Even after all those years, I don't think my dad had closure or finished grieving.

Recently another related question come up in a discussion that I had never considered before. In 1946 my father joined the Army and was in airborne training. One day his unit was asked for volunteers and he did. To his surprise they were sent to Trieste, Italy, to be part of the occupation forces guarding the border between Italy and Yugoslavia. Why had my father joined the Army and wanted to be a paratrooper? Was this choice a tribute to his brother? One person, I spoke with thought maybe Dad wanted to see if he could find out more about what happened to David. In fact, my father told me that when he was in the Army, I believe at Fort Bragg, he ran into someone who had known Uncle Dave. He told my dad that David had died crossing the

Why had my father joined the Army and wanted to be a paratrooper? Was this choice a tribute to his brother?

Rhine River. I believe that was a reference to the Waalcrossing because the 82nd Airborne never called the Waal River by that name. They always referred to it the Rhine because it was part of the lower Rhine.

My father's initial reticence to learn about the events surrounding Dave perhaps pointed out his long struggle with ambiguous loss and lack of closure.

Uncle Launie and PTSD

The story of Dave's brother, Launie, was briefly mentioned in Part 1. In addition to his ocean rescue from the *USS Chicago*, he was present during other major WWII battles, both before and after the sinking.

After the sinking of the *Chicago*, he and others were picked up by the *USS John Penn* (APA-23) and delivered to New Caledonia for reassignment.[68] After a one-month leave, Launie was stationed on the newly commissioned aircraft carrier, *USS Midway*. A few months later, the ship's name was changed to the *USS St. Lo*. About the same time, Launie was transferred to another ship, the *USS Fanshaw Bay*.

In late October 1944, during the Battle of Leyte Gulf, the *USS St. Lo* was the first American ship to be sunk by a Japanese Kamikaze attack. Uncle Launie was on the nearby *USS Fanshaw Bay*, defending the *USS St. Lo* during the attack.[69] So he was present during a battle when a ship he had been on only two months prior sank. He narrowly missed being on a sinking boat a second time and probably had friends on the *USS St. Lo* just like he did on the *USS Chicago*.

Besides PTSD, one wonders what the effect was from other psychological conditions such as trauma-related guilt (which includes survivor's guilt or survivor's remorse).

> *Feeling guilt after the experience of a traumatic event is serious, as it has been linked to a number of negative consequences. For example, trauma-related guilt has been found to be associated with* depression, *shame,* social anxiety, *low self-esteem, and thoughts of suicide. In addition, feeling a lot of trauma-related guilt has been connected to the development of PTSD. Given the potential negative consequences of trauma-related guilt, it is important that any such guilt is addressed in PTSD treatment.*[70]

My father said that on the *USS Chicago* one of the torpedoes hit the mess hall where Uncle Launie's friends were eating. This must have contributed to survivor's guilt and tremendous grief. World War II researcher and good friend, Jennifer Holik wrote the following in a recent article:

> *With all the studies on PTSD and veterans, one primary component, especially when we look at veteran suicide is GRIEF. Yet, grief has not been studied until recently. Grief also creates issues for not only the veteran but the family and friends close to the veteran.*

> *Unresolved, unacknowledged grief over what someone did in combat, or did not do, who they lost, survivor's guilt and sadness of being the only one left, and many other ways veterans hold grief all contribute to their state of mind, the*

life they live, the joy (or lack of) they feel. This unresolved grief also affects those closest to them.

Finally, the University of California Irvine conducted a study on grief in veterans. It is interesting what they discovered and how it deeply affects veterans, even separately from any PTSD they may have or had, and how it affects families.[71]

After reflecting over the denial and silent years, I now believe that the family was not talking about World War II for three reasons: Grandma's denial that Uncle Dave was dead, Uncle Launie's severe reactions to any mention of the details of the war, and a common belief after the war that the best way to cope with the pain was to not talk about it and try to get on with life.

CHAPTER TWENTY-TWO

WHAT WAS UNCLE DAVE LIKE?

The second type of closure is related to Uncle Dave's personality. As his nephew who never met him, I wanted to know what he was like. I eventually realized that my Aunt Janet (Goldie) also wondered what Dave was like as a soldier and as a person over the 32 months he was in the Army. It had not occurred to me that the family wondered about this too. They did get his letters home, but those were always written so that the censors would not have to blackout or cut information. Consequently, discussing battles, fellow soldiers, and other details about locations and actions didn't happen in the letters.

Two incidents brought closure in this area when I first found out what happened to Dave from Ted Finkbeiner. Around the same time I received Ted's phone number I also received Albert Tarbell's phone number. Albert told me many stories about what David was like as a soldier and as a person. For example, David was probably the only Sergeant in the 504 who did not swear profusely. He was helpful and supportive of replacements under his command and trained them as best he could to help them stay alive. Uncle Dave was also courageous.

Uncle Dave was also courageous.

After discussing Uncle Dave with several men who had known him, I called my Aunt Janet and was able to help bring some closure for her. She later called Albert and had a touching conversation.

In the book *Brave Men, Gentle Heroes* referred to earlier in the chapter about England, Albert related his conversation with Janet. His description reveals what appears to be some closure for her:

> *In the summer of 2000, his brother's son called me. The nephew said that he had been trying for 5 years or so to locate people that knew his uncle. Before that, they seemed to have never looked into the situation too much because they felt so bad about Rosie getting killed. I was so happy to hear from him because I had often wondered whatever became of the family.*
>
> *At the beginning of Hanukkah this past year, I got a call from Rosy's sister. This was the first time she made contact. I never knew that she existed.*
>
> *She was so happy. She was half crying. "I have to talk to somebody that knew my dear Rosy", she says. "He was so good to me." She was just over-joyed we talked for the longest time.*
>
> *Everybody loved him. Nobody ever had a bad word for him. He was a good soldier.*
>
> *She said that he was such a nice guy, and I told her that he was. Everybody loved him. Nobody ever had a bad word for him. He was a good soldier.*
>
> *She says the only thing I can think is that he went straight to heaven. That's why they couldn't find his body.*
>
> *I said, "He sure did. He sure did go to heaven." (Takiff, 2007, pp. 244-245)*

Janet told me how much it meant to her to learn about what David had done during the war, and it brought a lot of closure to her. Albert Tarbell was an exceptional person and stayed in touch with my aunt for years after that. They would talk on the phone occasionally and exchange Christmas cards.

The book signing and 504 reunion in Fond du Lac, Wisconsin in 2003 helped me gain some closure about Uncle Dave. Learning what those 17 veterans, all part of *The Greatest Generation.* (Brokaw, 2001) were like helped me know my uncle.

A third way to experience healing closure was by reading the letters he wrote home and the newspaper articles quoting him. It became obvious that Uncle Dave was a brave, humble person with an engaging personality.

CHAPTER TWENTY-THREE

BRINGING ROSIE HOME

Although we began to experience closure starting around 1999 when we learned what Dave was like and how he had died, his remains did not come home until 2018.

In March 2018, we were contacted by the Army that David's remains had been identified. That April William "Shorty" Cox, (Senior Mortuary Affairs Specialist-Identification Case Manager), personally met with our family to relate the details. He spent two hours telling us in detail the whole story of how Uncle Dave's remains had been found and their subsequent journey. Shorty then gave us a very brief understanding of what the process was for bringing him back for burial.

There were numerous details that had to be handled after the meeting, but the family was able to get some closure. This was the first time I had heard that the Canadians were involved with my uncle's remains. The description of the chain of events all made sense. A week before writing this chapter I noticed my photograph from the 2009 trip to Margraten of a grave dedicated to an unknown soldier. I don't recall taking the picture and certainly didn't have any thought that one of the unidentified graves could be Uncle Dave. In my mind, his remains were still somewhere in the Nijmegen area where he was killed. So even though his name has been on the wall of the missing at Margraten for many years, his remains were also at the cemetery a few hundred yards away. When I learned this, I wondered why DNA testing wasn't done earlier on the remains buried at Margraten. After reading the book *Soldier Dead* mentioned earlier, I now realize that locating and accurately

identifying dead soldiers is not as easy as just finding dog tags
or doing DNA tests.

*Twenty-five of Dave's relatives gathered at Phil & Judy's home on
April 14, 2018, to hear William "Shorty" Cox, Senior Mortuary
Affairs Specialist-Identification Case Manager, Past Conflict
Repatriations Branch (PCRB), describe the events and research
that led to the identification of Uncle Dave's remains.*

Shorty explained about the kind of research done to decide
which graves to exhume. They performed a historical analysis of
the remains, analyzing the records they had of where the
remains had traveled on their way to Margraten. They also
examined skeletal remains to either include or exclude names
based on dental records. In this case, they also had my uncle's
boot size, 7EEE. Selecting remains that had that boot size from
among those buried at Margraten helped narrow down the
possibilities. Finally, they performed DNA testing and
concluded that the remains belonged to my uncle.

Appendix A shows a timeline of events culminating in Uncle
Dave's return. The mysterious story reads almost like the tale of
lovers who crossed in the night and missed each other—not

being able to piece everything together for 73 years. Fortunately, on April 14th we finally learned the truth and had closure.

Bringing David Home – Arrival at Los Angeles International Airport

Many years ago I told myself that closure for me would be seeing Uncle Dave buried at the Riverside National Cemetery with his four brothers. On July 17, 2018, my uncle's remains were escorted from Offutt AFB near Omaha, Nebraska, to Los Angeles International Airport. My wife, Judy, our son, David, and I there waiting when the American Airlines plane arrived with his remains. This was more emotional than I expected. I had anticipated we would drive to the airport and then somehow be escorted to where the plane would arrive. Luckily for us, some accommodating people from the Risher Mortuary, an organization called Honoring Our Fallen[72], the Patriot Guard, and several veteran organizations were there to give us moral support and provide

...everyone in that area at the airport had stopped what they were doing and were paying their respects to the arriving fallen soldier.

transportation. Laura Herzog from Honoring Our Fallen came to our house and drove us to the airport. She was with us through all of the security procedures, entering the airport, and finally driving to the gate where the American Airlines jet would arrive.

As the plane pulled in you could see that everyone in that area at the airport had stopped what they were doing and were paying their respects to the arriving fallen soldier. We were told that none of the passengers would be able to deplane until after Uncle Dave's casket had been removed and placed in the coach. The plane captain exited the plane and personally gave us his condolences. The airport police also gave us their condolences along with the honor guard that escorted my uncle from Nebraska. Another military Honor Guard was present to help bring his casket off the plane and place it into the coach.

The process of bringing the casket off the plane was fascinating. Several soldiers entered the plane through the cargo hold and in private draped the casket with an American flag. Then the casket was brought down the ramp where my wife and I were allowed to spend a few moments mourning over it. I did not know my uncle personally, but this was one of the most emotional moments I have experienced, knowing he was physically home with the family after 73 years and what this would mean to his parents and siblings if they were still alive. We then escorted the coach back to the mortuary in Montebello where it was held for viewing later on.

S/Sgt David Rosenkrantz arriving at LAX from Offutt AFB in Nebraska on July 17, 2018.

The Funeral at Riverside National Cemetery

On July 20th, 2018 we buried Uncle Dave at the Riverside National Cemetery. His four brothers who also served in World War II or the Occupation Forces were already buried there. The funeral was at the amphitheater with over 130 people present;

34 of whom were his relatives. Dave's great-great nephew, Pastor Rudy Topete, gave a prayer at the beginning and end of the funeral service. Three paratroopers from the 82nd Airborne led by Lieutenant Colonel Joseph Buccino had flown from Fort Bragg to Riverside, California, to present Uncle Dave's medals and give him a long-overdue tribute. Lieutenant Colonel Buccino's tribute was very moving and showed how much Uncle Dave's service meant to our country and as an inspiration to thousands of paratroopers who followed in his footsteps. The Lieutenant Colonel's voice was both powerful and comforting as he spoke the following words:

> *You know we say when you serve in the 82nd Airborne, you walk in the footsteps of legends. Today one of those legends has returned home. David Rosenkrantz was among a small group of Americans who voluntarily jumped into battle to save the free world from Nazism. Today, 73 years after World War II, our nation has mastered the parachute assault. We do it safely over a thousand times each month. It was an example, an experiment—the concept of airborne paratroopers largely untested. The paratroopers themselves did not know if they would survive the landing.*

...when you serve in the 82nd Airborne, you walk in the footsteps of legends. Today one of those legends has returned home.

-Lieutenant Colonel Buccino

> *Nonetheless, men like David jumped into Sicily and Nijmegen because they always knew evil had to be defeated. From here forward, there is nothing but soft winds and safe landings for David Rosenkrantz. Over the past two years, I have spent some time in the towns liberated by our World War II paratroopers. I know some in here have as well. Unless you do so, you will never understand how grateful so many generations are to David Rosenkrantz and his fellow paratroopers.*

People in this country are surprised when I tell them that more than 100 paratroopers from the 82nd Airborne Division remain missing from World War II. Just this month another paratrooper, Willard Jenkins, was identified. Willard will be coming home next month. As a nation, we celebrate our war dead, and we cherish the accomplishments of our World War II veterans. But we sometimes lose sight of the fact that they have not all been found.

The 82nd Airborne Division is grateful to the Rosenkrantz family for the letters, photographs, memorabilia, and military uniform items provided in the effort to identify David Rosenkrantz. One of the most important things we do as an Army is recognize our soldiers for their service in combat. We do this with awards presented in formal ceremony. When an American soldier is missing those things are held in a place of honor ready for the day that soldier returns. It is now 74 years after his actions in the Netherlands that 1st Sergeant Douglas Smith will present Dr. Phillip Rosenkrantz with awards that could never before be presented. And I know the paratroopers in the auditorium here will know what I mean when I say? "David Rosenkrantz, we will see you at that final manifest call."

The following awards are presented on behalf of a grateful nation. The Bronze Star Medal second award for meritorious achievement in active ground combat against the enemy during Operation Market Garden in September 1944. Purple Heart second award for wounds received in action that led to his death on 28th September 1944. The European Campaign Medal for service during World War II's European campaign. The World War II Victory Medal for service during World War II. The Netherlands Orange Lanyard awarded to all soldiers who participated in the liberation of Holland during World War II. The Combat Parachutist Badge with two bronze stars for parachute assault into Sicily and the Netherlands. The 504th regimental coin. The 82nd Airborne Division Command Sergeant Major's Coin. And the 82nd Airborne Division Commanders Coin.

Military honors followed the tribute, beginning with a rifle salute accompanied by a bugle playing *The Last Post*. Hearing a bugle or bagpipes at a funeral always hits me square in the heart. Next was the folding of the American flag that adorned the casket. The folded flag was then presented to us.

Then I had to control my emotions long enough to deliver a nine-minute eulogy. My sincere hope was that my words honored Uncle Dave in some small way. The eulogy is copied in the Appendix, along with the obituary provided to Risher Mortuary. Uncle Dave's great-great nephew, Pastor Rudy Topete then gave a beautiful and poignant closing prayer that comforted and helped provide more closure.

Rabbi David Becker from the California National Guard was present and helped us escort Uncle Dave's remains to the graveside where he recited the Kaddish. Then with the assistance of the Rabbi, they lowered the casket into the grave.

The cemetery had asked if the family had any requests regarding where to locate David's grave within the cemetery and would try to honor our request. I asked if he could be buried as close to one of his four brothers as they could manage. Having visited all the graves several times, I guessed that their best chance of having an available plot would be to locate him near either his brother Jack or brother Lawrence. In fact, they were able to place Uncle Dave about 30 feet away from his brother Jack. Now, whenever I think about Uncle Dave, I usually think about all five of the brothers being together at Riverside. This brought yet another dimension of closure for the family.

The Army and the DPAA sent out press releases about my uncle all over the country as well as to Europe. There were articles about him in the Netherlands and Israel. I received email messages and calls about David and his funeral. It was gratifying to see how many people were concerned about his return and closure for the family. Quite a few people sent us copies of newspaper articles from their local papers. The front-page feature in the *Los Angeles Times* was one of my favorites; reporters Paloma Esquivel, Gina Ferrazi, and Laura Newberry collaborated to put together an awe-inspiring tribute followed by a thoughtful five-minute film a few months later.

Processional at Riverside National Cemetery (Photo by James "Woody" Woods)

The funeral was held at the amphitheater at Riverside National Cemetery

Receiving the folded flag

Lt. Col. Joe Buccino, 82nd Airborne Division from Ft. Bragg, NC, delivering a eulogy.

Below: S/Sgt David Rosenkrantz' grave marker

Below: Locations of the five Rosenkrantz brothers now buried at Riverside National Cemetery

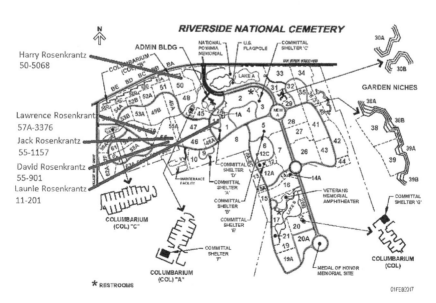

Final Closure – The Rosette Ceremony

On September 19, 2019, our family was joined by about 30 others for the Rosette Ceremony at The Netherlands American Cemetery in Margraten. When a soldier whose name is on the Wall of the Missing is found, a small medallion called a Rosette is placed next to the name. The placing of the Rosette can be done at a formal ceremony when desired. Superintendent Shane Williams and the staff at the Netherlands American Cemetery were very accommodating by scheduling our ceremony while we were in the Netherlands for the 75th Anniversary of Operation Market Garden. Ton Hermes of the Foundation for Adopting Graves American Cemetery Margraten made most of the arrangements and invited family members of the grave adopter, Eddie and Marion Gilissen (both the unmarked grave where Uncle Dave was *...it was my honor to place the Rosette on the wall next to Uncle Dave's name.* located for over 70 years and his name on the Wall of the Missing had grave adopters).

We were humbled and honored by the presence of so many of our friends who were also on the journey to find Uncle Dave and help bring him home. Ben Overhand and Frank van Lunteren were there. Frank kindly helped with the eulogy and described Uncle Dave's service history in North Africa, Sicily, Italy, and the Netherlands. I finally met World War II researcher and writer, Jennifer Holik in person after working with her online while researching and writing this book. Fellow 504 relatives were also there: Ray and Kathleen Buttke, Catherine Metropoulos, and Peter Smits. Many Dutch friends and grave adopters also attended. Finally, it was an honor to have some current 82nd Airborne paratroopers in attendance. Major Richard Ingleby from Fort Bragg and four paratroopers in his command drove from Nijmegen to the cemetery for the ceremony. After the eulogies by myself and Frank, it was an honor to place the Rosette on the wall next to Uncle Dave's name.

It was amazing and meaningful to finally achieve closure after so many years. Just as important is that the journey has taught me many things. I realize now families with lost or damaged loved ones from war suffer much more than we realize. Also, the suffering does not go away as quickly as we would like and can affect generations. We need to be more sensitive to Gold Star and refugee families we know and what they might still be going through. Reconciliation with war is possible, but not easy. Organizations like Honoring Our Fallen go a long way in helping families do more than just bring their loved ones home. They stay by their side and continue helping in the journey.

L: Judy, Phil, Liz & David at the Wall of the Mission after the Rosette Ceremony; R: Frank van Lunteren delivering his eulogy for Uncle Dave at the Rosette Ceremony

Top: Phil and Judy with Eddie and Marion Gilissen, members of the family who adopted Uncle Dave's grave while he was still unknown; Bottom: Phil placing the rosette next to Uncle Dave's name on the Wall of the Missing...a final act of closure.

CHAPTER TWENTY-FOUR

CLOSURE REQUIRED A LOT OF HELP

My wife and I and others in our family have commented numerous times about the many people who came to our side to help bring together the final events in July. Greg Welch, his wife Barbara Risher Welch, and Nancy Valdez from the Risher Mortuary were extremely helpful—going way above and beyond to make sure everything happened as needed. William "Shorty" Cox and Casualty Assistance Officer SFC Miguel Cesina were very helpful. Members of the Patriot Guard and several other veteran associations showed up and were very gracious in everything they did to help with the funeral and escorts. Laura Hertzog from Honoring Our Fallen drove us to LAX on July 17 to receive the casket and again on July 20 to help drive family members to and from the funeral in Riverside. Laura has even kept in touch with us since the funeral.

In searching for a place to hold a reception near the cemetery in Riverside my friend, Kevin Flye suggested that we contact Grove Community Church in Riverside a couple of miles from the cemetery. I called and spoke with Heather Tormey at the church to see if we could rent a space for my uncle's reception, bring in food, and put some of the memorabilia on display. They offered to host the full reception for us, including providing food. We were overwhelmed by their graciousness. During the gathering at the church, the Grove Community Church leadership came by to personally express their condolences. We have been overwhelmed by all those who came out of the woodwork to help us bring those final closing events to fruition.

PART FIVE

LEADERS EAT LAST

FAN organizers and supporters at the Waalcrossing Memorial prior to the Sunset March during the 75th Anniversary of Operation Market Garden. (Photo courtesy of Jaleesa Derksen/Jaleesa Freelance Fotografe ©)

From this day to the ending of the world,
But we in it shall be rememberèd—
We few, we happy few, we band of brothers

—Shakespeare (Henry V, Act IV)

CHAPTER TWENTY-FIVE

PARATROOPERS, BRAVERY, AND LEADERSHIP

Quote from an officer's manual:

A Captain cannot be too careful of the company the state has committed to his charge. He must pay the greatest attention to the health of his men, their discipline, arms, accouterments, ammunition, clothes, and necessaries. His first object should be, to gain the love of his men, by treating them with every possible kindness and humanity, inquiring into their complaints, and when well founded, seeing them redressed. He should know every man of his company by name and character. He should often visit those who are sick, speak tenderly to them, see that the public provision, whether of medicine or diet, is duly administered, and procure them besides such comforts and conveniences as are in his power. The attachment that arises from this kind of attention to the sick and wounded is almost inconceivable; it will moreover be the means of preserving the lives of many valuable men. (Baron Von Steuben 1785 Revolutionary War Officers Manual)

Except for the writing style, you might assume these instructions are from a present-day officers manual based on a leadership approach known as either servant leadership, inspirational leadership, emotional leadership, or transformational leadership. The goal is to produce a team of trained, self-motivated people committed to following leaders toward a common goal or vision. Surprisingly, this quote is well over 200 years old! It is taken from the Revolutionary War Officers Manual written by Baron von Steuben under the direction of General George Washington. The key phrase is,

"The attachment that arises from this kind of attention to the sick and wounded is almost inconceivable."

George Washington was one of the greatest leaders of all time. He was able to recruit a volunteer Army that left their families, followed him anywhere, suffered through a terrible winter at Valley Forge, and withstood many hardships. Washington ate his meals with the troops so he could get to know them and continue to drive home the importance of their mission. He used multiple sources of communication to maintain support.

In the book *The Founding Fathers on Leadership* by Ronald R. Phillips (Phillips, 1997) the author discusses George Washington's leadership style. A major leadership trait among George Washington and other founding fathers was passion for the mission. Passion is a vital ingredient to success because it drives you to look for alternatives and innovative solutions. Passion can force you to cultivate relationships as you talk to others and share the vision. Passion will move you to take risks that may be necessary for the success of high-risk, high-stake missions. Passion prevents you from dropping a project part way through just because the going gets a little tough.

> *"The attachment that arises from this kind of attention to the sick and wounded is almost inconceivable."*
>
> -Baron von Steuben

In addition to passion, our founding fathers possessed qualities of honor, integrity, and self-sacrifice in measures rarely seen these days. Their vision was quite uncanny considering the circumstances they were in. If you sum up the weapons they had at their disposal during the Revolutionary War, the only real weapon they had against the British was *shared vision*. Their vision of a people free of British domination was the only thing they could use to enlist troops to fight in the face of difficult odds. As the book pointed out, Washington stayed with his troops and had a high level of interaction because he knew he had to keep the vision alive and fresh in their minds. Today's leaders should take greater notice of this principle and spend a lot more time with the people in their charge. The book repeatedly pointed out the power of Thomas Paine's writings as they were distributed and read to the troops. Only the thought of someday being free of the British was keeping the troops motivated through difficult times. In the workplace, we desire people to have a deep sense of responsibility toward their fellow team members and the company's goals.

...our founding fathers possessed qualities of honor, integrity, and self-sacrifice...

This responsibility will most likely come from a shared vision that aligns with personal vision and goals.

Colonel (later General) James Gavin—commanding officer of 3400 paratroopers who jumped into Sicily—had many of the same challenges as our founding fathers. Gavin had one year to recruit and train volunteers (you had to volunteer to be a paratrooper) to do something that had never been done before in the history of the world. Paratroopers would be asked to jump out of an airplane at night behind enemy lines. If they survived the jump[73] they were to find their weapons, their buddies and their leaders. Then they needed to determine their location and figure out how to achieve their mission with the resources and people they had no matter what they were facing. Also, once they jumped out of the plane, there was no going back. The paratroopers in Sicily would be the only thing between the enemy and the beachhead where the Allied ground forces would be landing. They had to keep the enemy away from the beaches long enough for the ground forces to deploy. [74]

Gavin had to develop leaders that the men would respect and follow. The first thing he told junior level officers was, "*You will be the last to eat and the first one out of the plane.*" Gavin slept and fought with his troops. He participated with his men in the jumps in Sicily, Italy, Normandy, and Holland. It was discovered later that he had broken several vertebrae during one jump but continued in pain. In his book, *On to Berlin*, General Gavin says,

As a paratrooper I always made it a practice to sleep on the ground. Immediately following a parachute landing one would end up with a few paratroopers, or sometimes a larger number, and one had to live off the land. Parachute officers had to set an example and learn to live like other troopers. In any event it would have been unwise to succumb to the physical comforts of a bed and a permanent shelter. (Gavin, On to Berlin, 1978)

Gavin's paratroopers were well trained. One way to build a team is through training. People who train together form bonds and trust. Training leads to competence, which leads to confidence, which results in esprit de corps. Strong relationships and bonds among team members are built through a deliberate process and are not accidental. Training is also a strong signal that your leaders are investing in your growth and success, believe in you, and expecting you to step up.[75]

Paratroopers are first trained as infantry (ground troops). Then they are taught how to be a parachutist. After that, they are trained in strategy and tactics unique to chaotic conditions. They must be prepared mentally and physically to challenge the enemy in whatever circumstances they encounter. They are cross-trained in their roles, weapons, and even how to use the enemy's weapons if the occasion warrants. The men of the 82nd Airborne traveled by ship from the East coast of the US to North Africa, where they trained for three more months before jumping into Sicily. The paratroopers trained almost every day. Key road intersections in Sicily were duplicated so paratroopers could practice how to secure them. They learned about booby traps and weapons they would encounter. Uncle Dave's letters from North Africa describe this training. By this time, he was a sergeant leading other men and his attitude displayed maturity and sense of responsibility.

Paratrooper assault is the ultimate example of decentralized management.

Once the 247 planes took off from North Africa headed for Sicily, Colonel Gavin had very little control over his men. Their training, intelligence, and grit would be all he could depend on once they were airborne. Paratrooper assault is the ultimate example of decentralized management.

Many readers are familiar with the inspirational words uttered by King Henry V in an inspirational speech to his men in William Shakespeare's play, *Henry V, Act IV, Scene iii*, written around 1600.

> *From this day to the ending of the world,*
> *But we in it shall be rememberèd—*
> *We few, we happy few, we **band of brothers**;*
> *For he to-day that sheds his blood with me*
> *Shall be my brother; be he ne'er so vile,*
> *This day shall gentle his condition;*
> *And gentlemen in England now a-bed*
> *Shall think themselves accursed they were not here,*
> *And hold their manhoods cheap whiles any speaks*
> *That fought with us upon Saint Crispin's day.*[76]

Stephen Ambrose borrowed the phrase *Band of Brothers* for the title of his 1992 book about E Company of 506 Parachute Infantry Regiment in the 101st Airborne during World War II. The book was adapted into the 2001 miniseries *Band of Brothers*. I have watched the 10-part miniseries at least a dozen times, realizing that the characters symbolize my uncle and men he served with. Uncle Dave was part of a *Band of Brothers*.

Uncle Dave was part of a Band of Brothers.

The following was handed to each paratrooper before the invasion of Sicily:

Soldiers of the 505th Combat Team[77],

Tonight you embark upon a combat mission for which our people and the people of the free world have been waiting for two years. You will spearhead the landing of an American Force upon the island of SICILY.

Every preparation has been made to eliminate the element of chance. You have been given the means to do the job and you are backed by the largest assemblage of air power in the world's history.

The eyes of the world are upon you. The hopes and prayers of every American go with you. Since it is our first fight at night, you must use the countersign, and avoid firing on each other. The bayonet is the night fighters best weapon. Conserve your water and ammunition.

The term "American parachutist" has become synonymous with courage of high order. Let us carry the fight to the enemy and make the American Parachutist feared and respected through all his ranks. Attack violently. Destroy him wherever found.

I know you will do your job. Good landing, good fight, and good luck.

  - James M. Gavin

The term "American parachutist" has become synonymous with courage of high order. Let us carry the fight to the enemy and make the American Parachutist feared and respected through all his ranks.

-James M. Gavin

Like the speech from Henry V, Gavin's letter to his men was inspirational. He told them the whole world is watching and they were prepared. He also gave specific advice for survival as well as the goal to be feared and respected, and the charge to destroy the enemy. History has proven that the paratroopers of the 82nd Airborne Division lived up to General Gavin's expectations—including being called *Devils in Baggy Pants* by their enemy during the fighting at Anzio.

Leadership 101

Some experts teach that modern organizational leadership theory is based on the type of leadership examples presented in the previous section. It is worth looking at this claim briefly.

There are many sub-topics that could be addressed in the world of leadership study. These include types of leadership, purpose, values, ethical decision making, leadership styles and traits, leadership development, and leadership philosophy. In the interest of brevity, only three of these topics will be addressed: types of leadership, purpose, and values. A list of leadership books that include a significant reference to military leadership is included.

It should be noted that *The Army Leadership Field Manual 22-100* is 270 pages of the best leadership material I may have ever seen compiled in one document. It is referenced several places below. *FM 22-100* contains these topics and many more. (US Army, 1999)

Leadership Types

There are three types of leadership that encompass a wide range of existing leadership styles, Positional Leadership, Transactional Leadership, and Transformational Leadership.

Transformational leaders concentrate on getting people aligned with shared objectives, creating a teamwork culture, and focusing on continually improving the overall organization. Rewards are based on organizational success (e.g., profit sharing) and how well people contribute to team success. Leadership experts talk about various versions of this approach, such as inspirational leadership, visionary leadership, emotional leadership, participative leadership, servant leadership, and other similar names.

> *Transformational leaders concentrate on getting people aligned with shared objectives, creating a teamwork culture, and focusing on continually improving the overall organization.*

Where does military leadership fall? During a battle, it could be argued that military leadership is more like positional or transactional leadership. But when paratroopers jump out of planes, the transformational leadership approach is a better description of what Washington and Gavin used to prepare for battle. General Gavin was preparing his men to be self-starters, creative, courageous, physically fit, and technically competent.[78]

Leading with Purpose and Values

Revisiting the first question mentioned in the Preface: *Why volunteer to become a paratrooper?* What values and sense of purpose led David and others to volunteer to become paratroopers and—after having some idea of their destiny— continue to serve? Their leaders had to reinforce the paratroopers' purpose and inspire them to suffer through training and combat. The obvious intent of joining and fighting was to protect our country from the Nazi threat in the east and the Japanese threat in the west. The millions of young men and women who joined to fight wanted to keep the enemy from landing on our shores and occupying our land. Having a purpose is not enough. You need a plan and training to accomplish the plan provided by competent leadership.

Purpose is important. Purpose is referred to in various ways by leadership and management experts. Dr. W. Edwards Deming, for example, refers to the *Aim of the Organization*. Deming's first of his well-known 14 Points for Management is: *Create constancy of purpose toward improvement of product and service, with the aim to become competitive and to stay in business, and to provide jobs.* (Deming, 1986) Peter Senge wrote notably one of the best books on leadership and management in the last century, *The Fifth Discipline: The Art & Practice of The Learning Organization,* Senge refers to having a *shared vision.* (Senge, 1990) Dr. John Maxwell is one of the most recognized leadership gurus around today. In Maxwell's *Fifteen Laws of Growth,* he refers to the importance of *intentionality.* (Maxwell, 2012)

These books do not specifically mention military leadership. There are, however, some excellent recent books that explicitly discuss the contributions of military leadership in modern leadership teaching.

Simon Sinek in his bestselling *Leaders Eat Last* builds a solid case for the importance of knowing *why* at both the personal and organizational levels. (Sinek, 2017) He discusses the importance of clarifying the purpose, vision, and goals of an organization if you want people to invest themselves in striving for success. The title comes from the Marine Corps training for leaders about how to treat and inspire their troops.

Ed Ruggero is one of the leading experts on military leadership. The book *The Leader's Compass* by Ed Ruggero and Dennis F. Haley is a great story that uses the mental model of a compass aligning all aspects of leadership from philosophy to action, guiding everyone in the proper direction. (Ruggero, E. and Haley, D. E. , 2005) The authors use their Army and Navy backgrounds extensively in the book.

Be-Know-Do: Leadership the Army Way is an excellent book about leadership training by Frances Hesselbein and General Eric K. Shinseki (USA Ret.). Be-Know-Do comes right out of the *Army Leadership Field Manual 22-100* (US Army, 1999).

> *Character and competence, the Be and the Know, underlie everything a leader does. But character and knowledge— while absolutely necessary—are not enough. Leaders act:*

they Do. They bring together everything they are, everything they believe, and everything they know how to do to provide purpose, direction, and motivation. (Hesselbein, F. and Shinkseki, E. K., 2004)

The final book recommended here is *Leader of One* by Gerald Suarez. Combining systems thinking with knowledge and experience from many sectors, the author teaches a simple but effective approach for personal leadership. Purpose is refined through a process of contemplation and desire. (Suarez, 2014)

Underlying their sense of purpose, my uncles and father developed values over their short lifetimes. One of the best books on values is *#Values: The Secret to Top Level Performance in Business and Life* by Dr. Betty Uribe. Dr. Uribe interviewed 18 high-level leaders from both military and business organizations in depth. From her research, she identified their five top terminal values and the five top instrumental values:

The Army values are: Loyalty. Duty. Respect. Selfless Service. Honor. Integrity. Personal Courage.

(US Army FM 22-100, 1999)

After surveying the high-level participants in the study, the top five terminal values (what they would like at the end of their life) were family, health, spirituality, wisdom, and freedom. The top five instrumental values (those they use along their leadership journey) were honesty, courage, being responsible, helpful and loving). (Uribe, 2016)

The *Army Leadership Field Manual 22-100* also states what the Army values are: Loyalty. Duty. Respect. Selfless Service. Honor. Integrity. Personal Courage. (US Army, 1999) You can see many of these terminal, instrumental, and Army values underlying the motivation of both officers and enlisted personnel to sacrifice so much for their families and their country.

There is a subtlety there that we often forget. My high school friend, Colonel (ret.) Stan Phernambucq graduated from West Point and had a long career in the Army followed by another career in the construction industry. According to Stan, leadership training and development was everywhere in the Army. He said that one notable difference between his Army service and the private sector was that in the Army your mission included being prepared to die for your country.

CHAPTER TWENTY-SIX

GENERAL JAMES M. GAVIN AND FAN (FRIENDSHIP ALBANY NIJMEGEN)

Reflection on World War II, the millions of lives lost, the holocaust, and the devastation that occurred often leads to comments such as, *"How could this happen?"* and *"This should never happen again."* Out of extreme sorrow, we ask questions and make comments borne of frustration. However, we rarely go to the next step and do something in response. General Gavin provides a wonderful example of how to live out the last three of the five instrumental values mentioned by Dr. Uribe: *being responsible, helpful and loving.*

General James M. Gavin – Commanding Officer of the 82ⁿᵈ Airborne Division, US Army, World War II. He was called "Jumping Jim" and was the only US general to ever make four combat jumps. (www.warhistoryonline.com). He is reported to have fractured vertebra during Operation Market Garden on September 17, 1944 but continued to fight; not seeking treatment until almost two months after the campaign. (valor.militarytimes.com)

One of the most unfortunate *friendly fire* incidents of World War II was the accidental bombing of Nijmegen by American bombers on February 22, 1944. Operation Argument was intended to be a major bombing attack on German aircraft factories prior to D-Day. Bad weather prevented many of the bombers from completing their primary objectives, and on their return to England they focused on secondary objectives or *targets of opportunity.* There is some controversy about what happened, but most of the studies conducted since World War II concluded that some of the American bombers were trying to target the rail yards in Nijmegen because the Germans were using them during their occupation. For a variety of reasons, many of the bombs hit the city center, killing over 750 civilians. Poor communications in the air as well as on the ground, plus inaccurate target sighting are several reasons often cited for the accidental bombing of the city center and the high civilian death rate. Regardless, the tragic bombing has been a huge regret and received minimal attention after the war. [79]

Although he had nothing to do militarily with Operation Argument, General Gavin cared for the citizens of Nijmegen and always felt bad about the bombing tragedy and devastation from Operation Market Garden. After the war, he decided to try and do something about it. Enlisting the help of citizens from Albany, New York, a huge shipment of aid was organized. Below are excerpts from the Friendship Albany Nijmegen (FAN) website (http://www.stichtingfan.nl/en/):

> *The Albany Aid Campaign for Nijmegen in 1947 appears to be a more or less spontaneous relief action. This came about partially because of the Dutch roots in the region, but mainly thanks to the personal commitment and mediation by an American WWII commander: General James M. Gavin. His 82nd Airborne Division took part in Operation Market Garden and the infamous crossing of the Waal River at Nijmegen on September, 20, 1944. Gavin saw firsthand how the city of Nijmegen suffered during WWII. The US bombing of February 22, 1944 and the fighting that continued after the liberation wore the city and its population down to the bone. But he also saw how helpful the Nijmegen people were during the Liberation. Almost 800 US soldiers were buried at the temporary Military Cemetery at Molenhoek.*

The relief operation in 1947 led to a keen interest and contact between the two cities, including exchanges of letters among citizens.

In early July 1947 the SS Westerdam departed from the Port of Albany, via New York to Nijmegen. The Westerdam had an estimated 300 tons of relief goods on board, mostly collected by the citizens of Albany, as support for the hard-hit city of Nijmegen. [80]

During our 2019 trip to Nijmegen we were honored to attend many of the FAN events commemorating the 1947 relief effort and honoring General James M. Gavin for his involvement. FAN was founded by Anja Adriaans of Nijmegen, the current Executive Director. Several ceremonies were held and plaques dedicated to General Gavin were placed in commemoration. One of the most memorable events was participating in a Sunset Crossing March across de Oversteek Bridge on September 18 sponsored by FAN (March described pg. 191). General Gavin's daughter, Chloe Gavin-Beatty, and her son, James Gavin Beatty were in attendance and participated in all the ceremonies. We had the pleasure of dining with them several times.

FAN organizers and supporters at the Waalcrossing Memorial prior to the Sunset March during the 75th Anniversary of Operation Market Garden. (Photo courtesy of Jaleesa Derksen/Jaleesa Freelance Fotografe ©)

Albany, NY, and Nijmegen are now Sister Cities with many citizen-based exchanges. High school students from Albany have visited Nijmegen and in October 2019 32 high school students from Nijmegen visited New York and were able to meet the people in Albany.

Phil with Chloe Gavin-Beatty and James Gavin Beatty. Chloe and James represented General Gavin's family during at the 75ᵗʰ Anniversary of Operation Market Garden events.

General Gavin's actions to tangibly help the people of Nijmegen, and the dedication and hard work of people like Anja Adriaans to continue and preserve the relationship between Albany and Nijmegen are great examples of values in action. Even after tragedy there is usually something that can be done to help those left behind.

PART SIX

RESOURCES AND LESSONS FROM THE JOURNEY

CHAPTER TWENTY-SEVEN

LESSONS FOR FUTURE GENERATIONS – A SOCIAL STUDIES RESOURCE

A clear message from studying a war such as World War II is to ask ourselves how it started and what can we do to prevent something similar from ever happening again. People have been discussing World War II and asking related questions ever since. Sadly, events still occur today that are reminiscent of the decades before World War II.

Unfortunately, the lingering effects of the war on countries, societies, and families are often overlooked. This story amplifies what can happen to a family. We need to recognize damaged and suffering families and work together to try and minimize their pain. We will never eliminate the grieving and sadness that goes along with war, but we can try to do more to prevent war and more to reduce the hurt and bring some joy to families. The concept of ambiguous loss related to MIAs was new to me, although I had studied how to deal with grief. Organizations such as Honoring Our Fallen led by Laura Herzog are precious and doing all they can in this area. We need to support them and come alongside them.

As mention earlier, World War II was the most massive war in the history of the world and is one of the most significant world events. It behooves everyone to study World War II on some level. Hopefully, the stories and comments in this book will motivate and awaken the need to recognize and address the aftereffects of war.

Over the last year, I have started to take various national holidays and observances more seriously. If nothing else, I hope that future generations will recognize that they stand for and take time to remember and honor the men, women, and families who suffered during and after.

May 8 (in the US) – VE Day – Victory in Europe Day. The day Germany surrendered in 1945

Last Monday in May – Memorial Day – A day to remember those who died in service to the country

June 6 – D-Day – The invasion of France across the English Channel that began the liberation of Europe from the north in 1944

June 14 – Flag Day

July 4 – Independence Day. The day the Declaration of Independence was signed in 1776

September 2 (in the US) – VJ Day – Victory over Japan Day. The day Japan Surrendered in 1945

November 11 – Veteran's Day. Formerly Armistice Day. Major hostilities of World War I were formally ended at the 11th hour of the 11th day of the 11th month of 1918[81]

December 7 – Pearl Harbor Day. The day the Japanese bombed Pearl Harbor in Hawaii and brought the United States into World War II in 1941

CHAPTER TWENTY-EIGHT

FAMILY HISTORY AND THE JOURNEY TO ACHIEVE
CLOSURE

We hope this book will be of value to many people. First of all to our family; our history —especially as it relates to World War II—is compelling for many reasons. Also, we hope this book will be valuable to future generations in studying the impact of World War II from both the sizeable historical point-of-view as well as the individual family perspective. Finally, we hope that anyone who is on a similar journey with a family member who was MIA, KIA, or returned home suffering from PTSD will find some value here.

Two aspects of family history are worth looking at because they are linked together. The five Rosenkrantz brothers would not have served in World War II without first having the necessary character and a strong love for their country. It is significant that many of the men and women who defended our country in WWII were first- or second-generation immigrants.

The 20-year journey to discover what happened to Uncle Dave has helped connect our family in ways that would not have occurred otherwise. We have had family gatherings and shared many emails and posts on social media about him. I want to thank my cousins again who provided me with pictures, newspaper clippings, stories, old letters and other exciting artifacts that helped in the journey. I have accumulated several boxes of materials since this trek began. Only a few members of the family are still living who knew Uncle Dave, and they were just young children at the time. Those of us who grew up around his siblings could see the sadness that still encompassed the family even if we didn't entirely really realize it. I did not recognize the severity of grief at the time. Even if I had understood it, I would not have known what to do. Hopefully, reading this book will generate more respect and empathy for what people have gone through the last 75 years.

I also have more pride and respect for my family members who have served in the military and the war effort at home and the sacrifices they made for our country. At least one of our recent family members saw action in Iraq and did not come home unscathed. I encourage my family members (or anyone else who finds this book enjoyable) to visit the five Rosenkrantz brothers' grave markers at the Riverside National Cemetery: David (Army), Lawrence (Merchant Marine), Launie (Navy), Jack (Army Air Force), and Harry (Army).

Some people will be reading this book to help them achieve closure. Some may be just beginning their journey and others may be stalled along the way. Let me reiterate that when I started this journey after watching *Saving Private Ryan*, I only had a few pieces of information and no artifacts. I knew my uncle was a Sergeant in the 82nd Airborne, 504 Parachute Infantry Regiment, H Company. I did not personally own any pictures of him. Once I started to ask around, my Aunt Janet and various cousins began providing me with books, photos, old letters, military memorabilia, and other artifacts. I found some items among my father's and my grandmother's belongings that had ended up in our garage. The collection of information started to grow. Once there was enough exciting information, I created a website. People from the US and the Netherlands began to find the site and contact me. Many sent articles and photographs either by mail or digitally. Altogether I accumulated several boxes of materials plus other items, including seven books that mention my uncle or contain his photograph.

Many people have asked for advice on how they could find out more about their loved one. I had to confess to them that I was not an expert researcher and was lucky to learn what I had. However, I shared what I did. Several of the people I helped eventually came back and said they were able to discover what they wanted by doing the same thing.

It was surprising what was contained in my uncle's IDPF (Individual Deceased Personnel File). Some things I expected to see were missing, but some things that I did not expect were there. I empathize with those who are seeking closure and hope that in some way this book is helpful even if it is just to motivate you to start looking

I can't thank enough the Dutch researchers who came alongside and helped us along the way. Ben Overhand and Frank van Lunteren have been mentioned and will always be special to our family. I continue to receive new information about my uncle from Dutch contacts.

There are researchers who specialize in helping families navigate through the military records to find out information and write stories. One such person is Jennifer Holik from the World War II Research and Writing Center.[82] Besides offering personal assistance, she has many workshops, resources, and books on the subject available. Many veterans groups are helpful.

Someone once asked what our family would have been like if Dave had survived the war. It was a question I had never considered. We can only speculate about having Uncle Dave return, fall in love, get married, and once again be a part of his large, extended family. I do know that our lives would have been greatly enriched by knowing him. My friend, Jerry Carlos, pointed out something else: with Dave's nurturing personality and how—according to his mother— *"He could do anything,"* there is an immeasurable loss to our society because of positive contributions he never had the opportunity to make to future generations.

Uncle Dave was an integral part of the Rosenkrantz clan, and everyone loved him. But the sacrifice he made for his country has also left its mark. He has given us a deeper appreciation of our heritage, freedom, and liberty. After seeing much suffering, his parents came to America in hopes of providing a better life for their family. Dave went to war as a first-generation American in order to fight some of the same oppression his parents escaped. He fought valiantly in every battle he was engaged in. He was an integral part of the victory we witnessed when World War II ended.

Staff Sergeant David Rosenkrantz showed us firsthand that freedom comes with a high cost. It is not something that just happens. It's something that we fight to preserve. Since knowing the story of my Uncle Dave and more about my Uncle Launie, I stand taller when I say the Pledge of Allegiance. My voice is louder when I sing the National Anthem. I love my family deeper knowing how short life can be. Yes, David gave up his life for freedom on that little farm in far off Holland many years ago, but he lives on in our hearts as an example of a patriot and a hero. Thank you, Uncle Dave, for your unselfish sacrifice on our behalf. We love you even though we never got the chance to meet you and we hope to meet you one day in heaven.

Staff Sergeant David Rosenkrantz showed us firsthand that freedom comes with a high cost.

APPENDICES, GLOSSARY, REFERENCES, ENDNOTES, INDEX

APPENDICES

Appendix A - Timeline for S/Sgt David Rosenkrantz

Date	Unit	Location	David's Activities/ Actions	Others
10/31/1915		Los Angeles, CA	Born. Birth Certificate	
1934		Watts, CA	Graduated from David Starr Jordan High School	
1934-1941		California	Worked for Civilian Conservation Corps & General Motors Assembly, South Gate	
2/29/1942	Army	Ft. MacArthur, Los Angeles, CA	Inducted into the US Army	
		Camp Wolters, TX	Basic Training	
6/17/1942		Ft. Benning, GA	Parachute school	
7/25/1942		Ft. Benning, GA	Parachutist Certificate	
8/15/1942			First A/B Division Instituted	
8/17/1942		Los Angeles, CA		Sister, Frieda, buried in Los Angeles

Date	Unit	Location	David's Activities/ Actions	Other
9/30/1942	82nd A/B, 504 PIR, H Company	Ft. Bragg, NC	Moved to Ft. Bragg for Airborne training	
1/30/1943		Rennell Island, South Pacific		Sinking of the USS Chicago. Brother RM1C Launie Rosenkrantz rescued and survived
4/18/1943		Camp Edwards, MA	Preparing to go embark for Africa	
4/29/1943	*USS George Washington*	Travel to Africa		
5/10/1943			Arrived in Casablanca, Morocco	
			Marched 8 miles So. Of Casablanca	
			Moved to Kairouan, Tunisia	
7/9/1943	H Company	Sicily	Operation Husky	
7/10/1943			Captured 200 Italians	
(unclear)			Biazza Ridge	
7/13/1943		Drive NW 150 miles		
		Return to Kairouan		
	3rd Bn	To Bizerte	Prepare for beach assault	
Early Sept 1943	3rd Bn + 325th GIR + Rangers			

Date	Unit	Location	David's Activities/ Actions	Other
9/9/1943	H Co + Rangers	Maori	Beach landing. Seize Chunzi Pass and tunnel	
9/11/1943	G & I Co	Salerno	Beach landing	
9/13/1943	1st & 2nd Bn	Salerno	Night jump onto beach	
9/18/1943?	3rd Bn	Salerno	3rd Bn rejoins and drives Germans out	
10/1/1943	504	Naples	Regiment enters Naples	
10/9/1943	504 Regimental Combat Team	Comisco, Italy		
10/18/1943 – Nov. 1943			Fighting in hills	
1/4/1944		Naples	Pulled back to Naples	
1/9/1944	H Co	Naples	Morning Report –Into Hospital	
1/22/1944	H Co	Naples	Morning Report – Back to H Co on Light Duty	
1/22/1944	504	Anzio, 35 miles South of Rome	Operation Shingle Awarded Bronze Star for action on this date	
2/1/1944 – 2/16/1944	3rd Bn attached to 24th Brigade, 1st British Inf. Div.	Anzio		

Date	Unit	Location	David's Activities/ Actions	Other
2/4/1944- 2/8/1944	504?		Action resulting in Presidential Citation	
3/23/1944	3rd Bn	Naples	Returned to Naples	
4/10/1944	504	Board *Capetown Castle*	Travel to England	
4/22/1944	504	Liverpool, England	Arrived in England	1100 casualties in Italy. 25% occurred at Anzio
9/17/1944	504	Grave, Netherlands	Operation Market Garden. Drop Zone Overasselt, Netherlands	
9/20/1944	504, H Co	Nijmegen, Netherlands	Waalcrossing. Captured Nijmegen Bridges	
Abt 9/22/1944	H Co	Nijmegen, Netherlands	Interview with Foreign Corresp. Quaid	
9/27/1944	H Co	Heuvelhof, Netherlands	Platoon occupies Heuvelhof Farm	
9/28/1944	H Co	Heuvelhof, Netherlands	KIA during German counterattack	
10/1944				Family notified of death but listed MIA

Date	Unit	Location	David's Activities/ Actions	Other
11/3/1944				Letter sent to family confirming telegram notification of death in Holland 28 Sept 1944
Late 1944		Heuvelhof, Netherlands	Germans bury remains in a shallow field grave. Field grave hit by an artillery shell and dislodged. Dog tags dislodged from body.	
Early 1945			Farmer (Lamers) contacts authorities to collect body.	
Early 1945			Dutch Graves Ministry collects remains at Heuvelhof	
6/22/1945		Canadian National Cemetery	2nd Canadian Graves Registration collects remains labelled X-1234 near Heuvelhof	No mention of how they found the remains, but location was shown near Heuvelhof
7/28/1945		Netherlands American Cemetery, Margraten	X-1234 transferred to AGRC and interred at Margraten	

Date	Unit	Location	David's Activities/ Actions	Other
4/1/1947		Netherlands American Cemetery, Margraten	AGRC reprocessed X-1234 including size 7EEE boots. Plot LL, Row 11, Grave 274	
8/24/1948		Netherlands American Cemetery, Margraten	X-1234 disinterred	
9/20/1948		Belgium	Remains transferred to Belgium	
Summer 1950				AGRC investigates Heuvelhof and Den Heuvel searching for remains.
6/6/1950		Netherlands American Cemetery, Margraten	X-1234 interred Plot O, Row 22, Grave 16	
11/6/1950				AGRC declares remains of S/Sgt David Rosenkrantz as unre-coverable.
1952				Dutch Recovery Team gives dog tags to AGRC found in 1951 along with part of entrenching knife also found.

Date	Unit	Location	David's Activities/ Actions	Other
1952				AGRC reinvestigates Heuvelhof. The report includes a sketch of the field grave location.
1952				Dog tags stored in mausoleum in Griesham, Germany and forgotten until 2012.
Starting approx. 1985				Ben Overhand begins searching for the remains of S/Sgt David Rosenkrantz and other 504 MIAs at Heuvelhof and Den Heuvel.
1/22/2011				Rosenkrantz family attends DPMO Family Meeting in Scottsdale, AZ. Meet with Historian Heather Harris and requests renewed efforts in the search for S/Sgt David Rosenkrantz' remains. Sample DNA was given by Phil Rosenkrantz

Date	Unit	Location	David's Activities/ Actions	Other
3/12/2012				Dog tags rediscovered and returned to Phil Rosenkrantz
1/23/2013				Phil Rosenkrantz attends DPMO Family Meeting in San Diego. Meeting with Dr. Stephen Johnson. Evidence of body having been taken away by Dutch Graves Ministry presented.
2/2015				Netherlands Recovery & Identification Unit excavates Heuvelhof. No evidence of remains found — Ben Overhand present.
11/2015				DPAA Historians return to Nijmegen and meet with Ben Overhand and Frank van Lunteren and agree to look at records of known remains of unidentified American soldiers for possible retrieval and analysis.

Date	Unit	Location	David's Activities/ Actions	Other
2/17/2016				Letter to the Rosenkrantz family from DPAA that several remains at ABMC cemeteries were being investigated as possible matches
6/2017		Netherlands American Cemetery	Remains exhumed by DPAA & ABMC	
7/14/2017		Offutt Air Force Base, Nebraska	Remains transferred to Lab at Offutt Air Force Base	
1/3/2018		Offutt AFB, Nebraska	Remains Tested.	DNA from Dave's sister (Janet Norman) confirms identification
1/3/2018		Offutt AFB, Nebraska		Date of DPAA Summary Report of the finding of S/Sgt David Rosenkrantz remains
4/14/2018				William "Shorty" Cox visits the Rosenkrantz Family in Placentia, CA, and presents the story of how Dave's remains were identified and the next steps to bring him home.

Date	Unit	Location	David's Activities/ Actions	Other
7/17/2018		LAX, Risher Mortuary, Downey, CA		Remains flown from Offutt AFB to LAX. Patriot Guard Escort to Risher Mortuary.
7/20/2018		Riverside National Cemetery		Funeral at Riverside National Cemetery. Dave interred in Plot 55 901.
9/19/2019		Netherlands American Cemetery, Margraten, NL		Rosette Ceremony with Rosenkrantz Family & Friends. Rosette placed next to name on The Wall of the Missing

Appendix B

Excerpts from the Proposed Award Citation (Source: Italy 504 PIR After Action Reports received from the files of Frank van Lunteren)

The 504 Parachute Infantry Combat Team, composed of the 504th Parachute Infantry Regiment, 376th Parachute Field Artillery Battalion, and Company "C," 307th Airborne Engineers, is cited for extraordinary heroism and outstanding performance of duty for the inclusive period 22 January 1944 to March 23, 1944 on the ANZIO BEACHHEAD in Italy. After having completed over 60 days of the most arduous and stamina- exacting tenure of combat duty in actual contact with the enemy in the ISERNIA-COLLI-VENAFRO sector of the American 5th Army Front, 504th Parachute Infantry Combat Team was called upon, after an entirely inadequate rest, to participate in the assault landing on the ANZIO BEACHHEAD...(section omitted)

During the inclusive, February 1, 1944 to March 23, 1944 there were never less than two out of the three available infantry battalions representing the combat team on the line. From their OP's perched in the LIPINI MOUNTAINS which overlooked the entire area, the enemy was able to place accurately directed artillery fire of calibers ranging from railway guns to 77MM howitzers upon the troops below them. This fire was literally incessant, day and night. In addition to this harassing fire, 20MM flakwagons and SP artillery were used extensively,. The weather was rainy during a large share of this period, impairing air support and making the adjustment of counter-battery artillery fire most difficult. Daylight movement of personnel and supply vehicles was made most hazardous, as all supply routes and crossroads were perfectly "zeroed in" by enemy artillery observers. Food was poor consisting for the most part of "C" and "K" rations, and meals were uncertain. Days were made sleepless by constant artillery fire, and the nights were packed with action. In addition to repelling countless attacks by superior enemy forces, this physically exhausted nerve-strained group of parachutists was called upon to make nightly raids and patrols into heavily mined enemy territory in order to hide its true strength from the enemy. Had the enemy known how thinly held was the line opposite them, the results would have been disastrous. The aggressiveness and fighting spirit of this little band of men completely belied their true strength in numbers. When relieved from actual front-line duty, the men were forced through necessity to live, cramped together, and roofless houses approximately 1100 yards from the MLR on the canal and exposed to the ever-present artillery fire and dangers of the front lines which made any semblance of relaxation impossible. There was no rest for those in reserve as possibility of an enemy breakthrough of the precariously held line was ever-present, keeping the reserve battalion in a constant state of alert. This, for a period of 62 days contact with the enemy on the ANZIO BEACHHEAD, this Combat Team, at times numbering less than 1,000 fighting effectives, hurled back the best troops this enemy could place in the field, withstood prolonged periods of shelling, such as few troops have ever been called upon to endure, combated physical exhaustion and mental fatigue, fought with inadequate food and uncertain supplies, and took a grievous toll of many personnel and equipment, while holding intact and secure the most vitally strategic section of the entire Allied defense system on the ANZIO BEACHHEAD...(section omitted)

Together, this team, on the ANZIO BEACHHEAD, carved a brilliant chapter in blood and sweat which will ever remain outstanding in the annals of American Arms.

Appendix C – Obituary for S/Sgt David Rosenkrantz

David Rosenkrantz was born October 31, 1915, in Los Angeles. He was the middle child of eleven born to Hyman and Eva Rosa Rosenkrantz—Russian Jewish immigrants. Hyman and Eva Rosa came to the United States in 1902 by passenger ship, met and were married in New York. They moved to Los Angeles sometime after their second child was born. They eventually settled in Watts and raised their family there. David graduated from David Starr Jordan High School in Watts in 1934. He played football and was active in theater and glee club. He worked for the Civilian Conservation Corp and at the General Motors Plant in South Gate before finally joining the Army in February 1942. After basic training he completed Airborne training and was a member of the 82nd Airborne Division, 504 Parachute Infantry Regiment, H Company. Over the course of his time in H Company he rose to the rank of Staff Sergeant and was platoon sergeant at the time of his death. He led a mortar squad which had a pretty good reputation for their accuracy.

The Third Battalion of the 504 participated in the initial invasion of Sicily on July 9, 1943. David was mis-dropped like most of the other paratroopers but ended up helping to capture 200 Italian soldiers. After initially being captured by the Italians, David and Corporal Black from Tennessee convinced the Italians to surrender. The story was a huge media hit at home in Los Angeles and he received his first Bronze Star Medal for that event. David apparently was also involved with the Battle of Biazza Ridge, but the information about that is sketchy.

David was wounded later in Sicily but recovered to join his unit to fight in Italy at Salerno, Anzio, and Chunzi Pass. It was at Anzio that the Third Battalion earned the name "Devils in Baggy Pants" that has stuck with paratroopers of the 82nd Airborne and 504 PIR ever since. After recuperating in England, the 504 was involved with the liberation of the Netherlands in Operation Market Garden. The third Battalion jumped into the Nijmegen area and helped capture the bridges at Grave and over the Waal (Rhine) River. David was part of the famous Waalcrossing where paratroopers of the Third Battalion crossed the Waal River in daylight to capture the railroad and road bridges in Nijmegen. Many lives were lost in capturing the bridges, but David survived and helped capture both bridges. A week later on 28 September 1944, David's squad was on patrol in the Den Heuvel area a few miles south of Nijmegen. Unknown to them a large German counterattack swarmed over the squad and also, I Company which was positioned just north of them. David was killed from behind by German machine gun fire. The squad took cover and retreated at night unable to retrieve his body. When they went back for it, it was gone. His remains would be missing for the next 73 years.

Efforts were made to find David's remains at the farm where he was killed (Heuvelhof) with no success. His dog tags were found near where he was killed, but that knowledge did not help lead to the location of his remains. The report about the dog tags and the dog tags themselves got lost until March 2012. Starting around the mid-1980s a young Dutchman, Ben Overhand, started searching for David's remains. He was able to talk to eyewitnesses and had finally concluded the remains had been removed and buried somewhere else as an unidentified American soldier. He continued to try and help locate David's remains for the next 35 years. Also behind the scenes was author Frank van Lunteren who also continued to encourage the Defense POW MIA Organization (DPMO and later the DPAA) to search for and identify remains in their possession. Apparently, what happened was that the Dutch had recovered the remains from a field grave that had been hit by an artillery shell. They passed the remains to the Canadian graves team which passed by. The Canadians later passed the remains to the Americans after the Netherlands American Cemetery in Margraten was built. Finally DNA testing was conducted on some of the unidentified soldiers at Margraten and David was identified.

The Rosenkrantz Family would like to thank all of the people who helped locate our uncle and bring him home to be buried with his four brothers who were also part of WWII and are buried at Riverside National Cemetery: Lawrence (Merchant Marine), Launie (Navy), Jack (Army Air Force) and Harry (Army).

David was extremely close to everyone in the family and everyone who knew him loved him. His letters home while in the Army reflected how connected he was to everyone. He was very gregarious and a central figure in keeping the family close together. His loss was devastating to the family...especially to his mother. She never gave up hope that her son might still be alive.

Appendix D - Eulogy for S/Sgt David Rosenkrantz by Phil Rosenkrantz July 20, 2018

First of all, I would like to thank everyone for coming today to help honor our Uncle David for his service and sacrifice to our country. I want to thank everyone who has helped make this day possible from the Dutch and American researchers who helped find Uncle David, to everyone who helped bring him home to rest with his brothers here at Riverside. I want to thank my family—especially my wife, Judy—for their support and encouragement over the last 20 years as his story unfolded before us and we began to realize what Uncle David did during his time in the 82nd Airborne Division fighting in Sicily, Italy, and the Netherlands.

Much of David's story is already provided to you in the detailed obituary that has been handed out. I won't repeat all those details but will include some of them along with some other thoughts in the few minutes I have. What I want to talk about today are his story and the impact that David and his sacrifice had on our family and on our country.

David was the middle child of eleven children born October 31, 1915, to Hyman and Eva Rosa Rosenkrantz. Hyman and Eva Rosa were born in what is today Poland and immigrated to the US in 1902 where they met, married, and started their family. They moved to Los Angeles a few years later and eventually raised their eleven children in Watts. David was beloved by all his brothers and sisters and was the apple of his mother's eye. In high school he played football and participated in Theater and Glee Club. He worked for a few years after high school and joined the Army two months after the bombing of Pearl Harbor. He was tough enough to get through Airborne training become part of the 82nd Airborne, 504 Parachute Infantry Regiment, H Company. When they went overseas to Africa in 1943 before the invasion of Europe, he had attained the rank of sergeant. In his letters home he said a lot about their training and confidence. They were a tough bunch.

David was in the first wave of paratroopers that landed in Sicily as the invasion of Europe began. He and Corporal Black from Tennessee captured 200 Italians (well, they accepted the surrender of 200 Italians, but it is more dramatic say captured). The story was a huge hit back in the US and especially in Los Angeles. He received his first Bronze Star and Purple Heart in Sicily. He fought for many months in Italy at Anzio and Chunzi Pass. The 504 was recognized for their accomplishments and earned the nickname: Devils in Baggy Pants that remains part of their legacy today.

After recovering in England the 504 was part of the famous (or infamous) Operation Market Garden. David jumped into the Netherlands on September 17, 1944, to help capture the bridges in the city of Nijmegen. He was part of the famous suicide mission shown graphically in the classic war movie "A Bridge Too Far" where on September 20, 1944, paratroopers of the Third Battalion crossed the Waal River in canvas wooden row boats while under enemy fire to capture the two bridges. There were heavy casualties. David survived the crossing and helped capture both bridges earning his second bronze star which was presented posthumously today. My wife and I have had the honor of visiting Nijmegen three times when they commemorated that battle and honored those who died that day. A week later on 28th of September, 1944, while on patrol a few miles outside of Nijmegen, David's squad was overrun by a surprise German counterattack and he was shot and killed. His squad had retreated after the attack and when they went back to recover his body it was gone. His remains would not be recovered until 73 years later.

I will skip the details that are in the obituary of how we found out what happened and how his remains were recovered other than to thank two special Dutch friends that have worked on our family's behalf for many years to help us learn what happened and locate his remains: Ben Overhand and Frank van Lunteren. We had hoped they could be here today, but for various reasons that didn't happen.

I would like to get back to the themes I mentioned earlier about David's impact. I was born after WWII, but grew up knowing my grandmother, aunts, and uncles. David's death was a huge blow to the family. Because of his MIA status my grandmother would not accept David's death, and no one would talk about him or what might have happened. There certainly was no closure: No closure about what happened to him and no closure about where he was. By the time my grandmother died in 1960 the family was no longer talking about him. Whenever I asked about what happened to Uncle Dave, I got a different answer and none of them turned out to be correct.

In talking to my father, aunts, uncles and cousins over the years I can look back and say that David's loss had a major impact on the family that lasted many decades. That is huge. I think we greatly underestimate the impact on families when a loved one is lost in war. The positive side is that the journey to find out what happened to Uncle Dave has resulted in rich friendships with members of the 504, the Dutch people, other families of missing and dead paratroopers of the 504, and has brought our current generations of Rosenkrantz family members closer together.

On July 4 of this year—just 16 days ago—my wife, Judy, and I were on a trip to Europe and on that day we visited the Neuengamme Concentration Camp near Hamburg Germany. I won't go into detail but seeing the camp, going through the museums, and hearing what happened really helped me to understand the horrors of the holocaust. All those men and women who served in WWII were fighting to end that evil and prevent it from spreading around the world.

So please indulge me as I try to give this some historical perspective. One of the most significant centuries in world history is the 20th century. Probably the most significant event in the 20th century was WWII. Some of the most significant battles in WWII were battles our uncle fought in. He was indeed part of something large...in all of history and in making the world a better place for all of us.

We are extremely proud of our uncle and are honored to be members of the Rosenkrantz family. We want to thank all those who have served or are serving now for your sacrifice. Our prayers go out to all families who have lost loved ones while serving in the military. For those whose loved ones were missing and never returned, we hope this story brings you some hope that your loved one will somehow come home as well.

This is a day I have been hoping for over 20 years. We now have some closure. David is home. His brothers Lawrence, Launie, Jack and Harry who also served in WWII are already here at Riverside waiting for him. Thank you for attending today and helping honor our Uncle David.

Glossary of Paratrooper Weapons and Military Units

Paratrooper Weapons
The following are some of the most common weapons used by paratroopers during World War II. It is not an exhaustive list; they would jump with the weapons needed based on weight limitations, their role in the squad and the planned mission. A few of the weapons were specially designed for paratroopers. Modern day paratroopers have even more weapons available:

1911 .45 Automatic Pistol
The 1911 is a handheld semi-automatic pistol that has been around since before World War 1 and is still widely used today. The magazine holds 7 rounds plus one in the chamber. It is known for its stopping power, but not for accuracy compared to other handguns.

60mm Mortar
A mortar is usually a simple, lightweight, man-portable, muzzle-loaded weapon, consisting of a smooth-bore metal tube fixed to a base plate (to spread out the recoil) with a lightweight bipod mount and a sight. They launch explosive shells (technically called bombs) in high-arcing ballistic trajectories. Mortars are typically used as indirect fire weapons for close fire support with a variety of ammunition. Mortars have some advantages over conventional artillery. They are lighter weight, can hit targets that are at higher elevations, and can drop into the enemy trenches and machine gun nests. A mortar requires a small squad of soldiers to operate effectively for spotting, adjusting, preparing the shell, and dropping the shell into the tube to fire it. Excerpts from Wikipedia
https://en.wikipedia.org/wiki/Mortar_(weapon)
(accessed 6/21/2020)

Bazooka M1/M9
Bazooka is the common name for a man-portable recoilless anti-tank rocket launcher weapon, widely deployed by the United States Army. Also referred to as the "Stovepipe", the innovative bazooka was among the first generation of rocket-propelled anti-tank weapons used in infantry combat. Featuring a solid-propellant rocket for propulsion, it allowed for high-

explosive anti-tank (HEAT) warheads to be delivered against armored vehicles, machine gun nests, and fortified bunkers at ranges beyond that of a standard thrown grenade or mine. *https://en.wikipedia.org/wiki/Bazooka* *(accessed 6/22/2020)*

Bayonet
A long knife that can also be attached to the end of the rifle to use as a lethal stabbing weapon in close combat situations.

Browning Automatic Rifle (BAR) M1918
The Browning Automatic Rifle (BAR) served American soldiers in all major theaters of operation during World War II. Considered to be quite accurate, it could be carried into battle by one man. However, it could not be used for sustained fire because it was limited to its 20 round box magazine and the number of additional box magazines a soldier could carry. The Browning Automatic Rifle could be fired using a bipod (in later models), or from the shoulder.

Mk2 Hand Grenade
A hand grenade is a small exploding bomb thrown by the soldier at the enemy. It consists of a cast-iron case that has many grooves to improve the grip. It is filled with TNT or other explosive and has a fuse that delays the explosion by 4 or 5 seconds after the handle is released. There are many varieties of hand grenades, but the Mk2 was widely used and looked like a pineapple because of the grooves and hence had the nickname, pineapple.
Based on excerpts from Wikipedia
https://en.wikipedia.org/wiki/Mk 2 grenade
(accessed June 21, 2020)

M1918 Knife
Also known as a trenching knife, it was a very solid fixed blade knife with brass knuckles built into the handle. Versatile and deadly, it could be used for fighting or for digging a fox hole.

M1 Carbine and M1A1 Carbine with folding stock
The M1 Garand and M1 Carbine are two different rifles. the M1 Carbine is a pistol caliber rifle and is shorter and lighter than the M1 Garand. It is meant to fill the gap between the 1911

45acp pistol and the M1 Garand. The M1 Carbine also came with a wire folding stock in the M1A1 configuration for paratroopers.

M1 Garand
The M1 Garand is noteworthy. It is a .30-06 caliber semi-automatic rifle (each shot requires a trigger pull) that was the standard U.S. service rifle during World War II and the Korean War and saw limited service during the Vietnam War. It is sometimes called just the M1 or the Garand. The M1 Garand was made in large numbers during World War II and was used by every branch of the United States military. It generally performed well. General George S. Patton called it *"the greatest battle implement ever devised."* It is 43.6 inches (1,107 mm) long and weighs about 9.5 pounds (4.31 kg). The M1 Garand was designed for simple assembly and disassembly to facilitate field maintenance. It can be field stripped (broken down) without tools in just a few seconds. The M1 Garand held an internal eight round clip called an en-bloc that would eject with a "ping", once the last round was fired. It has a maximum range of 3,200 meters and maximum effective range of 400-500 meters. The M7 Grenade Launcher could be attached to the rifle, giving it the ability to fire grenades up to 250 yards using a special blank cartridge.
Excerpts from
Wikipedia: https://en.wikipedia.org/wiki/M1_Garand
(accessed April 4, 2020)

M2 Pocket Knife
The M2 is a folding knife activated by a push button and is usually carried by paratroopers in a hidden pocket at the top of their shirt. It has to be accessible for cutting the risers (ropes) on their parachute after jumping so they can release themselves as soon as possible and get to safety.

Machete
A machete is a fixed blade knife with a long, 18" blade. Often carried by mortar squads for clearing away brush so the mortar round had a clear path.

Rifle Grenades
Rifles with M7 and or M8 rifle grenade adapter could be used to launch the M17 fragmentation rifle grenade, M9 anti-armor rifle

grenade, or the M1 grenade adapter that held an Mk2 hand grenade, 100+ yards.

Sniper Rifle

A sniper rifle is used to shoot accurately at long distances to take out the enemy by surprise. These rifles are designed to be more accurate than the standard issue rifle and usually have a scope. They are only issued to top marksmen who usually have had special training. A sniper in Uncle Dave's platoon, Sgt Ted Finkbeiner, carried a Springfield M1903A4 .30 caliber rifle with a Stargazer barrel and a four power Weaver scope.

Thompson Submachine Gun (Tommy gun)

The Thompson submachine gun is an American submachine gun invented by John T. Thompson in 1918. It became infamous during the Prohibition era, being a signature weapon of various organized crime syndicates in the United States. It was known informally as the "Tommy Gun." The Thompson was favored by soldiers, criminals, police, FBI, and civilians alike for its large .45 ACP cartridge and high volume of fully automatic fire. In 1938, the Thompson submachine gun was adopted by the U.S. military, serving during World War II and beyond. There were two military types of Thompson SMG. The M1928A1 had provisions for box and drum magazines. The M1 and M1A1 had a barrel without cooling fins, a simplified rear sight, and provisions only for box magazines. In the European theater, the gun was widely utilized in British and Canadian commando units, as well as in the U.S. Army paratrooper and Ranger battalions, where it was issued more frequently than in-line infantry units because of its high rate of fire and its stopping power. This made it very effective in the kinds of close combat experienced by special operations troops. Both Military Police and paratroopers were fond of it, often "borrowing" Thompsons from members of mortar squads for use on patrols behind enemy lines.

Based on excerpts from Wikipedia:
https://en.wikipedia.org/wiki/Thompson_submachine_gun
(accessed April 4, 2020)

Glossary of Military Units

reference: [*https://www.britannica.com/topic/military-unit*](https://www.britannica.com/topic/military-unit) *(accessed 6/22/2020)*

Armies, navies, and air forces are organized hierarchically into progressively smaller units commanded by officers of progressively lower rank. The prototypical units are those of the Army.

Staff Sergeant David Rosenkrantz was in the Army, 82nd Airborne Division, 504 Parachute Infantry Regiment, Third Battalion, H Company, First Platoon. According to his letters he led a mortar squad and later a rifle squad. According to several men he served with, he was promoted to Platoon Sergeant before Operation Market Garden. He was leading his first platoon on his last mission because the lieutenant who was the new platoon leader had no combat experience.

Squad
The smallest unit in an Army is the squad, which contains 7 to 14 soldiers and is led by a sergeant.

Platoon
Three or four squads make up a platoon, which has 20 to 50 soldiers and is commanded by a lieutenant.

Company
Two or more platoons make up a company, which has 100 to 250 soldiers and is commanded by a captain or a major.

Battalion
Two or more companies make up a battalion, which has 400 to 1,200 troops and is commanded by a major or lieutenant colonel.

Regiment
Consists of two or more battalions and is commanded by a colonel or brigadier general.

Brigade
Several battalions form a brigade, which has 2,000 to 8,000

troops and is commanded by a brigadier general or a colonel. A brigade is the smallest unit to integrate different types of combat and support units into a functional organization. A combat brigade, for example, usually has infantry, armor, artillery, and reconnaissance units.

Division

Two or more brigades (or regiments), along with various specialized battalions, make up a division, which has 7,000 to 22,000 troops and is commanded by a major general. A division contains all the arms and services needed for the independent conduct of military operations.

Army Corp

Two to seven divisions and various support units make up an Army corps, or a corps, which has 50,000 to 300,000 troops and is commanded by a lieutenant general. The Army corps is the largest regular Army formation, though in wartime two or more corps may be combined to form a field Army (commanded by a general). Field armies in turn may be combined to form an Army group.

References

82nd Airborne Division. (n.d.). *Those Devils in Baggy Pants: Combat Record of the 504th Parachute Infantry Regiment.* US Army.

US Army. (1999). *Army Leadership Field Manual 22-100*

Baron Von Steuben, F. W. (1985). *Baron Von Steuben's Revolutionary War Drill Manual: A Facsimile Reprint of the 1794 Edition.* Dover Publications.

Brokaw, T. (2001). *The Greatest Generation.* New York: Random House Trade Paperbacks.

Burriss, T. M. (2000). *Strike and Hold: A Memoir of the 82nd Airborne in World War II.* Washington, D.C.: Brassey's.

Deming, W. E. (1986). *Out of the Crisis.* Cambridge, MA: MIT Press.

Elizabeth Hallum, et al. (1999). *Beyond the Body: Death and Social Identity.* London: Routledge.

Gavin, J. M. (1978). *On to Berlin.* New York: Bantam Books.

Gavin, J. M. (2014). *Airborne Warfare.* Pickle Partners Publishing (originally published in 1947).

Hesselbein, F. and Shinkseki, E. K. (2004). *Be-Know-Do: Leadership the Army Way.* San Francisco: Jossey-Bass.

Maxwell, J. (2012). *The 15 Invaluable Laws of Growth: Live Them and Reach Your Potential .* New York: Center Street.

Megellas, J. (2003). *All the Way to Berlin: A paratrooper at war in Europe.* New York: Presidio Press.

Outridge, P. (2007). *Baggy Pants & Warm Beer!: 504 Parachute Regiment of the US 82nd Airborne Division in Leicestershire UK, 1944.* Woodfield Publishing.

Phillips, D. T. (1997). *The Founding Fathers on Leadership: Classic Teamwork in Changing Times.* New York: Warner Books.

Ruggero, E. and Haley, D. E. . (2005). *The Leader's Compass: A Personal Leadership Philosophy Is Your Key to Success.* King of Prussia, PA: Academy Leadership.

Ruggero., E. (2003). *Combat Jump* (1 ed.). Harper.

Ryan, C. (1974). *A Bridge Too Far* (1 ed.). New York: Simon & Schuster.

Senge, P. (1990). *The Fifth Discipline: The Art & Practice of The Learning Organization.* New York: Doubleday Business.

Sharma, Neel K (et al). (2018). Role of Ionizing Radiation in Neurodegenerative Diseases. *Frontiers in Aging Neurosci, 10* , 134.

Sinek, S. (2017). *Leaders Eat Last: Why Some Teams Pull Togethre and Others Don't* . New York: Portfolio/Penquin.

Sledge, M. (2005). *Soldier Dead.* New York: University Press.

Suarez, J. G. (2014). *Leader of One: Shaping Your Future Through Imagination and Design.* North Charleston, South Carolina: Create Space Independent Publishing Platform.

Takiff, M. (2007). *Brave Men, Gentle Heroes.* New York, NY: Woodfield Publishing.

Uribe, B. (2016). *#Values: The Secret to Top Level Performance in Business and Life.* Las Vegas, NV: Next Century Publishing.

van Luntern, F. (2014). *Battle of the Bridges: The 504th Parachute Infantry Regiment in Operation Market Garden.* Havetown, PA: Casemate Publishers.

Welch, R. (1973). *The Romance of Education.* Belmont, MA: Western Islands.

End Notes

Preface and Introduction

[i] PTSD refers to post-traumatic Stress Disorder and is common among people who have experienced combat. PTSD is mentioned many times throughout the book. According to the Mayo Clinic: *Post-traumatic stress disorder (PTSD) is a mental health condition that's triggered by a terrifying event — either experiencing it or witnessing it. Symptoms may include flashbacks, nightmares and severe anxiety, as well as uncontrollable thoughts about the event. Most people who go through traumatic events may have temporary difficulty adjusting and coping, but with time and good self-care, they usually get better. If the symptoms get worse, last for months or even years, and interfere with your day-to-day functioning, you may have PTSD. Getting effective treatment after PTSD symptoms develop can be critical to reduce symptoms and improve function. Post-traumatic stress disorder symptoms may start within one month of a traumatic event, but sometimes symptoms may not appear until years after the event. These symptoms cause significant problems in social or work situations and in relationships. They can also interfere with your ability to go about your normal daily tasks. PTSD symptoms are generally grouped into four types: intrusive memories, avoidance, negative changes in thinking and mood, and changes in physical and emotional reactions. Symptoms can vary over time or vary from person to person.* https://www.mayoclinic.org/diseases-conditions/post-traumatic-stress-disorder/symptoms-causes/syc-20355967 (accessed 1/9/2020)

[1] Los Angeles Daily News, July 16, 1943, pg. xi

[2] Łódź - Omitting for the moment any focus on the fate of Jews of Łódź, Poland, during the holocaust, the briefest possible history is this: The second largest city in Poland, Łódź was chartered in 1423. Control was taken by Prussia in 1793, Russia in 1815, and reasserted by Poland in 1919. Łódź was occupied by Germany during World War II. The Jewish history of Łódź, reduced to one sentence, would tell of 150 years of robust growth (despite a myriad of anti-Jewish laws) followed by rapid slaughter at the hands of the Nazis (and, in part, an

unsupportive Polish population).

3 *Fiddler on the Roof* is a <u>musical</u> with music by <u>Jerry Bock</u>, <u>lyrics</u> by <u>Sheldon Harnick</u>, and <u>book</u> by <u>Joseph Stein</u>, set in the <u>Pale of Settlement</u> of <u>Imperial Russia</u> in 1905. It is based on *Tevye and his Daughters* (or *Tevye the Dairyman*) and other tales by <u>Sholem Aleichem</u>. The story centers on <u>Tevye</u>, the father of five daughters, and his attempts to maintain his <u>Jewish</u> religious and cultural traditions as outside influences encroach upon the family's lives. He must cope both with the strong-willed actions of his three older daughters, who wish to marry for love – each one's choice of a husband moves further away from the customs of their Jewish faith and heritage – and with the edict of the <u>Tsar</u> that evicts the Jews from their village. <u>https://en.wikipedia.org/wiki/Fiddler_on_the_Roof</u> (downloaded 2/17/2019)

4 <u>https://en.wikipedia.org/wiki/Watts,_Los_Angeles</u>

5 <u>http://www.wattstowers.us/</u> (accessed April 17, 2019)

6 I remember once my father receiving a phone call from the producers of the TV series Airwolf. They wanted to know if they could film on our desert property. My father told them it was OK and gave them permission to "blow it up" if they wanted.

7 A Four-Star Family had four children in the military. If a family lost a son or daughter, then that was a Gold Star Family and the star was colored gold. A Gold Star Mother had lost at least one child.

8 In 1997 we celebrated my parents 50th wedding anniversary. I was able to find my cousin, Bill and invited him to attend. It was a great reunion with most of the Rosenkrantz cousins. We have remained in contact ever since.

9 The influenza epidemic that swept the world in 1918 killed an estimated 50 million people. One fifth of the world's population was attacked by this deadly virus. Within months, it had killed more people than any other illness in recorded history. Young adults, usually unaffected by these types of infectious diseases, were among the hardest hit groups along with the elderly and

young children. The flu afflicted over 25 percent of the U.S. population. https://www.archives.gov/exhibits/influenza-epidemic/ (accessed 2/17/2019)

10 Watts riots. https://en.m.wikipedia.org (accessed February 19, 2019)

11 Julius Rosenkrantz Filmography. https://www.imdb.com/name/nm0742632/ (accessed 2/24/2019)

12 "William Henry Pratt (23 November 1887 – 2 February 1969), better known by his stage name Boris Karloff (/ˈkɑːrlɒf/), was an English actor who was primarily known for his roles in horror films.[2] He portrayed Frankenstein's monster in Frankenstein (1931), Bride of Frankenstein (1935) and Son of Frankenstein (1939). He also appeared as Imhotep in The Mummy (1932). In non-horror roles, he is best known to modern audiences for narrating and as the voice of Grinch in the animated television special of Dr. Seuss' How the Grinch Stole Christmas! (1966). For his contribution to film and television, Boris Karloff was awarded two stars on the Hollywood Walk of Fame." https://en.wikipedia.org/wiki/Boris_Karloff (accessed 5/6/2019)

13 Sidney Poitier. https://en.m.wikipedia.org (accessed February 19, 2019)

14 Rosenkrantz, Lawrence. (Lorenzo), b. September 29, 1913, Los Angeles, California, Jewish, CP, received passport# 27375 on April 30, 1937 which listed his address as 1633 East 92nd Street, Los Angeles, California, Sailed May 15, 1937 aboard the Georgic, Served with the Transport services, deserted and sought help from the American Consulate in Valencia April 1938, Returned to the US on June 13, 1938 as a work away aboard the Samaria, WWII Merchant Marine. http://www.alba-valb.org/volunteers/lawrence-rosenkrantz (accessed 2/23, 2019)

15 https://www.history.navy.mil/research/histories/ship-histories/danfs/c/chilton.html (accessed 11/16/2019)

[16] Sharma, Neel K (et al). *Role of Ionizing Radiation in Neurodegenerative Diseases*, Frontiers in Aging Neurosci. 2018; 10: 134.

[17] http://cms.sbcounty.gov/parks/Parks/CalicoGhostTown.aspx

[18] Eminent Domain Watch. https://emdo.blogspot.com/2005/08/eminent-domain-up-for-action-whittier.html (accessed 2/23/2019)

[19] "Dirty tricks are also common in negative political campaigns. These generally involve secretly leaking damaging information to the media. This isolates a candidate from backlash and also does not cost any money. The material must be substantive enough to attract media interest, however, and if the truth is discovered it could severely damage a campaign. Other dirty tricks include trying to feed an opponent's team false information hoping they will use it and embarrass themselves.

Often a campaign will use outside organizations, such as lobby groups, to launch attacks. These can be claimed to be coming from a neutral source and if the allegations turn out not to be true the attacking candidate will not be damaged if the links cannot be proven. Negative campaigning can be conducted by proxy. For instance, highly partisan ads were placed in the 2004 U.S. presidential election by allegedly independent bodies like MoveOn.org and Swift Boat Veterans for Truth." https://en.wikipedia.org/wiki/Negative_campaigning (accessed 5/5/2019)

[20] My father claims that when he was 14 years old, his sister, Goldie (Janet) was in the Hall of Records in Los Angeles for some reason and looked at his birth record. Apparently, no first or middle names had ever been recorded. The birth certificate simply said "(male) Rosenkrantz.". She asked him what name he wanted recorded for first and middle names and they would enter it. So he requested "Harry Phillip."

[21] Philip Hurlic. Wikipedia https://en.wikipedia.org/wiki/Philip_Hurlic (accessed 2/23/2019).

[22] The Adventures of Tom Sawyer (1938).
https://en.wikipedia.org/wiki/The_Adventures_of_Tom_Sawy
er_(1938_film). (Accessed 2/23/2019).

Part 2

[23] "Fort Wolters was a United States military installation four
miles northeast of Mineral Wells, Texas. Originally named
Camp Wolters, it was an Army camp from 1925 to 1946. During
World War II, it was for a time the largest infantry replacement
training center in the United States."
https://en.wikipedia.org/wiki/Fort_Wolters (accessed
5/5/2019)

[24] Battle of Crete https://en.wikipedia.org/wiki/Battle_of_Crete
(accessed 1/10/2020)

[25] *The Pike* was an amusement zone in Long Beach, California.
The Pike was founded in 1902 along the shoreline south of
Ocean Boulevard with several independent arcades, food
stands, gift shops, a variety of rides and a grand bath house. It
was most noted for the *Cyclone Racer* (1930–1968), a large
wooden dual-track roller coaster, built out on pilings over the
water. https://en.wikipedia.org/wiki/The_Pike (accessed
10/31/2019)

[26] *unlax* is apparently a word Dave invented to mean the
opposite of relax. Several times in letters he invents words and
displays his personality and sense of humor.

[27] The term "Hogan's Alley" is used generically to refer to any
shooting range devoted to tactical training.
en.wikipedia.org › wiki › Hogan's_Alley_(FBI) (accessed
6/16/20)

[28] Rosenkrantz Family Fruitcake Recipe:
    1 cup sugar
    1 cup butter (or shortening plus one teaspoon of salt
    2 cups applesauce
    1 pack of dates
    1 pack of raisins
    2 cups of nuts
    1/2 lb. citron

1/4 lb. orange and lemon peel & cherries
1 teaspoon cinnamon
1 teaspoon cloves
1 teaspoon nutmeg
1 teaspoon soda
2 tablespoons cocoa
2 1/4 cups flour
vanilla, brandy, brandy flavoring, or Rum extract.

29 https://en.wikipedia.org/wiki/Moroccan_Goumier

30 This idea was mentioned by Chris Hartley, author of *The Last Soldier: The ordeal of a World War II GI from the home front to the Hürtigen Forest*, during a streamed interview sponsored by the Institute for the Study of War and Democracy, Sept. 19, 2019, https://livestream.com/nww2m/events/8798891/videos/196577394

31 https://en.wikipedia.org/wiki/James_M._Gavin (accessed 4/10/2019)

32 *Combat Jump* by Ed Ruggero. Harper; 1 edition (October 21, 2003), ISBN-10: 0060088753, ISBN-13: 978-0060088750. https://www.amazon.com/dp/0060088753/ref=rdr_ext_tmb (accessed 2/24/2019)

33 Maria Montez Filmography. https://www.imdb.com/name/nm0599688/ (accessed 2/24/2019)

34 Operation Shingle is the name given to an amphibious landing by the Allies in Italy during World War II. It took place on January 22, 1944, under the command of United States Major General John P. Lucas. The object, which was successfully achieved, was to land sufficient forces to outflank the Germans along the Winter Line and set up an assault on Rome itself. The fighting which resulted after the landing is usually referred to as the Battle of Anzio http://totallyhistory.com/operation-shingle/ (accessed 4/27/2020)

35 I raised this question once with Frank van Lunteren. Because Sgt. Ted Finkbeiner was there, it is probable that Dave was there also because they were in the same platoon. By this time the platoon was quite depleted.

36 History of the name Devils in Baggy Pants. https://en.wikipedia.org/wiki/504th_Infantry_Regiment_(United_States)#Devils_in_Italy (accessed 2/24/2019)

37 History of the 82nd Airborne Division

38 History of the 82nd Airborne Division

39 Dave's personal effects from Europe included a presidential citation that had been worn. The bronze star and presidential citation indicate he did receive awards for the action at Anzio.

40 https://www.cpp.edu/~rosenkrantz/paratroop/sgtdave.htm

41 Peter Outridge, author of: *Baggy Pants & Warm Beer: 504 Parachute Regiment of the US 82nd Airborne Division in Leicestershire UK, 1944*

42 Bridge Too Far is a 1977 epic war film based on the 1974 book of the same name by Cornelius Ryan, adapted by William Goldman. It was produced by Joseph E. Levine and Richard P. Levine and directed by Richard Attenborough. https://en.wikipedia.org/wiki/A_Bridge_Too_Far_(film) (accessed April 12, 2019)

43 NAZIS DIED LIKE FLIES IN BATTLE OF NIJMEGEN BRIDGE, TOUGHER AND BLOODIER THAN SALERNO, Tuesday October 10, 1944, By B. J. McQuaid, Times Foreign Correspondent.

44 https://www.molendatabase.nl/nederland/molen.php?nummer=250 (accessed April 18, 2019)

45 MEMORANDUM FOR RECORD. *ASSOCIATION OF UNKNOWN X-1234 MARGRATEN WITH TWELVE UNRESOLVED WORLD WAR II CASUALTIES.* 30 September 2016

Part 3

46 https://en.wikipedia.org/wiki/Geneva_Conventions (accessed 4/5/2019)

47 https://en.wikipedia.org/wiki/Gettysburg_Address (accessed 5/18/19)

48 The *Final Solution* or the *Final Solution to the Jewish Question* was a Nazi plan for the genocide of Jews during World War II. The "Final Solution of the Jewish Question" was the official code name for the murder of all Jews within reach, which was not restricted to the European continent.[1] This policy of deliberate and systematic genocide starting across German-occupied Europe was formulated in procedural and geopolitical terms by Nazi leadership in January 1942 at the Wannsee Conference held near Berlin,[2] and culminated in the Holocaust, which saw the killing of 90% of Polish Jews,[3] and two thirds of the Jewish population of Europe. https://en.wikipedia.org/wiki/Final_Solution (accessed 5/8/2019)

49 In the summer of 2018, my wife and I visited the Neuengamme Labor Camp near Hamburg, Germany. It was our first visit to one of the camps. 100,000 people entered Neuengamme but only 50,000 survived. I will omit the details of how inmates were exterminated at Neuengamme, but I will never forget seeing the facility where they were executed and the impact of realizing what went on.

50 82nd Airborne Website: https://www.ww2-airborne.us/units/504/504.html (accessed 2/25/2019)

51 In fact, as of this writing today, March 11, 2019, it is Maggie's 102nd birthday!

52 The National Liberation Museum 1944-1945, Visiting address: Wylerbaan 4, 6561 KR Groesbeek, The Netherlands, Postal address: PO Box 144, 6560 AC Groesbeek, The Netherlands, Tel: +31 24 397 4404, Fax: +31 24 397 6694, E-mail: info@bevrijdingsmuseum.nl https://www.bevrijdingsmuseum.nl/basis.aspx?Tid=746#.XK5 WZ5hKjIU (accessed 4/10/2019)

53 2004, 2009, and 2014

54 Ducks (DUKW) https://en.wikipedia.org/wiki/DUKW (accessed 6/25/2020)

55 https://www.nytimes.com/2014/09/18/world/europe/a-dutch-town-honors-us-soldiers-wartime-bravery-at-germanys-edge.html (accessed 3/12/2019)

56 http://www.sunsetmarch.nl/en/welcome/ (accessed 3/12/2019)

57 In September 2019 I participated in two sunset marches and timed the lights. The lights were sequenced about 13 seconds apart. It takes a brisk pace to keep up with the lights, but very doable.

58 The Sunset March honors 48 lives lost

59 The Rhine Getaway from Basel to Amsterdam https://www.vikingrivercruises.com/cruise-destinations/europe/rhine-getaway/2020-basel-amsterdam/index.html#noscroll (accessed December 13, 2019)

60 In the ninth episode, Easy Company finally enters Germany in April 1945, finding very little resistance as they proceed. There they are impressed by the industriousness of the defeated locals and gain respect for their humanity. But the G.I.s are then confronted with the horror of an abandoned Nazi concentration camp in the woods, which the locals claim not to have known anything about. Here the story of Easy Company is connected with the broader narrative of the war—the ideology of the Third Reich and Hitler's plan to exterminate the Jews. https://images.history.com/images/media/pdf/BandofBrothers.9.pdf (accessed 2/22/2020)

61 https://en.wikipedia.org/wiki/Herzogenbusch_concentration_camp (accessed 1/22/2020)

62 https://en.wikipedia.org/wiki/Neuengamme_concentration_camp (accessed 1/22/2020)

63 https://yvng.yadvashem.org/ (accessed 1/22/2020)

64 https://www.imdb.com/title/tt0380615/ (Accessed 8/8/2020)

65 IDPF for S/Sgt David Rosenkrantz, 1952 report of dog tags found at Heuvelhof

Part 4

66 One variation of the six stages of grief model based on the Book of Job is: 1. Emotion (Job 1:20) and numb shock (Job 2:13), 2. Utter despair (Job 3:1-3, 11, 25), 3. Thinking of the past (Job 29), 4. Anger and resentment (Job 30:19-31), 5. New perspective (Job 38), 6. New beginning (Job 42)

67 Ambiguous Loss. Wikipedia https://en.wikipedia.org/wiki/Ambiguous_loss (accessed 5 March 2019)

68 https://en.wikipedia.org/wiki/USS_John_Penn_(APA-23) (accessed April 17, 2019)

69 https://en.wikipedia.org/wiki/USS_Fanshaw_Bay (accessed April 17, 2019)

70 Tull, Matthew. *Trauma-Related Guilt in People With PTSD.* Updated October 31, 2018. https://www.verywellmind.com/ptsd-and-guilt-2797537 (accessed April 17, 2019)

71 *UCI study is first to explore veterans' grief, an overlooked toll of war.* UCI News, Nov. 6, 2019 https://news.uci.edu/2019/11/06/uci-study-is-first-to-explore-veterans-grief-an-overlooked-toll-of-war/ (accessed 11/15/2019)

72 Honoring Our Fallen is an amazing organization founded by Laura Herzog that not only helps families of soldiers and first responders with the transportation and burial of the fallen and needs that arise during the grieving process https://www.honoringourfallen.org/ (accessed 12/17/2019).

Part 5

[73] It was expected that a percentage of paratroopers would not survive a combat jump due to enemy fire, equipment failures, dropping onto deadly terrain such as water, hanging up in trees, etc.

[74] Building a Winning Culture by Ed Ruggero (Video) http://edruggero.com/building-a-winning-culture (accessed 3/13/2019).

[55] Building a Winning Culture by Ed Ruggero (Video) http://edruggero.com/building-a-winning-culture (accessed 3/13/2019).

[76] https://en.wikipedia.org/wiki/St_Crispin%27s_Day_Speech (accessed April 12, 2019)

[77] The 505th Combat Team was comprised of the 505 Parachute Infantry Regiment and the 3rd Battalion of the 504 Parachute Infantry Regiment. Dave was in H Company of the 504, which was part of the 3rd Battalion.

[78] Building a Winning Culture by Ed Ruggero (Video) http://edruggero.com/building-a-winning-culture (accessed 3/13/2019).

[79] https://en.wikipedia.org/wiki/Bombing_of_Nijmegen (accessed 11/14/2019)

[80] http://www.stichtingfan.nl/en/ (accessed 11/14/2019)

[81] https://en.wikipedia.org/wiki/Veterans_Day (accessed 4/10/2019)

[82] http://wwiiresearchandwritingcenter.com/

Index

ABOUT THE AUTHOR

Dr. Phil Rosenkrantz is a devoted educator with a passion for lifelong learning and promoting student success. He especially enjoys traveling and annual backpacking trips anywhere in the Western US. Phil is an avid volunteer with many years of service to the San Gorgonio Wilderness Association (U.S. Forest Service), Boy Scouts, Eastside Christian Schools, the American Society for Quality, and Special Olympics. He is Professor Emeritus of Engineering at California State Polytechnic University Pomona, where he taught for over 35 years. Prior to teaching, Phil worked for General Motors for ten years in engineering and management. Phil and his wife, Judy, have four children: David, Julia, Sarah, and Debi. His other passions include World War II history, bluegrass, and Disneyland. Phil and Judy now divide their time between Southern California and Central Arizona.

Phil has been recognized professionally for his contributions to teaching and the engineering profession. He speaks regularly to schools and organizations on topics related to his Uncle David, study skills, teamwork, quality management, leadership, and backpacking on the John Muir Trail. Phil holds degrees from Kettering (BSME), Purdue (MSIA), UC Riverside (MS), and Pepperdine Universities (Ed.D).

To learn more, ask a question or book Phil as a speaker, please visit:

www.philrosenkrantz.com or
email him at phil@philrosenkrantz.com.

Made in the USA
Coppell, TX
03 October 2020